spirit of the earth

For Lucetta,
What a great pleasure
to see you again! Hope
you enjoy the book.
Much love/
Beverly

STEWART, TABORI & CHANG
New York

spirit of

the earth

NATIVE COOKING FROM LATIN AMERICA

Beverly Cox & Martin Jacobs

Maps and step-by-step illustrations by Glenn Wolff

Text copyright © 2001 by Beverly Cox and Martin Jacobs
Photographs copyright © 2001 by Martin Jacobs
Illustrations copyright © 2001 by Glenn Wolff

Published in 2001 by
Stewart, Tabori & Chang
A Company of La Martinière Groupe
115 West 18th Street
New York, NY 10011

Library of Congress Cataloging-in-Publication Data
Cox, Beverly, 1945–
    Spirit of the earth : Beverly Cox & Martin Jacobs
        p. cm.
    Includes index.
    ISBN 1-58479-024-5
1. Latin American cookery. 2. Native peoples of South and
    Mesoamerica—Food. I. Jacobs, Martin. II. Title.

TX715.C869397 2001
641.59'297—dc21   00-022480

Edited by Marisa Bulzone
Designed by Alexandra Maldonado
Graphic Production by Pamela Schechter

The text of this book was composed in Fairfield, the recipes were composed in Today.

Printed and bound in China by Toppan Printing

10 9 8 7 6 5 4 3 2 1

First Printing

Spirit of the Earth is dedicated to the memory of the late Sophie D. Coe. A noted anthropologist, food historian, and translator of ancient texts, she was a pioneer in recognizing the tremendous culinary contributions of the Maya, the Aztec, and the Inca. Though we never had the pleasure of meeting Sophie in person, through her wonderfully informative books, *America's First Cuisines* and *The True History of Chocolate*, co-authored with her husband, Michael D. Coe, she has inspired and guided us through this project.

CONTENTS

PREFACE

Writing *Spirit of the Earth* has been a wonderful adventure. Our travels have taken us from the lush jungles of the Yucatán peninsula to the arid highlands of central Mexico and on to the shores of Lake Titicaca, located at 13,000 feet in Bolivia's altiplano. We expected to find great food, but it has far exceeded our expectations. We have made many new friends along the way, and everywhere we have been treated with kindness and courtesy.

One thing has been obvious from the beginning: the native cooking of Mesoamerica and South America is a mammoth subject, far too rich and extensive to be covered in one book. Our goal has been to combine at least some of the fascinating food history of these regions with recipes that are both practical to make and appealing to the modern palate. With this in mind, we followed the lead of the late Sophie Coe, the author of *America's First Cuisines*, and focused primarily on the Maya, the Aztec, and the Inca, the dominant powers at the time of the Spanish Conquest in the sixteenth century. More is known about these highly evolved civilizations and their food than about those that preceded them and others who were their contemporaries. Though they suffered cruelly under the Spanish occupation, the people who made up these once-powerful empires survived. Today large numbers of their modern descendants continue to live and maintain many of their culinary traditions. These were the cooks we hoped to meet.

With the assistance of many generous and knowledgeable people on two continents, we have gathered enough luscious recipes to fill several vol-

umes and have learned much more about the extraordinary civilizations that gave the world such culinary treasures as corn, potatoes, beans, squash, chiles, tomatoes, pineapples, quinoa, amaranth, chocolate, and vanilla. We are sad to be near the end of the journey, but happy to be able to share this memorable experience with you.

We would like to thank our distinguished contributors: Carolyn Margolis, Chief of Exhibition Design for the National Museum of Natural History, Smithsonian Institution; Michael D. Coe, Professor Emeritus of Anthropology, Yale University, and author of many books on pre-Columbian civilizations; and Jack Weatherford, Professor of Anthropology at Macalester College in St. Paul, Minnesota, author and lecturer.

We would also like to acknowledge the support and advice of Clara Sue Kidwell, Director of Native American Studies, University of Oklahoma; Herman J. Viola, Curator Emeritus, National Museum of Natural History, Smithsonian Institution, author and lecturer; Betty Meggers, Archaeologist, Smithsonian Institution, specializing in Latin America; Donald Hazlett, ethnobotanist specializing in Mesoamerica and president of New World's Plants and People in Pierce, Colorado; and Rosario Olivas Weston, of Lima, Peru, food historian and award-winning author.

THE MAYA

Michael Coe has called the ancient Maya "the great innovators and culture-givers to the rest of the peoples of Mexico and South America." They studied the heavens and developed a calendar accurate to the day for a period of 374,400 years. They were agriculturalists, mystics, warriors, traders, and talented, refined cooks. Today more than 8 million Maya live on the Yucatán peninsula and in Mexico and Central America. They maintain many of the traditions of their ancestors.

Many thanks to our friends in the Yucatán, Guatemala, Honduras, and the United States who shared both their recipes and their time and made us feel welcome: Monica Hernandez, Anibal Gonzalez, and the staff at Hacienda Kantanchel in TixKoKob, especially Aida Dzul Coba, Maria Teresa Kep Mesh, Jorge Loeza, and Ezequiel Mendez Rosado; also Fiorentina Moguel Duran and family, Silvio Campos, Diana Cetina Aguilar, José Francisco Marrufo Rejón, Juanita Velasco, Soledad Marroquin de Palacios, Margoth Giron, Marta Zelaya de Hazlett, and Patricia Rain.

THE AZTEC

Mexico is amazing—rich in diverse indigenous cultures and cuisines. From the behemoth metropolis of Mexico City to Oaxaca and "the skirts of the Malinche" in Tlaxcala, where Huichol tribespeople live much as their ancestors did, we have been graciously received, nurtured, and nourished. Many thanks to all of the people in both Mexico and the United States who made important contributions to this chapter: Roger and Mary Wallace, Martha Medina, Eduardo Aceves, Josefina Luna Carrillo, Magdalena Carral, Marco Muñoz, Lila Lomelí, Guillermina Martinez, Marilyn Tausend, Ana

Elena Martinez, Amelia Woolrich, Beatriz Ramírez Woolrich, Yolanda Ramos Galicia, Gaston Melo Medina, and Carmen Ramírez.

THE INCA

Traveling in Peru and Bolivia is wonderfully exotic. A short flight takes you from the dense tropical rain forests of Amazonia to the intricately terraced foothills and towering, craggy peaks of the Andes. One constant is an unfailing tradition of courtesy and hospitality. We would like to thank the many generous people who made invaluable contributions to this chapter. In the United States: Mark and Emily Cox, Judy Boyd Tergen, Cindy Atkins, Martha Kreipe de Montaño, José Montaño, Joe Carrasco, and Douglas Rodriguez of Chicama and Pipa restaurants in New York City. In Peru: Irma Bacigalupo Henderson and Mike Henderson, Magaly Leon Bacigalupo, Luis Alberto Leon Bacigalupo, Celia Bedia de Ustua, Felicita PasaPera Villegas, Isabel Alvarez, Marisa Guiulfo Zender and Jorge and Lucía Palza, Jesús Aguirre, Román Viscarra, and Fielding Wood Viscarra and their children Suni and Tica, Tamia Serna Pérez, Jonny Pérez Burrios, and Víctor Serna Martinez. In Bolivia: Maria Cristina de Rojas, Teresa de Prada, Wilma de Velasco, Antonio Paredes Canbia, Lila de Palza, Javier Palza, Lucretia Palza, and Raul Garron Claure. In Cochabamba: Nelly de Jordan, José Maria Bakovic and Marcia Saavedra de Bakovic, Katica Bakovic, Tonci Bakovic and Duina R. de Bakovic, Lourdes Peñalosa Ramírez, and José and Elisabeth Lafuente.

This book could never have been completed without the hard work and dedication of the people who assisted in typing and organization, test cooking, and prop and food styling. Beverly would like to thank her husband, Gordon Black, who typed the manuscript and kept her on track. Judy Day, Marti Bressler, and Marta Hazlett cooked and recooked recipes to make sure that they were right and have embraced this project with great enthusiasm. Beverly's mother, Betty Cox, and sister-in-law, Dale Black, and the Day and Hazlett families have been helpful and patient and have acted as objective recipe tasters. Many thanks to Don Day Jr., who provided us with great fish and game for recipe testing and photography. Linda Johnson has, once again, done a great job with the prop styling.

We would like to thank our agent, Judith Weber, who encouraged our desire to take on this challenging project and has been supportive throughout. It has been a pleasure to work again with Leslie Stoker at Stewart, Tabori & Chang. We admire her vision and her desire to produce high-quality books. Our editor, Marisa Bulzone, has offered clear-headed advice and encouraged us to persevere. Our copy editor, Kathie Ness, has turned all of the pieces of a manuscript into a book that makes sense. And last, but very important, we have been fortunate to work with Alexandra Maldonado, a designer who produces consistently beautiful books.

Beverly Cox and Martin Jacobs

A New World, Full of Promise

CAROLYN MARGOLIS

When Columbus reached America's shores in 1492 he found a new world full of promise. It was not an empty and uninhabited land, nor one untouched by human activity—but compared to Europe, pre-Columbian America was pristine. This new Eden underwent rapid and profound transformations brought by the "seeds of change"—the plants, animals, and diseases that were introduced, sometimes deliberately, sometimes accidentally, by Columbus and those who followed.

This exchange was not one-way. Early explorers came seeking gold and silver, but in time the enduring treasure of the Americas proved to be the wealth of its native plants. Corn and potatoes, now two of the world's staple foods, originated in the Americas more than 5,000 years ago. Today they are cultivated more extensively than wheat or rice, and because they adapt to a wide variety of climates, they have helped to improve food production in developing countries. In the pre-Columbian Americas, corn was the most important crop, flourishing from what is now southern Chile to southern Canada. Corn could not, however, grow in the Andes. There, farmers cultivated hundreds of varieties of potatoes as their daily staple. Some have estimated that there were almost 80 million people in pre-Columbian America, many living in highly sophisticated societies, all nourished by corn and potatoes through trade networks that often spanned thousands of miles. Today the starches and sugars of both corn and potatoes contribute to thousands of products, from plastic to soft drinks to paints, and help support the world economy.

Corn was domesticated from native wild grasses in Mesoamerica at least 7,000 years ago and was grown by the great pre-Columbian cultures. The Inca made a fermented drink of corn (*chicha*) that was served in a special beaker often decorated with ears of corn. The Maya depicted the earth god as emerging from a cornstalk. Of all grains, corn converts the sun's energy into food most efficiently. It is the leading staple in many Latin American nations and is more widely grown in Africa than any other major crop. Ironically, it was the introduction of corn to Africa by Europeans that sparked the remarkable population explosion that fed the Atlantic slave trade.

While building their empire, the Inca of Peru absorbed thousands of years of farming traditions from the peoples they brought under their rule. For more than 2,000 years, and maybe as long as 15,000 years, Andeans have cultivated and eaten potatoes. Andean potatoes come in a dazzling range of colors, shapes, sizes, and flavors. In the highlands, farmers cultivate many tiny plots on steep mountain slopes. On these "staircase" farms, rainfall, sunlight, and soil type can vary within a few yards. As their ancestors did for centuries, farmers today raise many varieties of potatoes on these terraces, each adapted to their slightly different conditions. Potatoes today thrive all over the world and are grown in all fifty of the United States.

In my research to organize the 1991 exhibition *Seeds of Change* at the Smithsonian Institution National Museum of Natural History, I learned to look at foodstuffs and cuisines in a new way. I ate pure pre-Columbian meals with anthropologists from Mexico, and traveled to the International Potato Center in Peru to eat mashed bright yellow potatoes. At one food conference, I tasted the chocolate drink of Montezuma. I may have been sipping the drink of the gods, but I missed the sugar. I wished it had been the hot chocolate of the Maya, with the added honey. I saw the potato specimens from Monte Verde in South America that may force us to reconsider our dates for the first Americans. And I bought two *retablos* made out of potatoes from a Peruvian craftsman. I was able to touch the sculpted corn gods and goddesses of the ancient Maya people, and I learned about the great trade networks in Central and South America, where the cacao bean was king.

I saw how history could be interpreted through food—the growing of it, the storage of it, the trade in it, the feast and famine cycles. Sugar, for example, brought from Spain on Columbus's second voyage, fueled the slave trade, changed the ethnic makeup of the Caribbean, helped destroy the native vegetation on the islands, fed the markets of Europe, and in turn helped support the Industrial Revolution and set off trade wars that lasted hundreds of years.

In 1989, the National Research Council published *Lost Crops of the Incas*, about "little-known plants of the Andes with promise for worldwide cultivation." There were chapters on roots, grains, legumes, vegetables, fruits, and nuts; at the time most were completely unknown to North Americans. Many of these foods are ingredients in the recipes in this book and can now be found at your local market, quinoa being just one of them. This grain was so vital to the Inca that they considered it sacred. It is a major source of protein, and can take the place of meat in a diet—one reason that quinoa is finally generating tremendous sales in the United States.

We know that the Inca and those before them domesticated many varieties of potatoes, but did you know that it was the Spanish who took the potato back to Europe—from where it eventually made its way back across the Atlantic again to North America? We know about the potato famine in Ireland and about the thousands upon thousands who died or emigrated to the United States, but did you know that potatoes—safely planted under the ground out of reach of marauding armies—saved many Europeans from starvation?

Corn and potatoes, domesticated and grown by the predominant cultures of pre-Columbian America, have been the region's gift to the world. But these native Americans contributed much, much more: tomatoes, cacao, peppers, squashes, and vanilla are just a sampling. The Aztec and Maya used the tomato in sauces; Europeans brought it home and made ketchup and tomato sauce for pasta, while Latin Americans kept perfecting the original idea—and now salsa is the largest-selling condiment in the United States. Look at your next restaurant meal: Italian polenta, made of corn, sits beneath crabmeat from the Atlantic in a sauce made from cream from "Old World" cows. Next comes the traditional steak with *pommes frites*, and for dessert, a chocolate mousse mixing sugar originating in New Guinea with the cacao bean of the Aztec.

As immigrant plants took root in alien lands, diets and cuisines changed around the world. With New World peppers, Asians invented fiery curries. In Mexico, Asian rice is served side by side with corn tortillas. There's Andean potato in a European cheese pie. Every meal offers a chance to see cultural and biological exchanges in action. If you are what you eat, then we are truly a global community.

No one country or culture has a monopoly on good food. Pre-Columbian America gave much to our diet and well-being. When Hernán Cortés and his Spanish soldiers saw the great market in the Aztec city of Tlatelolco for the first time, one of his officers, Bernal Diaz del Castillo remarked: "On reaching the marketplace…. we were astounded at the number of people and the quantity of merchandise…. Each kind of merchandise was kept separate and had its fixed place marked out…. Some of our soldiers who had been in many parts of the world… said they had never seen a market so well laid out, so large, so orderly, and so full of people."

The Aztec were ahead of their time; it was just another day at the local farmers' market.

MAP

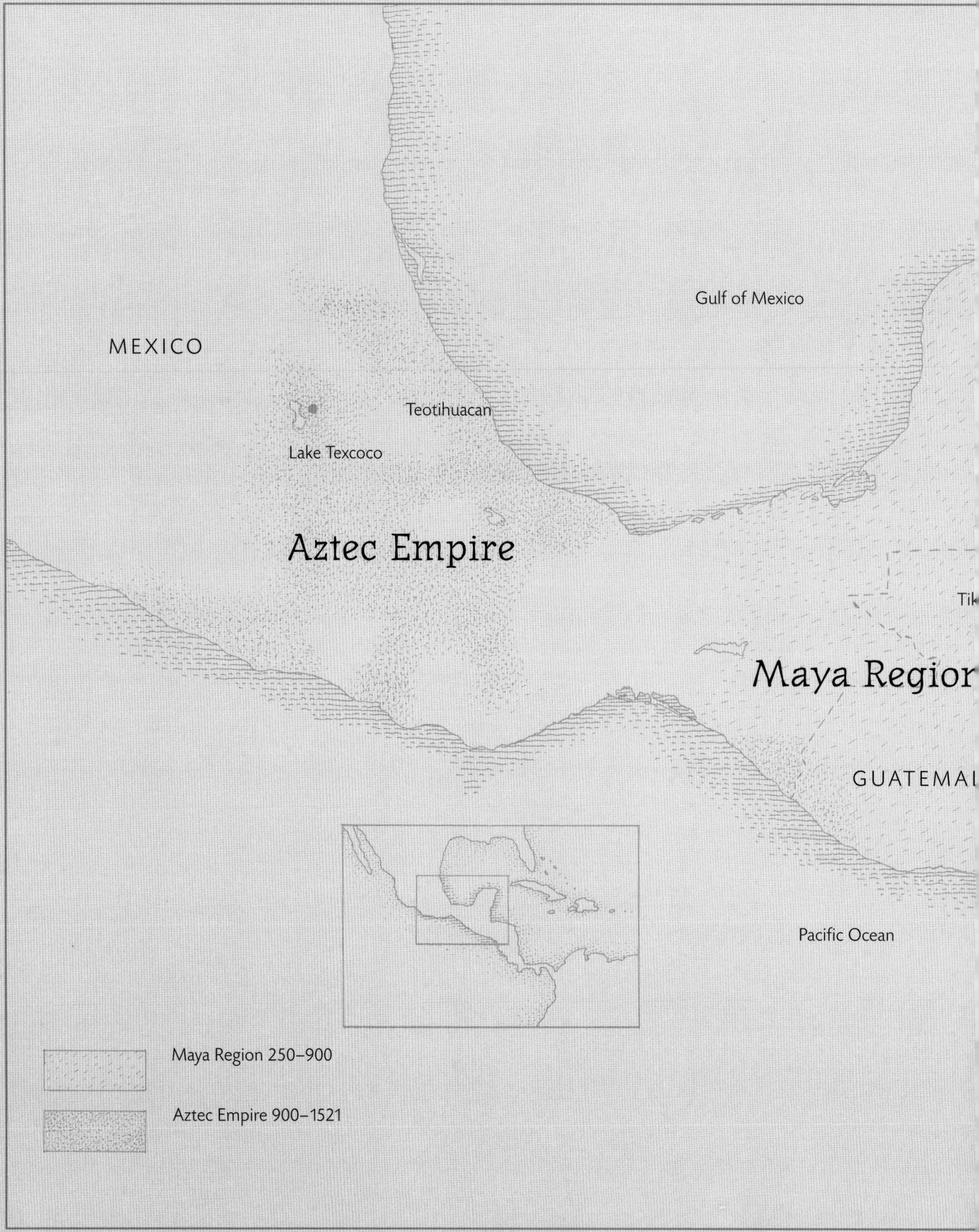

MEXICO

Gulf of Mexico

Teotihuacan

Lake Texcoco

Aztec Empire

Maya Region

Tik

GUATEMAI

Pacific Ocean

Maya Region 250–900

Aztec Empire 900–1521

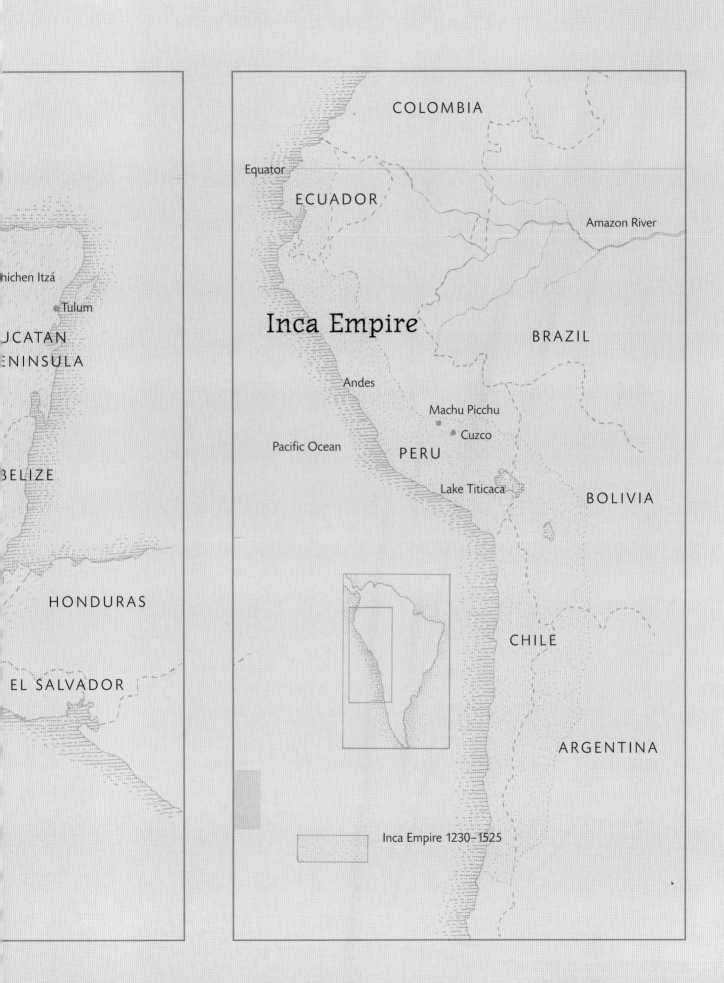

COLOMBIA

Equator

ECUADOR

Amazon River

hichen Itzá

Tulum

JCATAN

ENINSULA

Inca Empire

BRAZIL

Andes

Machu Picchu

Cuzco

Pacific Ocean

PERU

BELIZE

Lake Titicaca

BOLIVIA

HONDURAS

CHILE

EL SALVADOR

ARGENTINA

Inca Empire 1230–1525

the maya

chapter
one

A Living Civilization, a Living Cuisine

MICHAEL D. COE

We like to think of the ancient culture of the Maya as one of the world's "lost civilizations," but this notion is belied by the existence of the more than 8 million Maya who continue to live and work—and cook and eat—in the modern nation-states of Mexico, Guatemala, Belize, and Honduras. The famous Maya civilization did not die with the brutal Spanish Conquest, but it was transformed in many ways, not the least of which were changes in culinary habits.

Thanks in large part to the decipherment of the Maya hieroglyphic script that has taken place over the last half century, we now know a great deal about the Maya of the lowland forests during the Classic period, which lasted from about A.D. 250 until the ninth century. Unfortunately, we understand far less about the Maya of the highlands—the upland regions of Chiapas and Guatemala—since no Classic inscriptions have ever been found there: what we do know is largely based on "dirt" archaeology, rather than reading texts on stone monuments.

The lowland Maya—those living in the tropical region of southeastern Mexico, northern Guatemala, and the Yucatán peninsula—were organized into city-states, each headed by a family of hereditary rulers who claimed supernatural descent from the gods. The ruler (*ch'ul ahaw*, "holy king" in the ancient language), his queen or principal wife (*ix ahaw*), their children, and a vast retinue of retainers lived in grand masonry palaces, each consisting of many corbel-vaulted rooms arranged around courtyards. The principal business of this divine personage was to conduct war and to engage in royal rituals, including the worship of the deified former kings buried in sepulchers beneath the towering temple-pyramids that dominated the city. Such rituals might include the sacrifice of high-ranking captives, self-sacrifice by bloodletting, and the playing of a ball game slightly resembling modern soccer.

Warfare was endemic in the lowlands during the Classic period. Like those of Renaissance Italy, Maya city-states were relatively small but densely populated, and political rivalry between them often resulted in hostilities. Battles were fought with shields and spears, with one of the main aims being the capture of the enemy ruler—who, according to the inscriptions at several Classic sites, was usually beheaded. As the Classic period wore on, such warfare increased, with two of the most powerful city-states—Tik'al and Calakmull—in an almost continuous struggle for hegemony. Maya "super-states" like these achieved prominence not by the spear alone, but also by a combination of astute royal marriages and "big-power diplomacy."

We have vivid testimony about what life was like in these royal households from illustrations painted or carved on the surfaces of cylindrical ceramic vessels from Maya tombs. If we were to be admitted into the royal presence, what would we see? First of all, below a swagged curtain, the jade-and-feather-adorned "holy king" seated cross-legged on his stone throne, perhaps with his queen by his side. On the floor in front of him, various seated and standing officials, richly garbed. Standing to one side, a sarong-clad scribe, the "keeper of the holy books," the master of ceremonies, the librarian, and probably the king's chief advisor. But, most important for us, we would also see an array of offerings immediately below the throne, including precious quetzal feathers and seashells, bags of beans or cacao (the seeds from which chocolate is made), and other costly items of tribute brought by conquest or taxation.

But that would not be all. We would also observe a covered cylindrical vessel; and if we had that vessel in our hands, we would see a hieroglyphic text below its rim, stating that it contained the chocolate drink that was the all-important accompaniment to great Maya ceremonies and banquets. Next to it would be one or more flat-bottomed dishes containing corn tamales, not very different from those consumed today in Maya households throughout both highlands and lowlands. While we have never seen a drawing of the king actually drinking the foamy chocolate, or biting into a tamale (probably because no one was permitted to look upon the king while he was eating), we are sure that these were the basic foods for the ancient Maya elite.

Chocolate is an extremely ancient food in southern Mesoamerica. The secret of its preparation may have been discovered a thousand years before the Christian era by the mysterious Olmecs; the drink was forbidden to all but the elite—the royal house and the nobility. But maize (corn) is even more ancient, and is the staple food for all levels of ancient Maya society. The plant itself and all its products were sacred; the maize god was "First Father," the progenitor and protector of all. We know much about the Maya elite but little about the peasantry who planted and harvested maize. They lived in dispersed settlements throughout the countryside, annually invoking the rain god to bring moisture to their staff of life. According to recent carbon pathway studies on Classic skeletons, the upper crust supplemented their maize diet with game and fish, but the "common man" (and his family) probably ate little more than maize, beans, and chiles.

Unfortunately, the hieroglyphic inscriptions and pottery tell us about ceremonial occasions instead of the daily life of the elite, and there is almost no mention of the peasantry. Yet the palace cuisine of these highly sophisticated, artistically inclined people must have been very different from that of the farmers; one can imagine a veritable host of chefs and kitchen assistants producing dishes of the most refined delicacy, dishes comparable in elegance to the great Classic carvings and paintings that have survived the centuries. There may even have been cookbooks, but sadly, we have only four surviving books (screenfold manuscripts written on bark paper) for the entire pre-Conquest history of the Maya, and they are entirely ritual in content. Surely there were once thousands of books, and probably palace libraries, but all were destroyed, if not with the collapse of Classic civilization after A.D. 800, then centuries later with the arrival of European invaders.

The Spanish Conquest of the early sixteenth century truncated Maya society, lopping off the apex of the sociopolitical pyramid. With the exception of a few collaborating princes, the rulers and their palaces, together with the nobility, priests, and scribes, were virtually wiped out. But the peasants managed to survive both the sword and the foreign diseases, some fleeing into the deep forests, and others adapting to Spanish ways.

As we find with the immigrant populations of our own United States, traditional foodways are remarkably conservative, and the millions of Maya in Mexico and Central America today have retained many of the ancient ways of preparing food for everyday and festive consumption, as can be seen in Beverly Cox's wonderful collection of recipes. But the perceptive reader will also recognize the innovations that have come into the Maya cuisine, there to be readapted to new ends. Such ingredients as lamb, onions, garlic, sesame seeds, and cinnamon were unknown to the pre-Conquest Maya. But perhaps an even more fundamental change has been the introduction of oil and lard, and thus frying, into a cuisine that had previously cooked only by boiling, steaming, roasting, and pit-baking.

All of the world's great cuisines are the result of similar changes. For example, what would Thai or Indian food be like without chile peppers, an import from the New World? Or Italian cuisine without tomatoes or zucchini, both also gifts of the Western Hemisphere? All modern cuisines are hybrids: a deep, relatively unchanging cultural core (in the case of the Maya, a reliance on corn, beans, chile peppers, and squash seeds, as well as steaming and the use of the baking pit), with an overlay of introduced products and techniques. In Mayaland, the end product is still uniquely, and wonderfully, Maya.

PAPADZULES

ROLLED STUFFED TORTILLAS IN PUMPKIN-SEED SAUCE

The name of this popular Yucatecan *botana,* or appetizer, comes from the Maya words *papak',* to smear, and *sul,* to drench. (You may also see it spelled *Papa'Suules.*) With its sophisticated combination of colors, flavors, and textures, it has been considered a dish "fit for a lord" since early Maya times.

Don't be intimidated by the complicated-looking ingredients list. The *Recado de Pepita,* the *Chiltomate,* and the *Cebollas Encurtidas* may all be made well in advance. The secret to assembling *papadzules* quickly is to have all of the ingredients warm and ready before you begin.

1 white onion, peeled and quartered

3 cloves garlic, peeled and halved

1 habanero or jalapeño chile, seeded and sliced

3 sprigs fresh epazote or cilantro

4 cups water

1 recipe *Recado de Pepita* (pumpkin-seed seasoning, page 38)

12 small (4- to 5-inch) corn tortillas, preferably homemade (pages 51–52)

6 hard-cooked eggs, chopped

1 recipe *Chiltomate* (cooked tomato and chile salsa, page 31; see Note), warmed

2 cups *Cebollas Encurtidas* (pickled onions, page 49; see Note)

Fresh cilantro sprigs, for garnish (optional)

Place the quartered onion, the garlic, chile, and epazote in a saucepan, and add the water. Bring to a boil over high heat. Reduce the heat to low and simmer for about 15 minutes, until the water is well seasoned. Strain the liquid into a large measuring cup, discarding the vegetables and seasonings. Allow to cool slightly, then stir 2 to 3 tablespoons of the seasoned water into the *Recado de Pepita.* When the mixture is cool enough to handle, squeeze through your fingers until the seeds release some of their oil. Spoon the oil into a small bowl and set aside.

Gradually whisk more of the seasoned water into the *recado* mixture, until the sauce has the consistency of pancake batter. Keep this sauce warm in the top of a double boiler over simmering water. Stir it occasionally and do not allow it to boil, or it will curdle.

Prepare the homemade tortillas as described on pages 51–52, and keep them warm in a tortilla basket; or wrap packaged tortillas in aluminum foil and warm them in a 350°F oven for a few minutes.

To assemble the *papadzules:* Pour one-third of the warm pumpkin-seed sauce into a skillet. Dip the hot tortillas, one by one, into the sauce in the skillet. Place a heaping tablespoon of egg on each tortilla and roll it up like an enchilada. Place 2 or 3 *papadzules* on individual warmed plates. Cover them with warm pumpkin-seed sauce and top with the hot *Chiltomate.* Drizzle with the reserved pumpkin-seed oil and garnish with *Cebollas Encurtidas.* Place the completed dishes in a warm oven until all are assembled. Then serve immediately, garnished with cilantro (if using).

NOTES: *Chiltomate* will keep for up to a week in the refrigerator and may also be frozen.

Cebollas Encurtidas are best if prepared at least 2 days before serving. They will last for several weeks if stored in the refrigerator.

RIGHT: *Papadzules* topped with *Chiltomate,* accompanied by *Cebollas Encurtidas.*

PANUCHOS

CRISP TORTILLAS STUFFED WITH BLACK BEANS

When a practiced tortilla-maker cooks a tortilla on her *comal*, or griddle, it will usually puff up. When I was trying to acquire this skill, patient teachers like Maria Teresa Kep Mesh praised my better efforts by saying, "*Bueno!* That one will be for *panuchos.*"

Of all the Yucatecan *botanas*, or appetizers, *panuchos* may be the most popular. Ideally the tortillas should be homemade and should puff so you can split them open on one side to form a pocket to fill with refried black beans. However, if your tortillas don't puff or you prefer to use store-bought ones, simply fry them in a small amount of oil until crisp, and then spread the hot beans on top, followed by the chicken or turkey, shredded lettuce, diced tomato, and *Cebollas Encurtidas*. Serve these with *Xni Pec*, *Chiltomate*, or another favorite salsa.

12 small (4- to 5-inch) corn tortillas, preferably homemade (pages 50–51)

2 cups *Tsah Bi Bu'ul* (black bean puree, page 46), or one 15-ounce can refried black beans

3 to 4 tablespoons vegetable oil

2 to 3 cups shredded cooked chicken or turkey

1½ cups shredded lettuce

4 to 6 ripe plum tomatoes, diced

1 cup *Cebollas Encurtidas* (pickled onions, page 49)

1½ cups *Xni Pec* (roasted tomato and chile salsa, page 33), *Chiltomate* (cooked tomato and chile salsa, page 31), or another salsa

Prepare the homemade tortillas as described on pages 50–51, and use a small sharp knife to slit them along one side to create a pocket. Place about 1 tablespoon of the beans in each pocket, and press gently on the tortillas to spread the beans evenly. Dip the filled tortillas in the oil and place them on a griddle or in a skillet over medium-high heat. Cook, turning once, until crisp on both sides. Garnish the *panuchos* with the chicken, lettuce, tomatoes, and *Cebollas Encurtidas*. Top with the salsa and serve immediately.

Yucatecans love to snack, and *salbutes* are a favorite *botana* to buy at a stand in the market or to enjoy as an appetizer in a restaurant or bar. In Yucatec, *sal* means "light" and *but* means "stuffed" or "stuffing." Traditionally, a stuffing of cooked ground pork or shredded chicken is placed between two small, thin uncooked tortillas. The edges are pressed together and the *salbut* is gently lowered into hot oil to fry until crisp and golden.

Some Maya cooks we know add a pinch of baking powder to their dough to make the crust flakier, but this is a matter of taste. Though they may be drained on paper towels and kept warm in the oven, *salbutes* are at their best when hot and fresh. If you want to make them in quantity ahead of time, freeze the uncooked *salbutes* between sheets of aluminum foil or plastic wrap.

FILLING

2 tablespoons vegetable oil

½ pound ground pork

1 yellow onion, peeled and quartered

2 ripe tomatoes, peeled and quartered

¼ teaspoon ground cumin (optional)

Salt and freshly ground black pepper to taste

DOUGH

2 cups *masa harina*

1 teaspoon baking powder (optional)

½ teaspoon salt

1¼ to 1¾ cups lukewarm water (see Note)

Vegetable oil for deep-frying

GARNISH

1½ to 2 cups shredded green cabbage

1 cup *Cebollas Encurtidas* (pickled onions, page 49)

1½ cups *Eetch* (tomato and jalapeño salsa, page 32), *Xni Pec* (roasted tomato and chile salsa, page 33), or another favorite salsa

Prepare the filling: Heat the oil in a skillet over medium-high heat. When it is hot, add the pork and sauté until lightly browned, about 5 minutes. In a food processor or blender, finely chop the onion and tomatoes. Add this mixture to the pork, and stir in the cumin (if using), salt, and pepper. Simmer, uncovered, over medium heat until most of liquid has evaporated, about 5 minutes. Set the filling aside.

In a large mixing bowl combine the *masa harina,* baking powder (if using), and salt. Make a well in the center and add the water. Gradually mix the *masa harina* into the water to form a moist, pliable dough. If necessary add a bit more water, 1 tablespoon at a time. Roll the dough into 36 to 40 balls about the size of a large marble. Following the instructions on page 51, use your hands or a tortilla press to form 2 thin tortillas not more than 2½ inches across. Place 1 heaping teaspoon of the pork filling in the center of one round. Top with the other tortilla and press the edges together. If you like, use the tines of a fork to gently press down the edges

so the *salbutes* resemble miniature "suns." Continue to make more *salbutes* in the same manner until all the dough and filling are used. If you are not going to cook them immediately, place the salbutes on a baking sheet and cover them tightly with aluminum foil or plastic wrap. Refrigerate for up to 1 day or freeze for several weeks.

Into a deep-fat fryer or a deep skillet, pour enough oil to reach a depth of 2 to 3 inches. Heat the oil to 375°F on a deep-frying thermometer, or until a small piece of dough dropped into the oil browns in about 1 minute. Fry the *salbutes* a few at a time, turning them once, until golden brown, about 1 to 2 minutes per batch. Drain on paper towels. Serve hot, topped with the cabbage, *Cebollas Encurtidas*, and salsa.

NOTE: Depending on the brand used and the humidity in the air, *masa harina*—like flour—may absorb more liquid. Start with 1¼ cups liquid for 2 cups *masa harina* and add up to ½ cup more, 1 tablespoon at a time, as needed.

THE MAYA

SERVES 4 TO 6

When Juanita Velasco was a child, she used to gather large squash leaves and beautiful orange squash blossoms from her grandfather's garden to make this wonderful seasonal dish.

She remembers that sometimes, to make extra money for the family, she would offer to prepare *bosh boll* for tourists and other non-Maya residents of her village and would convince her grandmother and aunts to convert their home into a restaurant for the day. The young entrepreneur's enthusiasm for this venture caused her grandfather to complain, "If Juanita doesn't stop picking the blossoms, there will be no squash in the garden to harvest."

Although chayote squash leaves are traditional, they are not available commercially, and the leaves of other varieties vary in palatability. With this in mind, Juanita suggests that Chinese cabbage, kale, and Swiss chard may be prepared in the same manner. This is a delicious and unusal appetizer or main course.

24 large Chinese cabbage, kale, or Swiss chard leaves	1 fresh jalapeño chile, seeded and finely minced (optional)	1 cup *Recado de Pepita* (pumpkin-seed seasoning, page 38)
6 to 12 large squash blossoms	Salt to taste	1 cup *Eetch* (tomato and jalapeño salsa, page 32)
2 cups fresh *masa* or *masa harina*		

Wash the squash leaves in cold water and trim off all but about 1 inch of the stem. Gently rinse the blossoms and wipe out the insides with a damp paper towel.

Combine the *masa* or *masa harina* with enough lukewarm water to make a thick moist dough (see page 51). Add the chile (if using), and salt to taste.

In a small bowl gradually combine the *Recado de Pepita* with about 1 cup lukewarm water to make a creamy sauce; set aside.

Place a squash leaf, rib side up, on a cutting board. If the rib is thick, shave off some of it so that the leaf is more pliable. Place a rounded tablespoon of the dough on the leaf, about 1 inch from the top. With moistened fingertips spread the dough into an oval shape over the center of the leaf. Fold both long sides of the leaf over the dough, and then fold the leaf in half again to make a long tubelike shape.

To stuff the squash blossoms, roll a rounded teaspoon of dough into a ball about the size of a cherry. Place it inside the blossom and twist the ends of the petals slightly to enclose the dough.

Continue stuffing the leaves and blossoms in the same manner until they are all filled.

Place the leaves and blossoms in a steamer basket or on a rack in a roasting pan. Add boiling water to the pan, making sure it does not touch the leaves and blossoms. Cover tightly and steam until the dough is firm and the greens are tender, about 15 minutes. Serve the *bosh boll* topped with the *Recado de Pepita* mixture and salsa.

LEFT: *Bosh Boll*, served with a sauce made from *Recado de Pepita* and a bowl of *Eetch*.

THE MAYA

PUPUSAS DE CHICHARRON Y QUESO

HONDURAN PIES FILLED WITH CRACKLINGS AND CHEESE

In Honduras and El Salvador people often get together at their local *pupuseria* for a snack or a whole meal of *pupusas*, delicious little *masa* pies filled with meat, cheese, beans, or any combination thereof. Some cooks form the dough into a cup, place the filling inside, pinch the edges together, and then flatten it into a round disk. Our Honduran friend Marta Hazlett has an easier technique. Marta rolls her dough into small uniform balls and flattens them into individual thin tortillas. She places the filling between two tortillas and pinches the edges together. Though some cooks deep-fry *pupusas*, Marta usually cooks hers on a lightly greased *comal* or in a nonstick skillet.

FILLING

1 cup *chicharrones, tipo carnita* (meaty pork cracklings)

½ cup chopped yellow onions

1 fresh jalapeño chile, seeded

1 cup *queso fresco* or fresh mozzarella

DOUGH

2 cups *masa harina*

½ teaspoon salt (optional)

1¼ to 1¾ cups lukewarm water (see Note, page 25)

2 to 4 tablespoons lard, preferably home-rendered (page 217), or solid vegetable shortening

GARNISH

1 recipe *Salsa Casera* (Honduran cooked tomato sauce, page 29)

In a blender or food processor, puree the *chicharrones*, onions, and chile to make a paste. Crumble or finely chop the cheese. Place both fillings in small bowls; cover and set aside.

In a mixing bowl combine the *masa harina* and salt (if using). Gradually mix in enough of the water to make a moist, pliable dough. Roll the dough into 24 walnut-size balls. Using a tortilla press or your hands as described on page 51, flatten 2 balls of dough to form 4-inch tortillas. Place a heaping teaspoon of the *chicharrones* mixture and a heaping teaspoon of the cheese in the center of a tortilla. Top with the other tortilla and gently press the edges together to enclose the filling. Continue to form and fill the *pupusas* until all of the dough and filling is used. Cover the *pupusas* with a damp towel or with plastic wrap so they won't dry out.

Lightly grease a well-seasoned griddle or a nonstick skillet and place it over medium-high heat. Add the *pupusas,* 1 or 2 at a time, and fry until browned on both sides and hollow-sounding when tapped with a spatula, about 3 minutes per side, adding more lard or shortening as needed with each batch. Serve with the *Salsa Casera.*

SALSA CASERA
HONDURAN COOKED TOMATO SAUCE

Salsa casera (home-style sauce) is one of the most typical Honduran table sauces. It is less fiery than its Yucatecan cousin, *Chiltomate* (page 31), but it is just as flavorful and versatile. Marta Hazlett, who shared her recipe with us, likes to puree this salsa so that its texture is quite smooth. She serves it as a dipping sauce with *Pupusas de Chicharron y Queso* (page 28). It is so easy to make that it can be thrown together quickly for any occasion that calls for salsa.

2 ripe tomatoes, peeled and quartered

1 small white or yellow onion, peeled and quartered

1 clove garlic, peeled

1 fresh jalapeño chile, seeded and chopped

¼ teaspoon ground cumin

1½ tablespoons corn oil

1 tablespoon *masa harina*

Salt to taste

Place the tomatoes, onion, garlic, chile, and cumin in a blender or food processor. Pulse on and off until pureed.

Heat the oil in a skillet over medium heat. Add the *masa harina* and cook, stirring, until lightly browned, 2 to 3 minutes. Add the tomato mixture and cook, stirring, until the sauce is slightly thickened, about 5 minutes. Season to taste with salt. Serve warm or at room temperature.

In the Yucatán, salsa ingredients are often roasted on a hot *comal* (griddle). Roasting imparts a distinctive mellow flavor to the sauce. Traditionally, a *molcajete* and *mano* (stone mortar and pestle) are used to grind the roasted vegetables, but many modern cooks use a blender or food processor. The salsa is then cooked briefly to blend the flavors.

Chiltomate is a versatile sauce. It will keep for a week in the refrigerator and may also be frozen for up to 1 month. Whether used to prepare *Papadzules* (page 22) or *Huevos Montuleños* (page 45), two of the great specialties of Yucatecan cooking, or simply put on the table with a basket of tortilla chips, it is always great to have on hand.

1 or 2 fresh habanero or jalapeño chiles

1 large white onion, unpeeled, halved

5 or 6 medium-size, firm ripe tomatoes, or 12 plum tomatoes, unpeeled, halved

2 or 3 cloves garlic, unpeeled

3 tablespoons lard, preferably home-rendered (page 217), or vegetable oil

1½ teaspoons minced fresh oregano (preferably Mexican oregano), or ½ teaspoon dried

1 tablespoon minced fresh cilantro

Salt to taste

Preheat a griddle or a large heavy skillet over medium-high heat. Roast the vegetables and the garlic on the griddle for 6 to 8 minutes, turning them with tongs to brown all sides. Peel the chile and carefully discard the stem and seeds. (Be careful not to touch your face or eyes before washing your hands—these chiles will burn.)

Peel and dice the onion, tomatoes, and garlic. Place the roasted ingredients and the oregano in a mortar or in a blender or food processor, and grind or chop to the desired consistency.

Melt the lard in a large skillet over medium-high heat. Add the salsa and sauté for 2 to 3 minutes. Stir in the oregano and cilantro, and season to taste with salt. Serve warm or at room temperature.

LEFT: *Chiltomate* is shown here served in a traditional stone *molcajete*.

EETCH

TOMATO AND JALAPEÑO SALSA

Juanita Velasco is a charming and talented weaver from the highlands of Guatemala; she is also a great cook. Her salsa recipe has only three ingredients: tomatoes, chiles, and salt. It is easy to make and has a wonderful pure flavor. Four jalapeños may sound like a lot, but blanching them in boiling water seems to remove some of the heat. Juanita assures us that the real "fire eaters" she knows use seven jalapeños for eight tomatoes! This is the salsa that Juanita serves with *Ooben* (page 63), and with *Bosh Boll* (page 27), the masa-stuffed squash blossoms and greens that are a specialty of Nebaj, the ancient Maya city where she was born.

8 large ripe plum tomatoes   **2 to 4 fresh jalapeño chiles**   **Salt to taste**

Place the tomatoes and jalapeños in a large saucepan and add water to cover. Bring to a boil over high heat, and cook until the skin on the tomatoes begins to loosen, 1 to 2 minutes. Drain the tomatoes and chiles in a colander and rinse under cold water. When they are cool enough to handle, remove and discard the stems and seeds from the chiles, and if desired, remove and discard the skin from the tomatoes. Place tomatoes and jalapeños in a blender or food processor and puree. Season to taste with salt.

THE MAYA

MAKES ABOUT 3 CUPS

Xni Pec, which means "nose of the dog," is the most famous, and one of the hottest, Yucatecan salsas. After you eat some, your nose will be as damp as a puppy's—hence the name. Yucatecans serve it at almost every meal—with hot tortillas or over eggs at breakfast and with most anything else the rest of the day. Each cook has his or her own slightly different version. The best *Xni Pec* we have tasted was prepared for us by Yucatecan chef and cooking authority Silvio Campos at his home in TixKoKob (Nest of Serpents and Cenotes), an ancient Maya town in the lush jungle about fifteen miles east of Mérida.

Don Silvio's secret is to include both green and ripe tomatoes in the sauce. He roasts some of the ingredients, including the wickedly hot but addictive habanero chiles, to soften their flavors. Silvio also finds that, although you may certainly use a blender or food processor, the texture of the salsa is best when it is prepared by hand in a *molcajete* (stone mortar). His *Xni Pec* is just right—neither too chunky nor too smooth, and hot but mellow. Don Silvio likes to serve it as a dipping sauce with *chicharrones* (pork cracklings) instead of the usual tortilla chips.

2 large ripe firm tomatoes, roasted (page 217) and diced

1 fresh habanero or jalapeño chile, roasted (page 217), stemmed, seeded, and minced

1 large green tomato, chopped

1 white onion, peeled and chopped

⅓ cup fresh bitter (Seville) orange juice or fresh lime juice

3 tablespoons chopped fresh cilantro

Salt to taste

Place the roasted tomatoes, roasted chile, green tomato, onion, orange juice, and cilantro in a large mortar or in a blender or food processor. Crush and grind by hand, or pulse the machine on and off 2 or 3 times, until the ingredients are well blended but still slightly chunky. Add salt to taste. Serve at room temperature.

SI KIL PAK

TOMATO AND PUMPKIN- (OR SQUASH-) SEED SALSA

Squash has always been an important crop for the Maya. All parts of the plant are used, but the most valued edible portion is the seed. Toasted ground pumpkin or winter squash seeds are added as an enrichment in many Maya dishes. In this salsa (also called *Haskilpac*), the pumpkin-seed paste softens the acidity of the tomatoes and act as a foil for the heat of the habanero. The result is a wonderfully balanced sauce that you can eat with a spoon. Serve *Si Kil Pak* with tortilla chips, or as a sauce for grilled chicken or fish.

2 ounces (about ½ cup) hulled raw pumpkin seeds (*pepitas*), or ¾ cup *Recado de Pepita* (pumpkin-seed seasoning, page 38)

8 ripe plum tomatoes (about 1½ pounds)

½ to 1 fresh habanero chile, seeded and chopped

¼ cup chopped fresh cilantro

1 teaspoon salt, or to taste

Place the pumpkin seeds in a large skillet over medium heat. Toast, stirring constantly, until the seeds are fragrant and slightly puffed, 3 to 5 minutes. Then grind the seeds to a smooth paste in a blender, spice grinder, or with a mortar and pestle. Scrape the paste into a bowl and set aside. If you are using a blender, do not wash it. If you are using *Recado de Pepita*, omit this step.

Halve the tomatoes and place them, skin side up, on a baking sheet. Broil until the skin blisters, 8 to 10 minutes. Allow the tomatoes to cool slightly; then transfer them to a blender or food processor. Add the chile and cilantro, and pulse on and off until pureed. Transfer the mixture to a small saucepan and simmer over medium heat for about 5 minutes. Remove it from the heat and gradually whisk in the pumpkin-seed paste. Season with the salt and set the sauce aside to cool. Serve at room temperature.

Modern chefs and food companies seem to be outdoing themselves in creating new and different salsa recipes to satisfy the American consumer's taste for "heat." Chiles have become a passion, and the hotter they are the more we seem to like them. The ancient Maya understood this obsession; for them, doing penance meant eating foods without chile and salt. There are many wonderful Maya table sauces, from the very simple to those with sophisticated combinations of ingredients, like *Naranja Ik*. This unusual pumpkin-seed-based sauce is a good choice for spooning over grilled chicken or for eating as the Maya do, with a stack of hot tortillas.

Ik is the Yucatec word for "chile." The chile normally used to make *Naranja Ik* is *yax-ik*, a small green chile that is called *chak ik* when dried. Since it seems to be difficult to find this chile, fresh or dried, outside of the Yucatán, we experimented with some more readily available dried chiles and found that the crushed red chile called "Chile Caribe" works well.

1 small white or yellow onion, unpeeled, roasted (page 217)

2 ounces (about ½ cup) hulled raw pumpkin seeds (*pepitas*)

1½ to 2 teaspoons "Chile Caribe" or other dried hot red pepper flakes

2 tablespoons vegetable oil

½ teaspoon salt, or to taste

⅓ cup fresh orange juice

Peel and chop the roasted onion; you should have ½ to ⅔ cup. Set it aside.

In a medium-size skillet, toast the pumpkin seeds over medium heat, stirring constantly, until they begin to puff and make popping nosies, about 2 minutes. Add the chile and continue to stir for 1 minute, until the pumpkin seeds start to turn golden and the chile is lightly toasted.

Add the oil and onion to the skillet. Sauté over medium heat for about 2 minutes, until the onion begins to turn translucent. Stir in the salt and transfer the mixture to a blender or food processor. Add the orange juice and pulse on and off 2 to 3 times, until the sauce is coarsely chopped. Serve at room temperature.

RECADOS

THE SAVORY SECRET OF MAYAN COOKING

A visit to the spice section of a Yucatecan market is a feast for the senses. The artistically arranged produce stands attract us with their pyramids of chiles, exotic fruits, and vegetables, but we move on; drawn by the tantalizing aroma of vividly colored *recados*. These seasonings, which have been compared to the curries of India, make Maya cooking unique.

Like his father before him, José Francisco Marrufo Rejón is a spice vendor. Using recipes passed down for generations, Don Panchito, as he is known to his friends, prepares all the traditional *recados:* the red *Recado Colorado,* colored and flavored with annatto seeds; the black *Recado de Chimole,* which owes its inky hue to charred chiles; and the lovely celadon-colored *Recado de Pepita,* made from toasted squash seeds. The Maya word for *recado is xak',* which means something that is repeatedly ground. Traditionally this grinding was done by hand with a mortar and pestle, but modern cooks often use a spice mill or purchase their *xak'* from a vendor like Don Panchito.

In her wonderfully informative book *Mayan Cooking: Recipes from the Sun Kingdoms of Mexico,* anthropologist Cherry Hammon describes *recados* as "an early convenience food." She goes on to explain that since pre-Columbian times Maya women have taken advantage of the rare days when their chores were light to gather sweet herbs and aromatic spices and grind them on a *metate* to release their oils and flavor essences. The *recados* are then carefully wrapped in banana-leaf packets and hung from the kitchen rafters, out of the reach of marauding household pets and livestock. Adding a pinch or two of these precious seasoning mixtures to a marinade or a simple soup or stew turns an everyday meal into a gastronomic triumph.

Though over the centuries they have been stored without refrigeration for extended periods, we find that when stored in a tight container in the refrigerator, *recados* have a shelf life of several weeks and remain fresher in flavor.

RECADO COLORADO
ANNATTO SEED, GARLIC, AND SPICE SEASONING

MAKES ABOUT 1½ CUPS

Of all the *recados*, the most widely used and perhaps the most traditional is the red—*Chak Xak'* in Maya and *Recado Colorado* or *Rojo* in Spanish. For the ancient Maya, annatto seeds (*achiote*) were an important ceremonial offering to the gods. The tiny brick-red seeds of the *Bixa orellana* were associated with rain and were used by the Maya to season foods offered to the gods in agricultural rites. Maya priests painted their bodies, robes, and ceremonial ceramics with annatto. The seeds were also used as a form of currency. Today the custom of tinting and flavoring both ceremonial and everyday foods with annatto continues.

It is possible to purchase small blocks of prepared *Recado Colorado* (which may be labeled "Achiote" or "Yucatecan seasoning") in the Mexican food section of many supermarkets in the United States. If you have a spice mill or a small coffee grinder, however, it is easy to make your own.

Recado Colorado is a subtle and versatile seasoning. Once you have it on hand, you will find yourself adding a spoonful or two to marinades, soups, and sauces even when the dish you are preparing is not Maya.

- 1 white onion, unpeeled, roasted (page 217)
- 2 small heads garlic, unpeeled, roasted (page 217)
- 3 tablespoons annatto (*achiote*) seeds
- One 1-inch piece cinnamon stick (preferably Mexican cinnamon), crushed
- 1 tablespoon black peppercorns
- 8 whole cloves
- 6 allspice berries
- ½ teaspoon cumin seeds
- 1½ teaspoons dried oregano (preferably Mexican oregano)

Peel the roasted onion and garlic. Quarter the onion. Place the onion and the garlic cloves in a food processor or blender, and puree. Using an electric spice mill or a mortar and pestle, grind the annatto seeds, cinnamon, peppercorns, cloves, allspice, cumin, and oregano to a powder. Add the spice mixture to the onion and garlic, and blend to form a paste. Store the *recado* in an airtight container in the refrigerator. It should be good for several weeks.

RECADO DE PEPITA
PUMPKIN-SEED SEASONING

MAKES
ABOUT
2 ½ CUPS

Toasted ground pumpkin (or squash) seeds are an important flavoring in Mesoamerican cooking. They are the principal ingredient in the sauces for such traditional Maya dishes as *Papadzules* (page 22) and *Onsikil Bi Ceh* (page 72). Maya cooks often buy *Recado de Pepita* from the spice vendor at their local market, but it is not generally available in the United States. Hulled pumpkin seeds, however, are easily found.

Unhulled seeds are much less expensive and can be prepared the traditional way: Simmer the seeds in water until the hulls soften. When the hull is soft, it can be easily peeled away and removed. Then spread the seeds out on a tray and sun-dry them for one day (or place the tray in a 175°F oven for 3 to 4 hours) stirring and turning occasionally, then toast and grind.

**10 ounces (about 2 ½ cups) hulled
raw pumpkin seeds (*pepitas*)**

Place the hulled seeds in a large skillet over medium-low heat. Toast the seeds for 5 to 7 minutes, stirring frequently, until they begin to puff and make popping noises. Be careful not to burn them. While they are still hot, place the seeds in a blender or food processor and pulse on and off until they are so finely ground that they almost form a paste.

Press the ground seeds through a medium-mesh sieve into a bowl. Return any unground portions to the blender and pulse again until finely ground; pass through the sieve again. If you are not using it immediately, place the *recado* in an airtight container and store it in the refrigerator. It should keep for several weeks.

This wonderfully fragrant *recado* is made of lightly toasted pumpkin seeds, toasted sesame seeds, Mexican cinnamon, allspice berries, and whole cloves—a seasoning mixture that is typical of the Maya cooking of Guatemala. (Margoth Giron, who shared this recipe with us, comes from the town of Coban in northern Guatemala.) It is delicious as a flavoring for roasted meats and fish and is also used in the preparation of several different kinds of tamales. When stored in airtight containers in the refrigerator, this *recado* will keep for up to one year.

8 ounces hulled raw pumpkin seeds (*pepitas*)

One 1-inch piece cinnamon stick (preferably Mexican cinnamon), crushed

1 tablespoon allspice berries

¾ teaspoon whole cloves

4 ounces sesame seeds

Salt to taste

Place the pumpkin seeds, cinnamon, allspice, and cloves in a skillet over medium-low heat. Cook, stirring, for about 5 minutes or until the seeds puff slightly and make popping noises. In a separate skillet, cook the sesame seeds, covered, stirring often until lightly toasted, 3 to 5 minutes. (The sesame seeds will pop like popcorn, so the lid is important.) Mix together all of the toasted ingredients. In small batches, grind the mixture to a powder in a spice mill or blender.

(If too much is ground at one time, the mixture will turn to a paste.) When it is ground, press the powder through a medium-mesh metal kitchen strainer. Return any pieces that didn't pass through the strainer to the blender or spice mill and regrind; then pass through the strainer again. Salt to taste. Store the *recado* in an airtight container in the refrigerator.

SOPA DE LIMA
YUCATECAN CHICKEN AND LIME SOUP

MAKES
4 TO 6
SERVINGS

Sopa de Lima is a Yucatecan specialty that is served either as a first course or as a main dish. This fragrant and piquant chicken soup is flavored with the juice of the *lima*, the Mexican lime, and is garnished with wedges of crisp golden fried tortillas. *Limas* are not generally exported to the United States, but Key limes or the more common Persian limes sold in supermarkets are a good substitute.

When preparing *Sopa de Lima,* traditional cooks follow the old Maya custom of roasting the onion, tomato, and chiles to mellow their flavors. Younger or more hurried soup-makers eliminate this step or roast only some of the vegetables. Both versions are good, so whether you roast the vegetables or not is up to you.

This *Sopa de Lima* recipe is adapted from the excellent one served at Hacienda Kantanchel. Monica Hernandez and Hanibal Gonzales originally purchased this seventeenth-century plantation in a picturesque setting near TixKoKob as part of an ecological reforestation project. The old buildings were so beautiful that Gonzales, who is an architect, decided to restore them. The hacienda has become a very special hotel, staffed by local Maya people.

2 tablespoons butter or vegetable oil

1 white onion, roasted (page 217), peeled, and finely chopped

Juice of 2 limes (about ½ cup)

8 cups chicken broth

2 chicken breast halves, bone-in or boneless

Salt and freshly ground pepper to taste

Vegetable oil for frying

4 to 6 small (4- to 5-inch) corn tortillas, preferably homemade (pages 51–52), cut into wedges

1 fresh mild green chile, such as an Anaheim or Italian frying pepper, roasted (page 217), peeled, seeded, and diced

4 plum tomatoes, roasted (page 217), seeded, and diced

1 fresh habanero or jalapeño chile, thinly sliced (optional)

1 lime, sliced

Melt the butter in a large saucepan over medium-low heat. Add the roasted onion and cook, stirring occasionally, until softened, about 10 minutes. Add the lime juice and the chicken broth. Bring to a simmer over medium-high heat. Season the chicken breasts with salt and pepper and add to the broth. Reduce the heat to medium-low and simmer, uncovered, until the chicken is cooked, about 20 minutes. Remove the chicken from the broth and set it aside to cool. Reserve the broth.

Meanwhile, pour oil to a depth of ½ inch in a heavy 8- or 9-inch skillet. Heat the oil over medium-high heat until a test tortilla wedge lowered into the oil turns crisp and golden in

about 1 minute. Fry the remaining tortilla wedges. Remove them with a slotted spoon and drain well on paper towels.

Shred the chicken, discarding the skin and bones, and divide the meat among 4 to 6 soup bowls. Reheat the reserved broth and season it to taste with salt and pepper. Arrange the tortilla wedges, mild chiles, and tomatoes around the chicken. Place a slice of habanero chile (if using) in the center of each bowl. Ladle the broth over the ingredients and serve immediately, garnished with lime slices.

RIGHT: *Sopa de Lima,* garnished with lime.

TALL-A-KACH
GUATEMALAN CHICKEN-VEGETABLE SOUP

This chunky soup is the Maya equivalent of New England boiled dinner or French pot-au-feu: a complete meal in a bowl. It was one of the first dishes our friend Juanita Velasco's grandmother, Maria Ceto, taught her to prepare. It is an old recipe well suited to hurried modern times: the entire preparation and cooking takes only 45 minutes. Juanita likes the beautiful orange and yellow bell peppers that are sold in the United States and has added them to her version of Grandma's soup. Serve this with a basket of warm tortillas.

One 3- to 3½-pound chicken

10 cups water

1 tablespoon salt, or to taste

9 small new potatoes, unpeeled, scrubbed, and cut in half

2 cloves garlic, peeled and minced

2 ribs celery, coarsely chopped

1 medium zucchini, scrubbed and coarsely chopped

5 plum tomatoes, quartered

1 yellow or orange sweet bell pepper, seeded and coarsely chopped

1 small bunch Swiss chard, bok choy, spinach, or kale, well washed, tough stems trimmed, leaves coarsely chopped (3 to 4 cups)

1 bunch fresh cilantro, stems trimmed, leaves coarsely chopped (1 to 1½ cups)

Cut the chicken into 6 to 8 serving pieces and place them in a soup pot. Add the water and the salt. Place the pot over medium-high heat, cover, and bring to a boil. Reduce the heat to low and simmer for 30 minutes. As the chicken poaches, skim off and discard any foam that rises to the top.

Remove the cover. Add the potatoes and garlic and boil for 5 minutes. Stir in the celery and cook for 5 minutes. Add the zucchini and cook for 5 minutes. Then stir in the tomatoes, bell pepper, greens, and cilantro. Cook 5 minutes, then remove the pot from the heat and spoon the chicken, vegetables, and broth into large individual bowls. Serve immediately.

CALDO COLORADO DE CARNERO

GUATEMALAN LAMB SOUP

Although they are not native, the sheep introduced by the Spanish in the sixteenth and seventeenth centuries are ideally suited to life in the highlands of Guatemala. Highland Maya raise sheep both for meat and for wool, which is used to weave blankets. On chilly market days, vendors in picturesque mountain villages like Cunen and Cuchumatan do a brisk business selling this hearty, warming lamb soup spiced with *Recado Colorado* and fragrant with mint and cilantro. Serve it with warm corn tortillas.

2 pounds well-trimmed boneless lamb, cut into 2-inch pieces

8 cups water

1 to 3 tablespoons *Recado Colorado* (annatto-seed seasoning, page 37), to taste

1 teaspoon "Chile Caribe" or other dried hot red pepper flakes

1 pound red or white potatoes, peeled and cut into 1-inch cubes

1 small onion, peeled and chopped, or 3 to 4 scallions, sliced

4 tablespoons chopped fresh cilantro

1 tablespoon chopped fresh mint leaves, or 1 teaspoon dried mint

Salt to taste

Place the lamb in a large saucepan and add the water. Add 1 tablespoon of the *Recado Colorado* and the Chile Caribe. Bring to a simmer over medium heat; then reduce the heat to low and cook slowly for 1 hour.

Add the potatoes, onion, 2 tablespoons of the cilantro, and the mint. Taste, and add salt and more *recado* if desired.

Continue to simmer over low heat for 1 hour, until the liquid is reduced by one quarter and the flavors have intensified. Stir in the remaining 2 tablespoons cilantro and serve immediately.

SERVES 4 TO 8

The Yucatecan city of Motul was once the capital and an important religious center of the ancient Maya province of CehPech. The hearty egg dish named after this city is a popular breakfast item on restaurant menus throughout the Yucatán and is a particular favorite of ours. One of the best versions we have tasted was at the Hacienda Kantanchel near TixKoKob. This recipe is adapted from theirs.

The only difficult thing about preparing this Maya interpretation of *huevos rancheros* is having everything hot at the same time. To make it easier, prepare the sauce and beans ahead of time; then you can simply reheat them when you are ready to fry the tortillas and eggs and assemble the dish. Frying the tortillas makes them crisp, but it is optional. If you wish to omit this step, simply warm the tortillas. This recipe allows for generous portions.

1 recipe *Chiltomate* (cooked tomato and chile sauce, page 31)

2 cups *Tsah Bi Bu'ul* (black bean puree, page 46) or one 16-ounce can refried black beans

Vegetable oil for frying tortillas and eggs

8 small (4- to 5-inch) corn tortillas, preferably homemade (pages 51–52)

8 large eggs

¼ pound sliced baked or boiled ham, cut into thin strips

2 cups fresh or frozen peas, cooked, or canned baby peas, drained

2 cups crumbled *queso fresco* or shredded Monterey Jack, Colby, or mozzarella

1 or 2 fresh habanero chiles, thinly sliced (optional)

In separate saucepans, heat the *Chiltomate* and the beans; keep warm.

Pour oil to a depth of about 1 inch in a large nonstick skillet over medium heat. Fry the tortillas one at a time, turning once, until crisp, about 2 minutes on each side. Drain on paper towels. Pour off all but about 1 tablespoon of the oil from the skillet. Fry the eggs over medium-high heat until the whites are set but the yolks are still soft, about 3 minutes.

Arrange 1 or 2 fried tortillas on a warm plate. Spread a spoonful of beans over each tortilla and top with a fried egg. Spoon *Chiltomate* over the eggs, and garnish with the ham and peas. Sprinkle with the cheese. Top with a slice or two of habanero chile (if using). Place each finished plate in a warm oven until all are assembled. Serve immediately.

LEFT: The assembled *Huevos Motuleños* can be the centerpiece of a hearty breakfast or brunch.

TSAH BI BU'UL

MAYA-STYLE BLACK BEAN PUREE

SERVES

6 TO 8

MAKES ABOUT 8 CUPS

A bowl of creamy black bean soup sprinkled with fiery chiles and seasoned with a squeeze of fresh lime juice is a treat for the palate and makes a satisfying main course for lunch or dinner.

When we were first served *Tsah Bi Bu'ul* (*frijoles colados*) in the Yucatán, it seemed very thin compared to the refried beans of the American Southwest. We were confused. Was this a sauce or something to be eaten as a side dish? In fact, it is both. You may pour the puree over other foods, use it as a filling for *Panuchos* (page 24), tortilla dough (page 53), or tamales (pages 63 to 64), or eat it as is with a bit of tortilla or a spoon. Canned refried black beans, including an acceptable one flavored with lime juice, are now sold in the United States, but home-cooked beans always have better flavor and are easy to prepare. *Tsah Bi Bu'ul* freezes well, 2 to 3 months, so it's easy to have on hand.

One 16-ounce package dried black beans

1 fresh jalapeño chile, roasted (page 217), or 1 canned jalapeño

1 head garlic, roasted (page 217), left whole

½ cup lard, preferably home-rendered (page 217), or vegetable oil

1 white onion, roasted (page 217), peeled, and chopped

Salt to taste

1 or 2 habanero or jalapeño chiles, seeded and chopped, or 1 to 2 teaspoons "Chile Caribe" or other dried hot red pepper flakes

2 limes, cut into wedges

Pick over the beans to remove any debris, and rinse them under cold running water until the water remains clear. Place the beans in a large heavy nonreactive pot and add enough soft or distilled water to cover them by about 5 inches. Soak the beans overnight. (Or if you are in a hurry, bring the beans and water to a boil and simmer for 10 minutes; cover, turn off the heat, and allow to soak for 1 hour.)

Add the roasted jalapeño and garlic to the beans, and place the pot over medium-high heat. Bring to a boil, then cover and reduce the heat to maintain a steady simmer. While the beans are cooking, gently stir them every 20 minutes or so, and check to make sure there is adequate water—at least 1½ to 2 inches above the beans. (If you need to add more water, add boiling water, because cold water tends to toughen the beans.) Cook until the beans are nearly tender, about 2 hours. (At altitudes of 5,000 feet and above, allow 1 to 2 hours additional cooking time.)

While the beans are cooking, melt the lard in a large heavy skillet over medium heat. Add the onion and sauté until translucent, 2 to 3 minutes. Add the onion and lard to the beans and continue to simmer for about 1 hour more, until the beans are tender and the flavors have blended. Remove the garlic and chile. Season the beans with salt to taste.

The beans may now be served whole or pureed. To puree, press them through a sieve or place them in a food processor or blender and pulse on and off until pureed. If they are to be served as a soup, the mixture should be thinner than if they are served as a vegetable or refried. If the mixture is too thin, cook the puree over low heat, stirring often so the beans don't stick. If it is too thick, add more hot water. To serve, sprinkle the beans with the chopped chiles and garnish with a wedge of lime.

The Maya of the Yucatán celebrate the corn harvest by consuming the new corn in three different forms: roasted on the cob in a pit, ground and made into delicate tortillas, and ground and made into a deliciously fresh corn porridge called *Ak' Sa'*. Maize has always been the most sacred Maya crop and today the Maya, like their ancestors before them, give thanks and make special offerings of *Ak' Sa'* to the agricultural deities that make the harvest bountiful.

For ceremonial offerings *Ak' Sa'* is sweetened with honey, but for everyday eating, some people prefer to flavor their porridge with hot sauce. Cooked fresh whole corn kernels are sometimes stirred into the porridge before serving.

1 pound fresh or frozen corn kernels

Salt to taste

Honey or hot sauce, to taste

1 cup cooked fresh or thawed frozen corn kernels (optional)

Place the uncooked corn in a large saucepan and add water to cover (about 2½ cups). Bring to a boil, reduce the heat, cover, and simmer for 1 hour. Allow the corn to cool in the liquid. Puree the corn and liquid in a blender or food processor, and then press the puree through a sieve into a saucepan.

Simmer for 30 minutes, until slightly thickened. Season to taste with salt, and if necessary, add a little more water. The porridge should have the consistency of a thin cream soup. Drizzle with honey or hot sauce, and stir in the cooked corn kernels (if using). Serve in small bowls.

THE MAYA

XEC' DE NARANJA Y JÍCAMA

ORANGE AND JÍCAMA SALAD

This refreshing and colorful salad is one of the dishes traditionally served at the final meal of *Hanal Pixan,* the weeklong Maya holiday that honors and nourishes the souls of departed ancestors. The recipe for *Xec',* which is Maya for "mixed," varies somewhat according to the taste and customs of each family. The mix almost always includes either sour or sweet oranges, sugar, and dried red chile, but sometimes jícama, grapefruit sections, pickled onions, and chopped fresh cilantro are added. We like the contrasts of color, flavor, and texture in this version, which includes crunchy strips of jícama, cilantro, and *Cebollas Encurtidas,* those addictively tasty pickled red onion slices that garnish so many Yucatecan Maya dishes.

This recipe may be halved.

12 juice oranges

1 large jícama

1 lime, halved

1 cup *Cebollas Encurtidas* (pickled onions, page 49)

1 tablespoon sugar

½ teaspoon "Chile Caribe" or other dried hot red pepper flakes, or to taste

Salt to taste

⅓ cup chopped fresh cilantro

1 head romaine lettuce, separated into leaves

Peel the oranges, and using a sharp paring knife, cut them into sections. Work over a large mixing bowl to catch the sections and any juices as they fall. Peel the jícama and cut it into julienne strips. Add the jícama to the bowl. Squeeze the lime over the oranges and jícama. Garnish with *Cebollas Encurtidas* and sprinkle with the sugar, Chile Caribe, and salt; toss gently. Sprinkle with the cilantro. Refrigerate for 1 to 2 hours before serving to allow the flavors to blend. Serve on a bed of lettuce.

MAKES ABOUT 1 QUART

Yucatecan dishes like *Papadzules* (page 22) and *Cochinita Pibil* (page 69) would not be complete without a garnish of pickled red onion slices. They are easy to make and last for several weeks when stored in the refrigerator.

2 large red onions, or 1 red and 1 white, peeled and thinly sliced

1 cup cider vinegar or white vinegar

1 teaspoon salt

1 teaspoon ground allspice

1 teaspoon dried oregano (preferably Mexican oregano)

3 bay leaves

½ teaspoon black peppercorns

1 fresh habanero or jalapeño chile, seeded and sliced (optional)

Place the onions in a saucepan and add cold water to cover. Bring to a boil over medium-high heat. Immediately drain the onions thoroughly, and place them in a glass bowl. Toss with the vinegar, seasonings, and chile (if using). Allow to macerate in the refrigerator for at least 1 day before serving.

HOW TO MAKE TORTILLAS

Makes twelve to fourteen 4½-inch tortillas, or eight to ten 4½-inch *pim*

The lack of *comales* (griddles) in the excavations of Maya archaeological sites indicates that the original bread of the Maya was probably not the tortilla as it is made today, but the *pim*, a thicker cake that was cooked in the ashes of the hearth fire. Today *pim* are usually cooked on a *comal* instead of in the ashes. They may vary in thickness from ¼ inch to ¾ inch, and in diameter 3 or 4 inches to 8 or 9 inches. Sometimes ground toasted pumpkin seeds or chopped cooked black beans are mixed into the dough before the *pim* is formed and baked.

Tortillas, on the other hand, are very thin. It is a pleasure to watch a practiced tortilla-maker pat out perfectly round tortillas by hand. In Mexico and Central America we know many cooks who pat out their tortillas between two hands—patty-cake style. But mastering this technique requires both time and patience. We have found that—especially for novice tortilla makers—we prefer the method commonly used by Maya cooks in the Yucatán and described on the next page.

Maya tortillas are almost always corn. In the Yucatán they are usually small, 3 to 5 inches in diameter, and are normally patted out on a piece of banana leaf—or these days on a piece of a plastic shopping bag. When you first try hand-patting it seems difficult, but with a little practice it gets much easier. Buying a tortilla press is another option. Of course tortillas can be purchased at the market, but they won't be as good as homemade.

It is wonderful if you have a well-seasoned *comal,* but we have also had success using a small nonstick skillet to cook tortillas. The mark of a successful tortilla is that it puffs. Expert cooks accomplish this by pressing down on the tortilla with their fingers after it is turned for the third time. For less experienced tortilla-makers, or those with tender fingers, Southwestern cooking authority Huntley Dent suggests pressing down with the heel of your hand in a twisting motion, with a kitchen towel wrapped around your hand. This should be done as soon as the tortilla is flipped the third time; the towel should then be lifted away immediately. This is the method we use.

USING FRESH MASA

2 cups fresh *masa* (page 228)

¹/₂ teaspoon salt (optional)

1 to 4 tablespoons water, as needed

Knead the dough a bit. Tortillas are traditionally not salted, but some cooks like to add a small amount of salt to the *masa*. If the dough seems dry, gradually knead in the water, a few drops at a time, until the texture is firm, smooth, and pliable. One knowledgable tortilla-maker we know suggests controlling the amount of water by using a plant mister. Cover the dough with a damp towel to keep it from drying out.

USING MASA HARINA

2 cups *masa harina* (page 228)

1¹/₂ to 1³/₄ cups lukewarm water (see Note)

¹/₂ teaspoon salt (optional)

Place the *masa harina* in a large mixing bowl. Make a well in the center and pour in the water and salt (if using). Using your hands or a wooden spoon, gradually mix the *masa harina* into the water. Knead the dough until it is smooth and pliable. (You can also use a heavy-duty electric mixer fitted with the dough paddle.) Cover the dough with a damp kitchen towel to keep it moist.

NOTE: Depending on the brand used and the humidity in the air, *masa harina*—like flour—may absorb more liquid. Start with 1¹/₄ cups liquid for 2 cups *masa harina* and add up to ¹/₂ cup more, 1 tablespoon at a time, as needed.

TO FORM TORTILLAS BY HAND: Pull off a golf ball–sized piece of dough and roll it into a ball. Place the dough on a piece of banana leaf or a sheet of heavy plastic wrap. If you are right-handed, use your left hand to rotate the banana leaf counterclockwise, while the fingers of your right hand press the dough into a 4- to 5-inch round that is about ¹/₈ inch thick. (See picture.)

If you are making the thicker *pim,* use the same technique to form about ¹/₄ cup of dough into a disk that is ¹/₄ inch thick and 4¹/₂ inches in diameter.

TO USE A TORTILLA PRESS: Place a plastic sandwich bag or piece of waxed paper on the bottom section of the tortilla press. Place a golf-ball-sized ball of dough on the press, slightly above the center. Top the dough with a second sheet of plastic. Press the handle of the press down firmly. The trick is not to push down too hard—let the press do the work. Open the press and carefully peel off the top piece of plastic. Lift the tortilla from the press with the bottom plastic intact.

If you are making *pim,* form ¹/₄ cup of dough into a ball. Place it in the press, as described above, and press down gently.

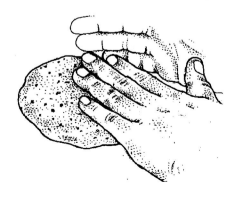

TO COOK TORTILLAS: Heat a well-seasoned griddle or skillet until a drop of water sizzles and jumps on it. Carefully invert the tortilla onto the palm of your right hand. With your left hand, carefully peel off the banana leaf, plastic or wax paper. Invert the tortilla back onto your left hand, and then invert it again, gently, onto the hot griddle. The side that was patted out by hand, "the face," is down.

Toast the tortilla for 1½ minutes. Flip it over and toast the other side for about 30 seconds. Turn it a third time, and press down on the tortilla with your hand or a folded dish towel and quickly lift away. This is done in one quick twisting motion as soon as the tortilla is flipped, and should cause the tortilla to puff. Continue to cook for another 20 seconds.

Cook *pim* the same way, allowing 2 minutes on each side and 20 to 30 seconds after it's flipped the third time.

As they are cooked, stack the hot tortillas on top of one another and cover them with a large pot lid or a plate. Tortillas are best when eaten fresh, but cooled tortillas may be placed in a plastic bag and refrigerated for a few days or frozen for several months. Separate individual tortillas with waxed paper if you are freezing a stack. To reheat, wrap the stacked tortillas in aluminum foil and place in a preheated 350°F oven for about 10 minutes; or wrap in paper towels and heat for 30 to 60 seconds in the microwave.

For variety, and especially for ceremonial occasions, the ancient Maya often added other ingredients, such as minced chiles, ground squash seeds, honey, annatto, or beans to the dough used to form tortillas and tamales. Bean doughs—usually made with the small Maya black beans—were especially popular.

Modern Maya cooks continue the tradition of making bean breads. This recipe comes from our Guatemalan friend Juanita Velasco. Her bean-filled tortillas are hearty and satisfying enough to be served as a meal with just salsa and a salad.

1 cup finely chopped white onion

5 tablespoons corn oil

1½ cups *Tsah Bi Bu'ul* (black bean puree, page 46), or one 15½-ounce can refried black beans

Salt to taste

4½ cups tortilla dough made with fresh *masa* or 2 recipes made with *masa harina* (page 51)

In a large nonstick or well-seasoned skillet, cook the onion over medium-high heat, stirring constantly, for about 1 minute, until most of the liquid evaporates. Add the oil and sauté until golden brown, about 2 minutes. Add the *Tsah Bi Bu'ul* and cook, stirring, for 2 to 3 minutes until the oil is incorporated and the bean mixture looks creamy and has thickened slightly. Season to taste with salt. Allow the bean filling to cool while you prepare the dough.

Roll ¼ cup of the dough into a ball, and pat or press it to form a 4½ inch round, following the directions on page 51. Place 1 tablespoon of the bean filling to one side of the middle of the tortilla. Fold the dough over the filling like a turnover, pressing the edges together. Use your fingertips to work the shape back into a round tortilla, about 4½ inches in diameter and ⅓ inch thick, with the filling inside. Ideally,

the bean filling should be completely enclosed, but if it does break through in spots, don't worry—the tortilla will still be fine.

Place a well-seasoned griddle or a nonstick skillet over medium-high heat. When the pan is hot (a few drops of water should sputter and dance on the surface), cook the tortillas for about 3 minutes on each side, until the outside is dry and nicely browned. Transfer the cooked tortillas to a basket lined with a napkin, and serve immediately.

NOTE: To reheat, wrap the stacked tortillas in aluminum foil and warm in a preheated 350°F oven for 10 minutes; or wrap them in paper towels and warm for 20 to 60 seconds, depending on the size of the stack, in the microwave.

THE MAYA

WAHI-TOP

TORTILLAS WITH TOASTED PUMPKIN SEEDS

The pre-Columbian Maya cooked with very little fat—it has even been suggested that they found animal fat repulsive. To enrich and add a "buttery" quality to tortillas and tamales, they sometimes mixed oil-rich ground toasted squash seeds into the dough.

½ cup hulled raw pumpkin seeds
(*pepitas*)

1 recipe tortilla dough made with
***masa* or *masa harina* (page 51)**

In a large skillet over medium-low heat, lightly toast the pumpkin seeds for about 5 minutes, until they begin to puff and make a popping noise. Stir constantly so that the seeds don't burn. Grind or chop them coarsely in a mortar with a pestle or in a spice grinder, and knead them into the prepared dough. Form and cook the tortillas following the instructions on pages 51–52.

The ancient Maya used red annatto (*achiote*) seeds to give a red or golden tint to ceremonial foods. Tamales made with annatto-tinted dough have a lovely golden color and a subtle but distinctive aroma and flavor. Some Maya cooks also like to add the heat of a minced green chile to their dough. The filling for tamales may generally be made a day or two in advance and refrigerated, but it is best to prepare the tamale dough shortly before you are going to use it.

USING FRESH MASA

4 cups (about 2½ pounds) fresh *masa* (page 228)

1 teaspoon salt

1 cup lard, preferably home-rendered (page 217), or solid vegetable shortening

2 tablespoons annatto (*achiote*) seeds

1 fresh jalapeño, serrano, or habanero chile, seeded and minced (optional)

Place the *masa* and salt in a large mixing bowl. Melt the lard in a skillet over low heat. Stir in the annatto seeds and continue to cook for 4 to 5 minutes, until the lard has turned a deep golden color. Pour the lard through a strainer into a bowl. Discard the seeds and allow the lard to cool.

Add the tinted lard and the chile (if using) to the *masa* and work the dough until it is pliable. This may be done in the traditional way, using your hands and mixing and kneading, or in a heavy-duty electric mixer fitted with the dough paddle. Cover the dough with plastic wrap or a damp kitchen towel to keep it from drying out.

Form the tamales according to the individual recipe directions.

⦿ ⦿ ⦿ ⦿ ⦿ ⦿ ⦿ ⦿ ⦿ ⦿ ⦿ ⦿ ⦿ ⦿ ⦿ ⦿ ⦿ ⦿ ⦿

USING MASA HARINA

1 cup lard, preferably home-rendered (page 217), or solid vegetable shortening

2 tablespoons annatto (*achiote*) seeds

4 cups *masa harina* (page 228)

1 teaspoon salt

2 cups lukewarm meat broth or water

1 fresh jalapeño, serrano, or habanero chile, seeded and minced (optional)

Melt the lard in a skillet over low heat. Stir in the annatto seeds and continue to cook for 4 to 5 minutes, until the lard has turned a deep golden color. Pour the lard through a strainer into a bowl. Discard the seeds and allow the lard to cool.

Place the *masa harina* and salt in a large mixing bowl. Add the broth to the *masa harina* and mix either with your hands or with a heavy-duty electric mixer fitted with the dough pad-dle. When thoroughly combined, add the tinted lard and continue to mix until a pliable dough is formed. Cover the dough with plastic wrap or a damp kitchen towel to keep it from drying out.

Form the tamales according to the individual recipe directions.

Mukbil Pollo is a large round tamale that is served at the final dinner in the weeklong celebration of Hanal Pixan, the Maya festival honoring departed souls. Hanal Pixan takes place at the end of October, near Halloween and All Saints' Day, but the origins of the Maya festival are pre-Columbian.

Unlike everyday tamales, which are steamed in a pot on the hearth, tamales prepared for ceremonial occasions are cooked in a *pib,* the Maya earth oven. *Mukbil* means "cooked underground," and *pollo* is the Spanish word for "chicken," the fowl most often used in modern times to make this special tamale. Recipes for *Mukbil Pollo* usually also include pork in the filling.

One of the best *Mukbil Pollos* we have tasted was prepared by Señora Fiorentina Moguel Duran, who lives in the Yucatecan city of TixKoKob. Doña Tini, as she is called by her friends, is the person to contact if you need tamales for a wedding or other special occasion. Many recipes for *Mukbil Pollo* call for poaching a chicken and a pork roast together. Doña Tini's version is a little more elaborate. She poaches the chicken but makes a separate *picadillo* of ground pork with tomato, onion, chiles, raisins, and capers. Though *Mukbil Pollos* normally are made only for Hanal Pixan, Doña Tini's customers like hers so much that she prepares them throughout the year. Traditionally, some of the chicken bones are mixed with the meat and enclosed in the tamale. The bones are symbolic and also add flavor, but they make serving and eating the *Mukbil Pollo* a bit more difficult, so we have made their addition optional.

Xec' de Naranja y Jícama (page 48) is a traditional accompaniment to *Mukbil Pollo.*

FILLING AND SAUCE

One 3½- to 4-pound chicken

Salt to taste

½ cup *Recado Colorado* (annatto-seed seasoning, page 37)

1 yellow onion, roasted (page 217)

1 head garlic, roasted (page 217)

1 or 2 fresh jalapeño chiles, roasted (page 217)

1 teaspoon dried oregano (preferably Mexican oregano)

2½ cups fresh prepared *masa* or 2 cups *masa harina*

PICADILLO

2 tablespoons vegetable oil

1 pound ground pork

1 medium yellow onion, peeled and chopped

1 clove garlic, peeled and minced

6 large ripe plum tomatoes, chopped

½ cup raisins

2 tablespoons capers (optional)

1 habanero or jalapeño chile, seeded and minced (optional)

1 teaspoon dried oregano (preferably Mexican oregano)

Salt to taste

2 recipes (about 10 cups) *Yucatecan Tamale Dough* (page 55)

3 cups *Xni Pec* (roasted tomato and chile salsa, page 33), for serving

To make this dish you will need 2 round or square 10-inch baking dishes, 2½ to 3 inches deep. To make the tamales you will need 4 or 5 large banana leaves prepared for cooking (page 224), or four 6 by 30-inch pieces of heavy-duty aluminum foil, plus four 30-inch lengths of kitchen string.

Rub the chicken inside and out with salt. Place it in a stockpot and add enough water to cover the chicken by at least 2 inches, about 10 cups. Add the *Recado Colorado,* onion, garlic, roasted chiles, and oregano. Bring to a simmer over medium-high heat. Cover, reduce the heat to low, and cook

(continued on page 58)

LEFT: A wedge of *Mukbil Pollos* is accompanied by *Xec' de Naranja y Jícama,* an orange and jícama salad (top).

THE MAYA

for about 1 hour, until tender. Remove the chicken from the broth and let it cool or, for a richer broth, if time permits and you have room in your refrigerator, place the pot in the refrigerator with the lid askew and allow the chicken to cool completely in the broth; when cool, remove the chicken from the broth.

Pull off the drumsticks and set them aside, if you wish to include the bones in the tamales. If you wish to avoid the bones, remove and discard the skin from the legs, and pull the meat from the bones. Remove and discard the skin from the rest of the chicken. Pull off the meat and shred it into bite-size pieces. Set the chicken meat aside.

Strain the broth and discard the vegetables. (The broth and chicken may be prepared to this point 1 or 2 days in advance and refrigerated.)

Next, make the sauce: Combine 2 cups of the cooled broth with the *masa* or *masa harina,* and whisk until the mixture is smooth. Pour the remaining cooled broth into a pot and bring to a simmer over medium-high heat. Place a fine-mesh sieve over the pot and, whisking constantly, gradually pour the *masa* mixture through a strainer into the simmering broth. Cook over low heat, stirring often until the sauce is smooth and has thickened, 20 to 30 minutes. Taste, and add salt if necessary. Set sauce aside.

Make the *picadillo*: Heat the oil in a large skillet over medium-high heat. Add the pork and cook until lightly browned, 5 to 7 minutes. Stir in the onion and garlic and sauté for 5 minutes. Add the tomatoes, raisins, capers (if using), chile (if using), and oregano. Season to taste with salt. Cover and simmer over low heat for 15 to 20 minutes, stirring often. The mixture should be fairly dry. Set the *picadillo* aside.

Assemble the tamales: Divide the tamale dough into 4 pieces and form them into 1-inch-thick rounds. Cover the rounds with plastic wrap to keep them moist. Place 2 lengths of kitchen string, crisscrossed, in one of the baking dishes. Place 2 pieces of banana leaf or aluminum foil in the pan, forming an X. Place 2 more pieces in the dish, criss-crossed, so that the inside of the dish is completely lined and there is enough overlap to enclose the tamale.

Place 1 round of dough in the dish and use your fingers to press it evenly up the sides like a pie crust. As you work, gradually rotate the dish counterclockwise with your other hand. Place half of the shredded chicken in the crust, with the drumstick tucked in the middle if you are using it, and spoon about 1½ cups of the sauce over the chicken. (Reserve some of the sauce to serve later with the cooked tamales.) Top with half of the *picadillo*.

Working on a sheet of plastic wrap, pat another round of dough out to form a 10-inch round (or square) and place it on top of the baking dish like a lid. Pinch the edges of dough together to completely enclose the filling. Then fold the edges of the banana leaves or foil up over the tamale and tie the whole package together with the strings. Repeat the process to make a second tamale. (The tamales may be wrapped in aluminum foil and frozen for up to 1 month at this point.)

Preheat the oven to 325°F. Place the two baking dishes with the *Mukbil Pollos* on a rack in a large roasting pan. Pour hot water halfway up the sides of the pan, and cover it tightly with a lid or heavy aluminum foil. Check every 30 minutes and add more water if needed. Bake for 1½ hours. (If frozen, bake for an additional 20 to 30 minutes.)

Remove the *Mukbil Pollos* from the roasting pan, and allow them to cool in the baking dishes for 10 to 15 minutes. Meanwhile, gently reheat the reserved sauce.

Carefully transfer the *Mukbil Pollos* to serving platters. Cut the strings and open the tamales at the table. Cut the tamales into wedges (this is difficult to do neatly if you have chosen to include the whole drumstick, but it is part of the tradition). Serve immediately, with the remaining sauce alongside.

SERVES 12

Like most agricultural societies, the Maya have always known the importance of rain. To ensure that the life-giving rains will come, inhabitants of farming villages join together in July for Chaachak. During this three-day ceremony, offerings are made to the gods of agriculture and hunting.

The traditional Chaachak feast includes *saka'*, a porridge made from dried corn; *balche'*, a honeyed bark liquor; *Pavo en K'ol Indio*, turkey simmered in a subtly spiced *masa*-thickened sauce (page 75); and *tutiwahs*, large firm tamales filled with a delicate pistachio-colored pumpkin-seed seasoning.

Because the Maya heavens are believed to consist of thirteen layers, a *Tutiwah* prepared by the village shamen is often an elaborate affair made up of thirteen layers of dough and filling. Our version is tasty and visually interesting, but much easier to assemble. Serve these with salsa or as an accompaniment to *Pavo en K'ol Indio*.

1 recipe *Yucatecan Tamale Dough* (page 55)

¾ cup *Recado de Pepita* (pumpkin-seed seasoning, page 38)

26 lightly toasted hulled pumpkin seeds (*pepitas*), for garnish

To make this dish you will need 2 large banana leaves, prepared for cooking (page 224), or 4 sheets cooking parchment or heavy-duty aluminum foil.

Preheat the oven to 325°F.

Divide the dough into 4 pieces and form them into rounds about 1 inch thick. Cover the rounds with plastic wrap to keep them from drying out.

Place two 22- to 24-inch-long sections of banana leaf side by side, rib down, on a work surface. Arrange the leaves so that they overlap by about 2 inches and form a rectangle that is approximately 16 x 22 inches.

Place 1 round of dough in the center of the rectangle and pat it out to form an 8-inch circle about ½ inch thick. Gently spread all but about 2 tablespoons of the *Recado de Pepita* over the dough. Pat out another circle of dough and place it on top of the first, like a layer on a cake. Then gently press the edges together, being careful not to distort the shape.

Form a Maya cross (+) in the top of the tamale with 13 indentations, beginning with 1 in the center and 3 for each branch of the cross. Place a bit of the *recado* and a pumpkin seed in each indentation. Fold the banana leaves up around the tamale as if wrapping a package, and tie it securely with string (page 218). Make another tamale in the same way. (The tamales may be refrigerated for up to 1 day or tightly unwrapped and frozen for up to 1 month.)

Place the tamales on a rack in a large steamer or deep roasting pan. Pour boiling water into the pan, making sure it does not touch the bottom of the tamales; there should be at least 2 to 3 inches of water below the rack so that the pan does not boil dry. Cover the pan tightly with a lid or with aluminum foil and place in the oven. Check every 30 minutes and add more water if needed. Bake for 1½ hours, or until the tamales are firm to the touch. (If frozen, allow 20 to 30 minutes additional steaming time.) Open the *Tutiwahs* at the table and cut them into wedges.

THE MAYA

UVEN
POTATO TAMALES

Tamales made of mashed potatoes instead of corn are typical of Quetzoltenago in eastern Guatemala. This recipe was given to Margoth Giron by the mother of a school friend from that region.

Uven are usually made for special occasions, such as Christmas and weddings. The filling may be either chicken or pork. Though they may be made smaller, normally *Uven* are about 6 inches long and 2½ to 3 inches wide. If banana leaves are not available, Margoth suggests wrapping the tamales in cooking parchment and tying them with unflavored "ribbon" dental floss, or simply wrapping them in aluminum foil. Margoth's family likes these tamales so much that she usually makes 8 to 10 dozen at a time! We cut the recipe down to make about 30 tamales, but it may be doubled or tripled if desired. Two to three tamales, served with a salad and a basket of hot tortillas, makes a great lunch or dinner.

One 5- to 6-pound chicken, or 2½- to 3-pound boneless pork roast

Chicken broth or salted water

1 pound plum tomatoes

1 white onion, peeled and quartered

2 heads garlic, peeled

1 pound red bell peppers, seeded and quartered

1 pound fresh tomatillos, papery husks removed

½ pound (about 1⅓ cups) lard, preferably home-rendered (page 217), or 1 cup vegetable oil

2 cups *Juy'vil* (pumpkin-sesame seed seasoning, page 39)

¼ cup *Recado Colorado* (annatto-seed seasoning, page 37)

2 tablespoons salt, or to taste

5 to 6 cups fresh bread crumbs

5 pounds russet, red, or white all-purpose potatoes, peeled

10 to 12 fresh jalapeño chiles, seeded and cut into thin strips (optional)

1 pound (4 cups) diced or shredded *queso fresco* or fresh mozzarella

For this recipe you will need two 16-ounce packages of banana leaves, prepared for cooking (page 224), or 30 12 x 15-inch sheets of cooking parchment or aluminum foil.

Place the chicken or pork in a large kettle, and add chicken broth or salted water to cover. Cover, bring to a boil, then lower the heat and simmer until cooked and tender, about 1 hour. Remove the kettle from the heat and allow the meat to cool in the broth. When it is cool enough to handle, remove the chicken or pork from the kettle and slice or shred the meat (discard the skin and bones from the chicken). Set the meat aside and strain the broth. Reserve 4 to 5 cups of the broth and set it aside. (The recipe can be prepared to this step 1 day in advance and refrigerated.)

Place the tomatoes, onion, garlic, bell peppers, and tomatillos in a vegetable steamer basket over hot water, or in a 2- to 3-quart saucepan with a little water. Cover and steam until the vegetables are just tender and the tomato skins have split, 15 to 20 minutes. Drain, and set aside to cool. When the vegetables are cool enough to handle, remove and discard the tomato skins and, if desired, trim off the tougher stem end of the tomatoes. Place the vegetables in a blender or food processor, and puree.

Place 4 cups of the reserved broth in a large (4- to 6-quart) saucepan. Stir in the pureed vegetables, the lard, *Juy'vil,* and *Recado Colorado.* Bring to a simmer over medium-high heat, stirring until throughly combined. Taste, and season with salt. (The mixture should taste a little salty at this point.) Stir in 5 cups of the bread crumbs. Reduce the heat to low and simmer, stirring often to keep the mixture from sticking, until it is as thick as oatmeal, about 30 minutes.

Meanwhile, bring a large pot of water to a boil and add the potatoes; cook until tender, then drain and mash them.

Stir the vegetable mixture into the potatoes and allow to cool. The potato mixture should have the consistency of firm mashed potatoes. If it seems too soft, add more bread crumbs; if it seems dry, add a little broth.

To make the tamales, simply set the pieces of banana leaf, parchment, or foil on your work surface.

Place ½ cup of the potato mixture in an oval mound in the center of the rectangle. Press 2 or 3 pieces of the meat into the potato mixture, and top with a few strips of jalapeño (if using) and 2 tablespoons of the cheese. Wrap the tamale up in a tight, neat rectangular package, and tie it with banana-leaf strings or kitchen string (page 218). If you are using aluminum foil, just fold and seal the edges.

Place the tamales in a large steamer or on a rack in a large roasting pan. Add boiling water to the pan, making sure it does not touch the bottom of the tamales. Cover tightly with a lid or foil, and steam for 40 minutes in a 350°F oven. Remove the tamales from the steamer and let them rest for about 10 minutes before serving. Open the wrappings carefully to avoid being burned by the steam. Leftover tamales may be refrigerated for 1 to 2 days, or frozen. Reheat them in a steamer or in the microwave.

GUATEMALAN BLACK BEAN TAMALES

In her landmark book *America's First Cuisines,* anthropologist and food historian Sophie D. Coe describes a kind of tamale often depicted in the painted designs on pottery from the Maya Classic period, A.D. 250 to 900. These paintings show a woman holding a plate of round objects with dark spirals on their upper surfaces. Coe explains that to form this kind of tamale, "the dough was spread on a piece of fabric, the filling spread on the dough, and then the whole thing rolled up like a jelly roll, using the fabric to help in the process. Sections of the roll could then be cut off, wrapped in leaves, tied and cooked." We were fascinated by this concept and were delighted to find a modern Maya cook who makes these "jelly roll" tamales.

Juanita Velasco, who shared several of her wonderful recipes with us, comes from the highlands of Guatemala but now lives in New York City. Since freshly ground *masa* is sometimes difficult to find in the United States, Juanita has converted her recipe to use *masa harina.* She recommends Maseca Instant Corn Masa because it is very finely ground. Modern Maya sometimes enrich their doughs with salt, meat broth, and/or lard, but Juanita's recipe calls only for *masa*—or *masa harina*—and water, just as it would have hundreds of years ago. Juanita pats out the dough on a board dusted with *masa harina,* instead of spreading it on fabric. We also have had good luck patting the dough out on sheets of plastic wrap.

These tamales make a wonderful first course, and if they are made smaller they are a great hors d'oeuvre. Serve them with *Eetch,* Juanita's fiery fresh tomato salsa (page 32). For variety, mix ½ cup well-drained chopped cooked spinach into the dough.

One 8-ounce package dried corn husks

1 large white onion, peeled and finely chopped

½ cup corn oil

3 cups *Tsah Bi Bu'ul* (black bean puree, page 46), or two 16-ounce cans refried black beans (see Note, page 64)

1 tablespoon salt, or to taste

6 cups *masa harina,* plus additional for the work surface

4 to 5 cups lukewarm water

Thoroughly rinse the corn husks under hot water, then place them in a pan or bowl. Cover with boiling water and set aside to soften for 45 minutes to 1 hour. Meanwhile, prepare the filling and dough.

In a large nonstick skillet, cook the onion over medium-high heat, stirring constantly, until most of the liquid evaporates, about 1 minute. Add the oil and sauté until the onions are slightly golden. Add the bean puree and salt. Cook, stirring, until the oil is incorporated and the mixture looks creamy and has thickened. Allow the bean filling to cool while you prepare the dough.

Prepare a tortilla dough with the *masa harina* and water as described on page 51. The dough should be moist but not sticky. Cover it with plastic wrap or a damp towel.

Spread the corn husks out on paper towels and pat dry.

Dust the work surface with extra *masa harina* or cover it with plastic wrap. With moistened hands, pat half of the dough into a 14 x 16-inch rectangle about ¼ inch thick. Spread half of the bean filling over the dough, leaving a 1-inch border on all sides. Roll up the dough from one long side, like a jelly roll, and press gently to seal the ends and edges.

(continued on page 64)

LEFT: *Ooben is formed by making a jelly roll of tortilla dough and a puree of black beans.*

So the spiral pattern shows clearly in each slice, use a thin meat-slicing knife or a length of thread to cut the roll into slices about 1½ inches thick. With the smoother (inner) side of a corn husk facing up, carefully place a slice near the wide end of the husk. Wrap both sides of the husk over the slice to enclose it, and fold the narrow pointed end over. The tamale will remain open on the wide end (page 222). Repeat with the remaining slices. Prepare and slice another tamale roll, using the remaining ingredients, and wrap the slices in the remaining corn husks.

Carefully arrange the tamales, seam side down, in a steamer or on the rack of a roasting pan. (It is all right to layer them.) Add boiling water to the pan, making sure it does not touch the bottom of the tamales. Cover tightly and steam on top of the stove or in a 350°F oven for 20 to 30 minutes, until the tamales are firm to the touch. Remove the tamales from the steamer with tongs, then let them rest for about 5 minutes. Serve tamales warm in their husks.

NOTE: If you are using canned refried black beans, use only 3 cups for the filling. Do not overfill the dough.

BATCHA
GUATEMALAN STUFFED FISH

This recipe—a whole fish seasoned with a pumpkin- and sesame-seed *recado* and stuffed with a flavorful mixture of cilantro, scallions, and ripe red tomatoes—originated in the highlands of Guatemala. Traditionally *Batcha* is roasted in a *pib*, the Maya earth oven. Since this is a highland dish, the fish most often used is one of the firm-fleshed freshwater varieties. Margoth Giron, our Maya friend who now lives in New York, makes *Batcha* with catfish or bass and sometimes a saltwater fish like porgy. We tested the recipe with a beautiful large rainbow trout and found it to be delicious. Serve the fish with a basket of hot tortillas or over rice.

One 2- to 3-pound whole fish (catfish, bass, trout, or other firm-fleshed variety) cleaned and scaled, with or without head

1 cup *Juy'vil* (pumpkin-sesame seed seasoning, page 39)

Salt and freshly ground black pepper to taste

1 bunch fresh cilantro, coarsely chopped

1 bunch scallions, coarsely chopped

½ pound cherry tomatoes, quartered

2 or 3 cloves garlic, peeled and minced

1 fresh jalapeño chile, seeded and minced, or 3 or 4 dried pequin chiles, mashed

For this recipe you will need 1 large banana leaf prepared for cooking (page 224) or two 12-inch-wide sheets of cooking parchment and string, and one 12 x 25-inch sheet of heavy-duty aluminum foil.

Preheat the oven to 350°F.

Rinse the fish carefully inside and out with cold water and pat dry. Rub the fish all over with the *Juy'vil,* and season it with salt and pepper. Lay out a rectangle of overlapping banana leaves (or two overlapping sheets of parchment) that is large enough to completely enclose the fish. Place the fish on the leaves.

In a mixing bowl, gently combine the cilantro, scallions, tomatoes, garlic, and chile. Stuff the fish body cavity with this mixture, and scatter any remaining mixture under and on top of the fish. Wrap the fish securely in the leaves and tie it like a package (page 218), using strings cut from the ribs of the banana leaves or kitchen string. Enclose the wrapped fish in the aluminum foil, and place it on the middle rack of the oven. Bake for 1 hour.

Remove the fish from the oven and let it rest for 10 minutes. Then remove the foil, being careful not to get burned by the steam.

Carefully transfer the leaf-wrapped fish to a serving platter. Cut the strings, and open and fold back the leaves. Pull off and discard the fins. Gently push aside the vegetables. With the point of a fish-serving knife or a metal spatula, make a horizontal cut just to the bone behind the head and above the tail of the fish. Do not cut off the head or tail. Then cut lengthwise down the center of the fish just to the bone, separating the two top fillets. Use the knife or spatula to gently lift aside the fillets and the stuffing, revealing the skeleton. Starting with the tail, gently lift out the whole skeleton. Gently push the stuffing and fillets back into place. Cut the boned fish into 4 to 6 servings, and serve immediately. Though most should now be removed, be careful to watch for bones when eating.

PESCADO EN TIKIN-XIC'
GRILLED FISH WITH *RECADO COLORADO*

On a sunny morning in January, Telchac Puerto is sleepy and uncrowded. It is off season at this popular seaside resort near Mérida—a great time to visit. We've come here to meet Diana Cetina Aguilar and to taste *Tikin-Xic'*, a Yucatecan specialty. As we approach Doña Diana's restaurant, Via del Mar, the aroma of freshly caught fish being grilled over a hardwood fire tickles our noses and makes our mouths water. The catch of the day is *huachinango,* red snapper.

We sit at a table on the terrace and watch the waves roll in from the Gulf of Mexico. The *Tikin-Xic'* is presented on a platter colorfully garnished with *Cebollas Encurtidas* (page 49), sliced tomatoes, and lime wedges. We wrap luscious, flaky morsels of fish in fresh tortillas and dip our "tacos" in a simple but incendiary sauce made of habaneros, lime juice, cilantro, and salt. A bowl of hot fluffy rice on the side helps put out the fire.

¾ cup *Recado Colorado* (annatto-seed seasoning, page 37)

2 tablespoons vegetable oil

1 cup bitter (Seville) orange juice, or ½ cup sweet orange juice combined with ½ cup lime juice

1 teaspoon salt, or to taste

Two 1½- to 2-pound whole red snappers, scaled and split lengthwise, or 2 pounds snapper or grouper fillets

4 to 6 bay leaves

1 cup *Cebollas Encurtidas* (pickled onions, page 49)

4 plum tomatoes, sliced

2 or 3 limes, cut into wedges

In a mixing bowl, dissolve the *Recado Colorado* in the vegetable oil, then stir in the orange juice. Season with salt. Place each fish in a large glass or ceramic dish and rub the flesh generously with the seasoning mixture. Scatter the bay leaves over the fish and marinate, refrigerated, for at least 1 hour or overnight.

Prepare a wood, charcoal, or gas grill.

Remove the fish from the dish, reserving the marinade. If you have a grilling basket, place a banana leaf, rib side down, in the basket and arrange the fish on top, skin side up. Or, instead of a banana leaf, oil a piece of aluminum foil and place it, oiled side up, in the basket and arrange the fish on top. Place the basket on the grill and cook for 15 minutes. Then turn the basket over, baste the fish with the reserved marinade, and cook on the other side for 15 minutes. The fish should flake easily with a fork.

(If you don't have a basket, place the leaf or foil directly on the grill rack and arrange the fish on it, skin side down. Grill, basting frequently with the reserved marinade, until the fish flakes easily, 20 to 30 minutes.)

Starting at the tail, gently lift out the backbone and pull off the fins. Discard the bones and arrange the fish on a platter. Garnish with *Cebollas Encurtidas*, tomatoes, and lime wedges, and serve immediately.

NOTES: If you don't have a grill, you can prepare this dish in the oven. Preheat the oven to 375°F. Place the fish in an oiled baking pan and bake, basting frequently, until it flakes easily, 20 to 30 minutes.

This fish is spicy, but if you'd like it even hotter, do as the Maya do and make a quick table salsa. Combine ¼ cup lime juice with a little chopped onion and cilantro, 1 or 2 slices of a habanero chile, and salt to taste. Habaneros are among the hottest of chiles, so be cautious when you drizzle this fiery potion on your food!

RIGHT: *Pescado en Tikin-Xic'* is served with a garnish of *Cebollas Encurtidas* and lime wedges.

THE MAYA

PESCADO CON PLATANO CAMULEAN
FISH FILLETS SIMMERED WITH PLANTAINS

SERVES
4 TO 6

Although they are not native, plantains and bananas have been a staple in the diet of indigenous peoples in the tropical regions of Central and South America for centuries. They were introduced, early in the Conquest, from the Canary Islands and have thrived in the New World. Plantains are eaten in different ways at different stages of ripeness. A green plantain, *platano macho,* is boiled in its skin, then peeled, sliced, and fried; a ripe plantain, *platano maduro,* is used to make desserts; and the ripe but firm *camulean* is just right for sautéed and simmered dishes like this one.

Just about any firm fish fillet will work well in this Honduran recipe. It is also a great way to prepare boneless chicken breasts and pork chops. When cooking chicken or pork, substitute chicken broth or water for the fish stock.

1½ pounds red snapper or other firm white fish fillets

Salt and freshly ground black pepper to taste

2 to 4 tablespoons corn oil or solid vegetable shortening

1 rounded tablespoon *pinole* (pinole) or yellow cornmeal

1 yellow onion

2 large ripe tomatoes, peeled and

diced, or one 14½-ounce can diced tomatoes

1 orange, yellow, or green bell pepper, seeded and chopped

2 fresh mild green chiles, such as Anaheim or New Mexican, seeded and diced

½ to 1 fresh jalapeño chile, seeded and finely chopped

1 cup fish stock (see Note) or water

2 slightly firm ripe plantains, or 2 or 3 green bananas

Hot cooked rice

1 tablespoon chopped fresh cilantro or parsley

Pat the fish fillets dry with paper towels, and season with salt and pepper. Place 2 tablespoons of the oil in a large sauté pan or deep skillet, and place over medium-high heat. Add the fillets and brown lightly on both sides, 4 to 5 minutes total. (Do not crowd the pan. If necessary, brown the fish in two batches, adding more oil as needed.) Remove the fillets and set them aside, leaving the oil in the pan.

Add the *pinole* to the pan and cook, stirring, over medium heat for 1 to 2 minutes, until golden brown (if using cornmeal, cook for 1 to 2 minutes more). Stir in the onion, tomatoes, and mild and hot chiles. Reduce the heat to medium-low. Cook, uncovered, stirring often, until the vegetables have begun to soften, about 15 minutes. Add the fish stock and simmer for another 15 minutes.

Meanwhile, peel the plantains, cut them in half, and then slice them lengthwise. Place the plantains on top of the vegetables, cover the pan, and simmer for 10 minutes. Return

the fish fillets to the pan and simmer until the fish is hot and cooked through, about 10 minutes. Place the fish fillets on a bed of hot fluffy rice. Surround them with the sliced plantains, and spoon the sauce over all. Sprinkle with the cilantro and serve.

NOTE: To make a quick fish stock, place fish skeletons, with heads attached, in a large pot and add cold water to cover. Add 1 peeled quartered onion, 1 peeled carrot, 1 rib celery with leaves attached, a few peppercorns, and 1 to 2 teaspoons salt. Bring to a boil, then reduce the heat to low and simmer for at least 30 minutes. Strain the broth, discarding the bones and vegetables.

THE MAYA

68

Pit-cooking in the Yucatecan fashion produces meat that is flavorful, moist, and succulent. The pit (*pib*) also has religious significance for the Maya. Thanksgiving offerings of food—whether meat, special tamales, or the roasted ears of new corn—are not considered appropriate fare for Maya agricultural deities unless they are cooked in the bosom of the earth.

A *pib* is a rectangular pit about 18 inches deep and wide enough to accommodate whatever is being roasted. It is lined with a hardwood kindling, such as oak. The wood is covered with an even layer of stones; in the Yucatán, they use limestone, which won't shatter when heated. The wood is ignited, and when the stones are red-hot, pans of food are placed on top. The pit is then covered, first with leafy oak branches and then with a large sheet of corrugated metal. A space is left at one end to open the *pib* after cooking. It is covered with a piece of canvas tarp. Dirt is shoveled over the pit so that no smoke escapes. Depending on the thickness of the meat being prepared, it is left to cook for 1 to 2 hours. When the *pib* is opened, a delectable aroma wafts through the air.

Nothing quite duplicates the flavor of *pib*-roasting, but the method described here achieves a similar effect in a home oven. If desired, the same method may be used to cook the pork over indirect heat in a covered grill. In that case, sprinkle some damp wood chips over the coals to give the pork some of the smoky flavor of a traditional *pib*.

¼ cup *Recado Colorado* (annatto-seed seasoning, page 37)

⅓ cup bitter (Seville) orange juice, or 2 tablespoons sweet orange juice combined with 3 tablespoons lime juice

Salt to taste

One 3½ to 4-pound boneless pork loin roast

6 cloves garlic, peeled and slivered

16 small (4- to 5-inch) corn tortillas, preferably homemade (pages 51–52)

1 recipe *Cebollas Encurtidas* (pickled onions, page 49)

1 recipe *Xni Pec* (roasted tomato and chile salsa, page 33)

For this recipe you will need 2 large banana leaves prepared for cooking (page 224), or 3 or 4 sheets of cooking parchment, or 3 or 4 sheets of wide heavy-duty aluminum foil.

In a small bowl combine the *Recado Colorado* with the orange juice, and add salt to taste. Place the pork in a shallow roasting pan. With a sharp knife, make 1-inch-deep incisions all over the roast to allow the seasonings to penetrate. Rub the pork all over with the *recado* mixture and place the garlic slivers in the incisions. If desired, cover the pan tightly with aluminum foil and allow to marinate, refrigerated, overnight.

Preheat the oven to 325°F. Arrange overlapping banana-leaf pieces to form a 24 x 26-inch rectangle. Place the seasoned pork in the center, and pour any remaining *recado* mixture over it. Wrap the leaves around the roast like a package (page 218). Tie it with strings cut from the banana-leaf ribs or with kitchen string. Place the package on the rack of a broiler pan. Fill the pan about halfway with boiling water. Cover the pan tightly with a tent of aluminum foil, being sure to seal the edges. Bake until the pork is tender, 3½ hours. Halfway through the roasting time, wearing oven mitts, carefully lift the foil and add more boiling water as needed.

Transfer the roast to a serving platter or large cutting board. Cut the strings and open the leaves, being careful not to get burned by the steam. Slice the pork and serve in tacos made with hot fresh tortillas. Garnish with *Cebollas Encurtidas* and top with the *Xni Pec*.

COSTILLAS DE CERDO A LA YUCATECA
YUCATECAN-STYLE PORK RIBS

SERVES
4 TO 6

There are many fine cooks in the town of TixKoKob, but perhaps the most renowned is Silvio Campos. Don Silvio is famous for his *Cochinita Pibil* (page 69). He sells his pork at the market in TixKoKob and is often called upon to cater weddings and other feasts.

A few years ago, celebrity chef and respected Mexican cooking authority Rick Bayless visited TixKoKob and met Silvio. Rick was so impressed by Silvio's cooking that he invited him to Chicago to appear as guest chef at his restaurant, the Frontera Grill. Since then many other well-known cooks have made their way to Silvio Campos's door.

We visited Don Silvio on a Friday, somehow expecting to find a venerable old gentleman with a walking stick. Instead we were greeted by a vigorous young man who served us a cold drink and escorted us into his kitchen. Silvio was busy seasoning pork to be baked in the *pib* for Saturday's market. He took a break to chat with us, as his friend and neighbor Carmen Mendoza patted out perfectly round corn tortillas. We shared a light lunch of these grilled baby back ribs seasoned with *Recado Colorado* (page 37), accompanied by Doña Carmen's fresh hot tortillas and a bowl of *Xni Pec*, the fiery tomato, onion, and habanero salsa (page 33).

3 racks baby back ribs (about 3 pounds)	1 fresh mild green chile, such as Anaheim	¼ cup *Recado Colorado* (annatto-seed seasoning, page 37)
1 white onion, unpeeled, roasted (page 217)	2 teaspoons dried oregano (preferably Mexican oregano)	¼ cup bitter (Seville) orange juice, or 3 tablespoons sweet orange juice combined with 1 tablespoon lime juice
1 head garlic, unpeeled	Salt	

Place the ribs, vegetables, oregano, and 1 teaspoon salt in a large pot or Dutch oven. Add enough water to cover the ribs by 2 inches. Bring the water to a boil over high heat. Reduce the heat to low and simmer, covered, for about 45 minutes, until the ribs are tender. Remove the ribs from the broth and drain well.

Meanwhile, prepare a wood, charcoal, or gas grill.

In a small bowl, combine the *Recado Colorado* and orange juice to make a thin paste, and season to taste with salt. Rub the ribs generously with the *recado* mixture. (The ribs may be prepared to this point and refrigerated for up to 2 days before grilling.) Grill the ribs over a medium-hot fire for about 15 minutes, turning them once, until hot and slightly charred.

LEFT: Yucatecan-style Pork Ribs are accompanied by *Xni Pec* and a fresh tortilla.

ONSIKIL BI CEH
VENISON IN PUMPKIN-SEED SAUCE

Because of its abundant game, the Yucatán peninsula was once known as "the Land of the Turkey and the Deer." The Yucatán deer, a small white-tailed variety, was very important to the pre-Conquest Maya in this region, many of whom were hunters. The deer is associated with god M, the god of hunting and war. Two ceremonies were held each year to honor the deities who protected the animals. The first ceremony asked their blessing for a successful hunt, and the second asked forgiveness for having taken the animal's life. Unfortunately, in modern times the deer have not been treated with the respect accorded to them by the ancients. Overhunting and man's encroachment on their grazing land have taken a heavy toll on these beautiful animals and measures are now being taken to protect them. In fact, although venison is a local specialty, it is no longer legal to serve it in restaurants in the Yucatán.

Onsikil Bi Ceh, or *Pipian de Venado,* is one of the most traditional venison recipes of the Yucatecan Maya. The addition of toasted ground pumpkin seeds and fresh corn *masa* gives the sauce for this exotic stew a velvety richness and a slightly nutty flavor. It is also a wonderful way to prepare pork or lamb.

3 pounds boneless venison, pork, or lamb (loin, leg, or shoulder)

2 tablespoons lard, preferably home-rendered (page 217), or vegetable oil

6 cups water

1 head garlic, unpeeled, roasted (page 217)

1 white onion, unpeeled, roasted (page 217)

Salt and freshly ground black pepper to taste

1½ teaspoons dried oregano (preferably Mexican oregano), crumbled

1 cup *Recado de Pepita* (pumpkin-seed seasoning, page 38)

1 cup *Recado Colorado* (annatto-seed seasoning, page 37)

1 cup fresh *masa* and ½ cup lukewarm water, or 1 cup *masa harina* and 1 cup lukewarm water

4 large tomatoes, quartered

3 tablespoons chopped fresh epazote or cilantro, plus additional for garnish

2 limes, cut into wedges

Cut the venison into 2½- to 3-inch cubes and pat dry with paper towels. Melt the lard in a large Dutch oven over medium-high heat. When the lard is hot, add the venison and brown on all sides. (Do not crowd the pan or the venison will not brown properly. If necessary, brown the meat in two or three batches.) Add the water, garlic, the onion, and oregano. Bring to a boil, cover, and reduce the heat to medium-low. Simmer for 30 minutes, or until the venison is tender. Season to taste with salt and pepper.

Meanwhile, in a medium-size bowl, whisk the *Recado de Pepita* and the *Recado Colorado* with enough water (about 1½ cups) to make a mixture with the consistency of pancake batter. Set aside. In another mixing bowl combine the fresh *masa* or *masa harina* with enough water to make another mixture with the consistency of pancake batter. Set aside.

Strain the venison, pouring the broth into a large mixing bowl. You should have about 5 cups of broth. Discard the onion and garlic. Reserve the meat. Return the broth to the Dutch oven. Pour the *recado* and *masa* mixtures through a strainer, and whisk them into the venison broth.

Return the meat to the pot, and add the tomatoes and 3 tablespoons epazote. Bring to a simmer over medium heat, stirring constantly. Reduce the heat to low and simmer for 25 to 30 minutes, until the sauce thickens. Spoon the stew into shallow soup bowls and garnish each serving with a wedge of lime and chopped epazote.

RIGHT: A bowl of *Onsikil Bi Ceh* is served with a lime-wedge garnish and a stack of warm tortillas.

THE MAYA

GALLINA EN PINOL

HEN IN CORNMEAL-THICKENED BROTH

When Marta Hazlett was a little girl growing up in the village of San Louis in central Honduras, *Gallina en Pinol* was a favorite dish that her mother, Eva Oviedo, and grandmother, Maria de los Angeles Oviedo, often prepared for Sunday lunch. During the week, Marta's family, like most Hondurans, ate a mostly vegetarian diet of corn porridge, tortillas, beans, rice, fresh vegetables, and fruit, with some eggs and cheese. But for Sunday lunch there was always meat—here, simmered in a corn-thickened broth. Unlike the fresh masa-thickened sauces of the Yucatán, however, the corn used in this recipe is first parched and then ground to make a product called *pinol*.

Though her grandma's recipe calls for a flavorful but tough and long-cooking "stewing hen," Marta usually selects a more tender and readily available young chicken. To give the broth more intense flavor, she adds some chicken broth to the poaching liquid. If you do use a hen or stewing fowl, increase the initial simmering time by at least 1 hour and omit the chicken broth in the recipe. Since *pinol*, also called *pinole*, is not always available in the United States, Marta suggests substituting yellow cornmeal. The cooking method is the same, but when using cornmeal, allow it to toast a bit more in the oil to achieve a subtle "nutty" flavor similar to that of *pinol*. Serve this stew with hot corn tortillas.

One 3½- to 4-pound chicken, cut into 8 pieces

3 large ripe tomatoes, peeled and chopped, or one 14½-ounce can diced tomatoes

1 green bell pepper, seeded and chopped

1 yellow onion, peeled and chopped

4 tablespoons chopped fresh cilantro

2 large cloves garlic, peeled and minced

1 quart chicken broth

1 teaspoon salt

¼ teaspoon freshly ground black pepper

¼ teaspoon ground cumin

3 tablespoons corn oil

1 cup *pinol* (*pinole*) or yellow cornmeal

Place the chicken, tomatoes, bell pepper, onion, 2 tablespoons of the cilantro, and the garlic in a large pot. Add the chicken broth and about 4 cups water—enough to cover the chicken and vegtables. Stir in the salt, black pepper, and cumin. Bring to a boil over high heat, then reduce the heat to low and simmer, covered, for about 45 minutes, until the chicken is tender and cooked through.

Meanwhile, heat 1 tablespoon of the oil in a large nonstick or well-seasoned skillet. Add the *pinol* and cook, stirring, over medium heat, until it is lightly toasted, 2 to 3 minutes (about 5 minutes for cornmeal). Remove the *pinol* and set aside. Add the remaining 2 tablespoons oil to the skillet. Remove the chicken from the broth with tongs, and brown, a few pieces at a time, in the skillet. Do not crowd the pan or allow the pieces to touch, or they won't brown properly. Return the browned chicken to the broth and stir in the reserved *pinol*. Cook, stirring, over medium-low heat for about 10 minutes, until the broth thickens to a sauce-like consistency. If the sauce seems thick, add a little chicken broth or water. Spoon the chicken and sauce into shallow bowls. Sprinkle with the remaining cilantro, and serve.

PAVO EN K'OL INDIO
TURKEY SIMMERED IN *MASA*-THICKENED BROTH

The turkey is a native bird of the Americas. The ancient Maya knew and domesticated the species we are most familiar with today (*Meleagris gallopavo*) and hunted the wilder ocellated turkey (*Meleagris ocellata*). Because they are considered a sacred fowl, symbolic of rain, turkeys are important even today in the ritual world of the Maya.

Pavo en K'ol Indio—turkey simmered in a delicate, flavorful broth thickened with corn dough—is served at special ceremonies for healing, planting, and praying for rain. This is a wonderful dish, fit for the gods but easy enough for mere mortals to prepare. It is usually served with a wedge of *Tutiwah* (page 59), but you can also simply serve a basket of warm tortillas on the side.

One 12- to 14-pound turkey

Salt to taste

1 or 2 fresh jalapeño or other hot green chiles, roasted and left whole (page 217)

2 heads garlic, unpeeled, roasted (page 217)

1 large yellow onion, unpeeled, roasted (page 217)

1 cup *Recado Colorado* (annatto-seed seasoning, page 37)

3 cups *masa harina*

1 cup *Xni Pec* (roasted tomato and chile salsa, page 33) or other salsa

Fresh cilantro sprigs, for garnish

Rinse the turkey under cold running water. Rub it inside and out with salt, and place it in a large stockpot, with enough water to cover. (If your pot is not large enough hold a whole turkey, cut it into more manageable pieces.) Add the roasted vegetables. Stir enough water into the *Recado Colorado* to make a pourable liquid, and add it to the stockpot. Bring to a simmer over medium-high heat. Cover, and reduce the heat to low. Cook the turkey in barely simmering broth until tender, about 3 hours. If time permits and you have space in your refrigerator, place the pot in the refrigerator with the lid askew when the broth is still warm, and allow the turkey to cool completely in the broth. Cooling the poached poultry in its broth will make the meat more moist and juicy.

Remove the turkey from the broth and pull the meat from the bones. Shred the meat, or cut it into bite-size pieces. Strain the broth, discarding the vegetables. (The recipe may be made ahead to this point 1 to 2 days in advance and refrigerated.)

Skim off any fat that has gathered on top of the broth. (If you plan to make the *Tutiwah*, reserve the fat and 2 cups of the broth to make the tamale dough. This fat may be substituted for some of the lard used in the recipe on page 59.)

Reserve 1 quart of the broth and return the remaining broth to the pot. There should be at least 10 cups; if not, add some water.

When the reserved quart of broth has cooled, whisk in the *masa harina*, stirring until the mixture is smooth. Gradually whisk the *masa harina* mixture into the broth in the stockpot, and cook over medium heat, stirring, until the sauce has thickened enough to coat the back of a spoon. Return the turkey meat to the pot, and add salt to taste. Simmer over low heat, stirring often, for 15 to 20 minutes to blend the flavors. Serve, topping each portion with a spoonful of *Xni Pec*. Garnish with the cilantro.

IS-WAHES DULCES
SWEET FRESH CORN TORTILLAS

MAKES
ABOUT 30
TORTILLAS

To celebrate the young corn, the Maya, like the other great corn cultures of the Americas, prepare special dishes that are eaten only during the time of the harvest, in early autumn. *Is-wahes* are delicate fresh corn tortillas that are prepared for *La Promicia,* the Promise, the thanksgiving ceremony that honors and nourishes the deities and spirits responsible for a bountiful harvest. *Is-wahes* are traditionally served accompanied by *Pibilnales,* fresh ears of corn roasted in an earth oven, and by *Ak'Sa'* (page 47), a fresh corn porridge.

The classic *Is-wahes* are made from sun-dried fresh corn *masa,* salt, and a little water. The corn is ground and sun-dried for 2 to 3 days. It is then ground again, pressed through a sieve and mixed with salt and water to form a sticky dough. Tortillas made from fresh *masa* are like a naturally sweet cornbread. Over the years, especially in larger towns, some cooks have added lard, sugar, flour, and eggs to the original recipe and have cut the sun-drying time down to a day. These *Is-Wahes Dulces* are sweet like shortbread.

Though both the traditional and the sweet versions of *Is-wahes* are delicious, we have chosen to include the sweet one, because the dough is easier to handle. Purists may want to grind their corn by hand or in a food mill and sun-dry the *masa,* but in experimenting with this recipe we came up with a couple of time- and labor-saving techniques. We tried both fresh corn purchased at the farmers' market and the supermarket and frozen corn niblets. Because of the differences in starch levels in different varieties of corn, we had the best and most consistent results when using the frozen corn. We dried the niblets at a low temperature in the oven and then pureed them in the food processor and added the remaining ingredients.

Though *Is-wahes* are best when served fresh, Maya cooks sometimes make extra, and punch a hole through the middles while they are warm. When thoroughly cooled and then sun-dried for one to two days, the leftover *Is-wahes* are strung on a string and hung from the rafters, out of reach of animals and children, to be reserved for later use.

One 16-ounce package frozen corn kernels

½ cup lard, preferably home-rendered (page 217), butter, or solid vegetable shortening, plus additional for the skillet

1 ⅓ cups all-purpose flour

2 eggs, beaten

4 tablespoons sugar, or to taste

¼ teaspoon salt

Preheat the oven to 200°F.

Spread the corn out on a baking sheet and dry in the oven, stirring occasionally, for 3 hours. Remove the corn from the oven and allow it to cool to room temperature. Place the corn in a food processor fitted with the steel knife blade. Pulse on and off until the corn is thoroughly chopped. Add the lard, flour, eggs, sugar, and salt. Pulse on and off until a soft, slightly sticky dough forms. Allow the dough to rest for about 5 minutes.

Lightly grease a well-seasoned or nonstick griddle or large skillet and place over medium heat. An electric pancake griddle works well if you have one.

With lightly floured hands, roll the dough into a walnut-size ball. Place the ball on a sheet of plastic wrap and pat it out to form a tortilla about 5-inches in diameter, following the instructions on pages 51–52. Gently peel away the plastic wrap and place the tortilla on the griddle, with the side that was next to the plastic facing up. Reduce the heat to medium-low and cook the tortilla for about 5 minutes, until golden brown on the bottom. Using a spatula, carefully flip the tortilla and cook for 5 minutes on the other side. Remove to a rack and repeat with the remaining dough. Serve at room temperature.

DULCE DE CAMOTE
CANDIED SWEET POTATOES

While walking through the market in the Yucatecan city of TixKoKob we noticed a pretty young woman selling candied sweet potatoes. The *camotes* were swimming in a rich amber-colored syrup flavored with cinnamon sticks and a few slices of bitter orange. We watched as the vendor used tongs to remove sweet potato quarters from the syrup. She wrapped them in brown paper cones and handed them to happy customers, who walked off eating *camotes* as we would eat ice cream cones.

In talking with other Maya cooks we found that *Dulce de Camote* is popular not only as street food but also as a proper dessert. Candied sweet potatoes are delicious served warm or cool in their syrup and outstanding when topped with crème fraîche or spooned over vanilla ice cream. Peeled chunks of pumpkin and winter squash are often prepared and eaten in the same manner.

These days most cooks prepare these *dulces* using *piloncillos*, cones of unrefined brown sugar, but originally the syrup was probably made with Maya honey.

1½ pounds red or yellow sweet potatoes or yams	**1 to 2 pieces Mexican cinnamon or 1 small cinnamon stick**	**1 slice lime, with peel**
1 cup honey or firmly packed light or dark brown sugar	**1 slice orange, with peel**	

Peel and quarter the sweet potatoes. In a large wide-bottomed saucepan combine either honey and ¼ cup water or brown sugar and ½ cup water. Add the sweet potatoes and cinnamon. Cover the pan and bring to a boil over medium heat, then reduce the heat to low. Cook the sweet potatoes, uncovered, turning and basting occasion-ally with the syrup, for about 2 hours, until they are tender but still hold their shape. The syrup should be fairly thick. Turn off the heat and add the orange and lime slices. Allow the sweet potatoes to cool in the syrup. Serve alone or with vanilla ice cream or crème fraîche.

HA TSIKIL KAB
HONEY AND PUMPKIN-SEED CANDY

In 1517 Francisco Hernández de Cordóba led an expedition to the island of Cozumel and the Yucatán peninsula. He was impressed by the Maya's extensive honey production and described seeing thousands of beehives and sampling the excellent white honey.

The question of whether the pre-Conquest Maya were also candy-makers is open to debate. Some authorities claim that confectionary techniques were first introduced by the Spanish, who were notorious for their sweet tooth. We do know, however, that the Maya cooked down watery honey to make it easier to store and that both honey and squash seeds were frequent Maya offerings to the gods. Whether the recipe that follows is pre-Columbian or post-Conquest, these golden candies are delicious, easy to make, and very Maya.

2 cups hulled raw pumpkin seeds (*pepitas*)	**1 cup honey**

In a large skillet over medium-low heat toast the pumpkin seeds, stirring constantly to keep them from burning. When the seeds start to puff and make popping noises they are done. Transfer the seeds to a heavy saucepan and stir in the honey. Cook over medium heat, stirring constantly, until the honey begins to foam and bubble. Reduce heat to medium-low and continue to stir and simmer for 10 minutes more.

Drop the candy by tablespoons onto a lightly oiled baking sheet and allow to cool. Store the candies in an airtight container for up to 1 month.

The Americas have given the world many important foods, but none more fascinating than chocolate. For many, chocolate is not a food but a passion. It is said that the Aztec emperor Motecuhzoma so craved *Chocoatl,* the sacred beverage made from cocoa beans, that he consumed fifty golden goblets of it in a day.

The first cocoa trees probably grew in the tropical lowlands of Mexico and Central America. Ancient Toltec myth credits the feathered serpent god Quetzalcoatl with planting these trees and bringing chocolate, food of the gods, to man. The blossoms that grow in clusters on the main branches and on the trunk of the cocoa tree produce pods about eight inches long. These pods are harvested and split open to reveal amethyst-colored seeds, or beans, embedded in a pale pink pulp. The beans, after being fermented, cleaned, roasted, and ground, eventually become chocolate or cocoa powder.

Both the Maya and the Aztec treasured chocolate. The Aztec bagged the beans in standard weights and used these bags as their primary form of currency. In both cultures, *Chocoatl* was consumed during religious rites and was also considered to be a potent aphrodisiac and a source of quick energy.

In pre-Columbian America, chocolate was prepared by roasting the cocoa beans on a hot *comal* (griddle) until they darkened and began to exude their oil. The roasted beans were allowed to cool, then rubbed over a hair sieve to separate them from the hulls. The shelled beans, or nibs, were ground with a *mano* (pestle) in a heated *metate* (stone mortar) to form a paste, and then were shaped into small cakes and allowed to cool and harden. Sometimes a cinnamon-like spice (probably allspice), dried red chile, and annatto (*achiote*) seeds, which gave the mixture a reddish tinge, were ground with the beans. To prepare *Chocoatl,* the chocolate cakes were melted in boiling water, brought to a boil again, and then beaten with a *molinillo* (wooden whisk) until frothy. The Aztec apparently preferred to drink *Chocoatl* cold and unsweetened, though the beverage was sometimes flavored with a vanilla bean. The Maya were skilled beekeepers and often added honey to their hot version of *Chocoatl.*

(continued on page 82)

RIGHT: The chocolate of the Maya frequently included dried chile, while *Chocoatl,* their sacred hot chocolate drink, was sweetened with honey. The wooden *molinillo* was used to whisk the froth.

CHOCOATL
MAYA HOT CHOCOLATE

Hernando Cortès brought chocolate to Spain in 1519. Following the Maya lead, Spaniards sweetened their chocolate. They ground the nibs with sugar and added cinnamon and ground almonds to the mixture. They also, on occasion, prepared hot chocolate using milk instead of water. By the seventeenth century, the lust for chocolate had spread throughout Europe.

Modern commercially produced Mexican chocolate is similar to the original Spanish mixture. It is sweetened with coarse sugar, flavored with cinnamon, almonds, and vanilla, and shaped into rounds. Though this convenient form of chocolate is widely available, traditional native people throughout Mexico and Central America continue to roast, grind, and flavor their own chocolate much as their ancestors did.

We have been fortunate to find a mail-order source for both high-quality cocoa nibs (roasted shelled cocoa beans) and pure unsweetened chocolate (see Sources). Though it will not be as good, unsweetened baking chocolate may be substituted in the recipe that follows.

1 quart water or milk

⅓ to ½ cup honey, to taste

1 vanilla bean, split or 1 teaspoon pure vanilla extract

One 2-inch cinnamon stick (preferably Mexican cinnamon)

½ teaspoon annatto (*achiote*) seeds, ground (optional)

⅛ teaspoon dried ground *guajillo* or other red chile (optional)

¼ pound cocoa nibs, ground, or pure unsweetened chocolate or unsweetened baking chocolate

In a large saucepan combine the water, honey, vanilla, cinnamon, annatto (if using), and chile (if using). Bring the mixture to a boil over medium-high heat. Remove the pan from the heat, add the chocolate, and stir until melted and thoroughly combined. Return the pan to the heat and bring the mixture to a rolling boil (if you are using milk, bring it to just below the boiling point). Remove the pan from the heat for a moment, then return it to the heat and bring it to a boil (or almost to a boil) a third time. Remove the pan from the heat and beat with a whisk or rotary beater until frothy on top. Pour three-fourths of the chocolate into 4 cups. Beat the remaining chocolate in the saucepan until a thick froth forms. Spoon the froth on top of the chocolate in the cups and serve.

NOTE: If you choose to grind your own chocolate nibs, a modern alternative to the *metate* is a small clean electric coffee grinder. Grind the nibs, 2 tablespoons at a time; if desired, add a few annatto seeds and a pinch of dried chiles to each batch. Grind together to a fine powder. Remove powder from the grinder and warm it over a hot-water bath for about 5 minutes or at low temperature in a microwave oven for 1 to 2 minutes. Stir mixture until it becomes a smooth, glossy paste. While still warm, form the paste into small round cakes and allow to cool until firm in the refrigerator. When cool, the cakes may be stored in an airtight container. Two tablespoons of nibs make one ½-ounce cake of pure, unsweetened chocolate. You will need 2 homemade cakes to equal 1 ounce for each serving of hot chocolate.

X-TANCHUCHUA
CHOCOLATE AND MAIZE DRINK

In pre-Columbian times chocolate was a beverage of the nobility and the upper classes of Mesoamerica. The average Maya or Aztec would drink chocolate only on special ceremonial occasions, such as at a birth, wedding, or funeral. To stretch this precious commodity, and also to make it easier to transport from one place to another, cocoa beans were often ground and mixed with toasted ground corn or nuts. Chocolate mixed with either fresh or toasted ground corn was made into a thick hot drink that the Maya of the Yucatán call *X-Tanchuchua*. It is traditionally served at the festival of Ok Na, a celebration held in late December during which temples are cleaned and repaired and prayers are offered to the gods of agriculture for abundant spring rain.

⅓ **cup honey or dark brown sugar**

3⅔ **cups water or milk, or a mixture of the two**

1 **cinnamon stick (preferably Mexican cinnamon)**

Pinch of salt

⅓ **cup *masa harina* and ⅓ cup unsweetened cocoa powder or ⅔ cup *pinolillo* (finely ground toasted corn combined with cocoa)**

½ **teaspoon pure vanilla extract, optional**

In a heavy saucepan combine the honey and 3 cups water. Add the cinnamon and salt and place over medium-high heat. Bring to a simmer, stirring to dissolve the honey. In a small mixing bowl combine the *masa harina* and cocoa. Gradually stir in the remaining ⅔ cup water to form a paste.

Whisk the *masa* mixture into the simmering honey mixture in the saucepan. Add the vanilla, if using. Bring to a boil and cook, stirring, for about 5 minutes, until the chocolate is smooth and has begun to thicken. Pour through a strainer into cups and serve.

Though the Maya city-states of the Classic period (A.D. 250 to 900) were often at war with one another, they maintained good trade relations with neighboring groups such as the Totonac of Veracruz. The Maya were accomplished beekeepers, and one of their articles of trade was honey. Veracruz was the source of another rare luxury item, vanilla, which the Totonac traded for Maya honey and cocoa beans.

Vanilla (*Vanilla planifolia, Vanilla fragrans, or Vanilla aromatica*) is the fruit of a climbing orchid indigenous to southeastern Mexico, the West Indies, Central America, and northern South America. The Totonac are credited with being the first to discover wild vanilla—which they called *xanath*—and to cultivate it.

Vanilla is among the most labor-intensive agricultural product in the world. Demand is far greater than supply. The average retail price of a high-quality bean is between two and three dollars. This may sound like an extravagance but a bean may be used more than once. After steeping, remove the bean and rinse and dry it. Beans may be stored in an airtight bottle, or in a canister of sugar. Keep vanilla extract capped in a cool, dark place.

When traveling abroad, beware of bargain vanilla even if it is labeled "pure." Labeling laws vary from one country to another. Synthetic vanilla extract, particularly in Mexico and the Caribbean, may contain coumarin, used in blood-thinning medicines as an anticoagulant.

The recipe that follows combines the honey of the Maya and the vanilla of the Totonacs with fruits like peaches, plums, and cherries that originated in the Old World but have thrived in the New World.

1½ cups honey	6 to 8 small, ripe but firm peaches (about 2 pounds)	2 to 4 thin slices of lime, halved
3½ cups water		
1 vanilla bean, split, or 1 tablespoon pure vanilla extract	6 to 8 small, ripe but firm plums	
	½ pound fresh cherries with stems	

In a three-quart saucepan, combine honey and water. Place pan over medium heat and bring to a simmer, stirring to dissolve honey. Place vanilla bean in syrup and reduce heat to low.

Meanwhile bring another large saucepan of water to a boil. Plunge peaches into boiling water for a few seconds, then remove and peel. With a small sharp knife make 4 vertical slices in the peeled peaches and in the plums so they may absorb the syrup. Add peaches and plums to simmering syrup and poach fruit, stirring gently from time to time for 15 minutes. Add cherries and continue to poach for an additional 10 to 15 minutes or until fruit is tender but still holds its shape. Allow fruit to cool in the syrup. Remove vanilla bean, and rinse, dry, and store as recommended above. Serve compote chilled or at room temperature. Garnish with thin slices of lime.

LEFT: A refreshing compote of peaches, plums, and cherries, poached in a honey-vanilla syrup.

the aztec

A Culture and a Cuisine Misunderstood

MICHAEL D. COE

If any people have received bad press through the ages, the Aztec certainly have. Defeated by both European microbes and advanced military technology, the process of defaming and belittling them began with their Spanish conquerors and has continued down to our day. But we know that they had a side considerably more benevolent than that of bloodthirsty cannibals; for example, Aztec intellectuals and even one of their kings created some of the world's most beautiful poetry. They were great farmers and botanic experimenters, and gave to the world a host of important domesticated plants, including maize, beans, squash, tomatoes, and chile peppers. Not the least of the gifts bestowed by the Aztec has been their cuisine, one of the most sophisticated ever developed.

The Aztec began as semi-nomadic barbarians, arriving in central Mexico during the fourteenth century from a homeland in the north, and they never forgot their humble roots. They were always frugal eaters with a somewhat puritan ethic, and wild animal and plant foods continued to play an important part in their diet through the Conquest and into the Colonial period. When they came into the beautiful Valley of Mexico, eventually to found their island-capital, Tenochtitlan, they took over many of the customs, domesticated plants, and foodways of older, more settled civilizations; yet they typically remained ambivalent about such luxuries. The use of chocolate, for instance, was restricted to the nobility and the warriors, and was always used as a religious drink. That is the major reason why one never finds chocolate used in Aztec cookery (unlike in the *mole poblano* of Colonial and modern Mexico).

We have a few precious ethnographic accounts of Aztec cuisine, mainly from the pen of the sixteenth-century friar Bernadino de Sahugún. While these records tell us much about what was sold in the enormous Aztec markets, and give us the names and general ingredients of a host of dishes, there are no real recipes as we know them. The basis of the Aztec diet, of course, was maize, considered an entirely sacred substance because they believed the gods had manufactured human beings from maize dough. There were many kinds and colors of maize, just as there are in today's Mexico. This staple food was a major ingredient in stews, and was ground into dough for tortillas and tamales. Maize dough could also be mixed with water to make the gruel known as *atolli*. Sahagún mentions an amazing number of names for different tamale dishes, suggesting to me that even the myriad ways of making tamales in modern Mexican kitchens are a poor reflection of what the Aztec knew and ate. But if a nutritionist could analyze the typical diet, probably most of what an Aztec family actually consumed was in the form of tortillas.

Many books describe the triad of maize, beans, and squash in the native diet, but just as important were chiles in innumerable forms and degrees of hotness. The Aztec often fasted for religious reasons, and a truly severe fast called for abstinence from salt and chile, an indication of the high esteem in which this vitamin-laden food was held.

Almost no animal food source in the Valley of Mexico was neglected by the Aztec cook. Venison and wild migratory waterfowl formed an important part of the cuisine. In contrast to the diversity of domesticated plants utilized by these people, the array of domesticated fauna available as food was very limited; besides turkeys, Muscovy ducks, and stingless bees, dogs were a source of meat. The latter may not appeal to modern Americans, but even the Spaniards came to appreciate Aztec dog meat, which came from a special breed fed exclusively on vegetables, rather than on meat and kitchen scraps. And any traveler in backcountry Mexico knows that all kinds of insects are still eaten enthusiastically; we know that this was also the case with the Aztec.

Most food was prepared by toasting on griddles, stewing, steaming, or roasting, but never by the frying introduced by the conquistadors. In fact, the heavy use of oil and lard so prominent in modern Mexico and other former Spanish colonies was unknown in the pre-Columbian New World.

I have said that Aztec culture was somewhat on the puritanical side, at least in theory. But we know that elaborate banquets did take place among some elite groups (such as the traveling merchants) during religious festivals. The conquistador Bernal Diaz del Castillo gives us an especially vivid description of a royal banquet in Motecuhzoma's palace: the emperor was presented with hundreds of dishes, from which he partook frugally behind a gilt screen. Although women prepared all the food, these feasts were strictly stag events, ending up with the Aztec equivalent of brandy and cigars: the chocolate drink, followed by the smoking of tubes of perfumed tobacco. The most highly valued part of the chocolate, which was always taken cold, was the frothy head on the drink, prepared by pouring the liquid from a height. Many kinds of flavoring ingredients could be added to the drink, including allspice, honey, and chile (surprisingly good in chocolate). The sugar and cinnamon found in Mexican chocolate today are Spanish innovations.

Alcohol, in the form of *pulque*, the fermented juice of the century plant, was allowed, but only under the strictest rules. Chronic drunkenness was punishable by death (Aztec laws were draconian), but old people could drink as much as they wished.

All in all, the Aztec nation, from the emperor down to the common man, was remarkably well nourished—probably far better than the Spaniards, with their heavy reliance on meat and oils and their disinterest in vegetable foods. The sophisticated native cuisine underwent many changes during the Conquest, especially with the introduction of such useful animals as pigs, cattle, and chickens, along with citrus and other fruits. But far more foods traveled back across the Atlantic to Europe than had been brought from Spain. From the point of view of foodstuffs and ways of preparing them, the New World in reality conquered the Old World.

AHUACA-MULLI
GUACAMOLE

The modern Mexican word *aguacate* (avocado) is a combination of two Nahuatl words: *ahuacatl*, meaning "testicle," and *cauhuitl*, meaning "tree." Avocados were regarded as an aphrodisiac and provided a good source of fat, as well as protein and vitamins, in the traditionally low-fat diet of pre-Columbian America.

According to the late anthropologist and food historian Sophie D. Coe, avocados either grew wild or were cultivated in Oaxaca and the Tehuacan valley of Mexico as early 8000 to 7000 B.C. The cold- and drought-resistant avocados of this region are small and thin-skinned. Both the leaves of the trees and the pit of the fruit have a distinctive anise scent and flavor. The leaves and pits, as well as the fruit itself, are used in cooking.

One of the few recorded pre-Columbian recipes for avocados is *ahuaca-mulli*, "avocado sauce," known today as guacamole. Depending on the cook and the occasion, guacamole may be chunky or smoothly pureed and thinned with a bit of vinegar or lime juice. The distinctive version that follows, made with the tart, green husk tomatoes native to Mexico, is typical of Oaxaca. To give a hint of the anise flavor of Oaxacan avocados, we like to add a tablespoon or two of minced fennel tops.

3 or 4 fresh tomatillos, papery husks removed

2 large ripe Hass avocados

½ teaspoon salt, or to taste

1 or 2 fresh jalapeño or serrano chiles, seeded and chopped

⅓ cup minced white onion

⅓ cup minced fresh cilantro

2 tablespoons minced fresh fennel tops (optional)

Bring a saucepan of water to a boil and add the tomatillos. Boil for 5 minutes over medium-high heat, then drain and set aside to cool.

Peel and pit the avocados, and place them in a mortar or a small serving bowl. Mash coarsely, and season with the salt.

Place the tomatillos, chiles, onion, cilantro, and fennel greens (if using) in a blender, and pulse on and off a few times until blended but not completely pureed. Stir the tomatillo mixture into the mashed avocado. Taste, and add salt if needed. Serve immediately, or place the avocado pit into the guacamole to stop it from discoloring, cover directly with plastic wrap, and refrigerate for up to 1 hour.

We first learned about *chilapitas* many years ago in Cuernavaca. Walking along the street near the Zócalo, we noticed a young woman selling plastic sleeves filled with stacks of crisp, thin, delicious-looking *masa* shells. She was doing a lively business and seemed to have many steady customers. We bought a couple dozen to take home before returning to the United States.

The shells froze well and were a wonderful appetizer or snack, even when filled with a spoonful of simple refried beans or guacamole. Long after the last one had been gobbled up, *chilapitas* stayed on our minds, and we hoped to learn to make them one day. Fortunately, we met a wonderful cook named Guillermina Martinez, who comes from the Mexican state of Guerrero. She explained that *chilapita* comes from the Nahuatl word meaning "stream near the chile field" and that they are a specialty in Guerrero. She generously shared her recipe and spent a morning demonstrating how to make them.

Fill your *chilapitas* with refried beans topped with crumbled cheese; refried beans, shredded chicken, lettuce, tomato, and sour cream; or guacamole topped with whole shrimp, a dollop of sour cream, and a sprig of cilantro.

---

2 ½ **cups *masa harina***

1 **tablespoon all-purpose flour**

½ **teaspoon salt**

¼ **teaspoon baking powder**

1 ¼ **to 1 ¾ cups lukewarm water**

Lard, preferably home-rendered (page 217), or vegetable oil, for deep-frying

---

In a large mixing bowl, combine 1 ¼ cups of the *masa harina*, the flour, salt, and baking powder. Gradually mix in water. Knead the dough until it is smooth and supple, 2 to 3 minutes, adding more *masa harina* as needed. Divide the dough into about 20 equal pieces and roll them into balls. Cover them with a clean damp kitchen towel to keep them from drying out. The dough, wrapped in plastic, can be kept in the refrigerator for up to 1 day.

Place a ball of dough on a lightly oiled work surface. Press your thumbs into the center of the ball, and using your thumbs on the inside and your fingers on the outside, form the dough into a thin-shelled shallow cup about 3 ½ inches in diameter with sides about ¾ inch high. This may sound difficult, but it is really like playing with clay. After you make one or two, you'll find that it is not hard and that your *chilapitas* are fairly uniform in shape. As you complete each shell, slide a spatula underneath it to loosen it in case the bottom has stuck to the work surface.

Line a baking sheet with paper towels, and set aside.

Heat the lard in a deep, heavy frying pan or in a deep-fat fryer; the fat should be at least 1 ½ inches deep. It is hot enough when the oil reaches 375°F on a deep-frying thermometer, or when a small piece of dough dropped into the fat turns golden brown in about 1 minute. Fry the *chilapitas*, one at a time, until they turn a deep golden color and the edges are lightly browned, 1 to 2 minutes. Using a slotted spoon, carefully transfer the fried shells to the baking sheet.

Blot the bottom of each shell, then turn them rim side down to drain. Serve immediately, or allow the shells to cool completely and then store them in the refrigerator for 1 to 2 days or in the freezer, wrapped tightly in plastic wrap, for up to 1 month, until needed.

NOTE: If you made them in advance, reheat the *chilapitas* right-side up in a preheated 350°F oven for 15 to 20 minutes if stored in the refrigerator, 20 to 25 minutes if frozen, until hot and crisp. Blot with paper towels.

QUESADILLAS DE HUITLACOCHE

CORN MUSHROOM QUESADILLAS

SERVES

4 TO 6

MAKES 12 TO 14 QUESADILLAS

Huitlacoche is an intriguing- (some might say alarming-) looking "mushroom" that sometimes grows on ears of corn. Farmers in the United States consider it a blight, but to the Aztec and their descendants it is a delicacy as prized as the truffles of France and Italy. *Huitlacoche* is expensive, even in Mexico, and quite addictive once you develop a taste for it. A few farmers in the United States are beginning to produce it for fine restaurants. We have included one of these suppliers in the Sources section of this book. Canned *huitlacoche* from Mexico is sold at some specialty food stores, but if you can get it, the fresh or frozen product is superior.

Huitlacoche filling is often used in quesadillas, as in this recipe, or as a filling for soft rolled tacos. Making quesadillas from *masa* produces a different result from using premade corn tortillas. The outside of the *masa* quesadillas is crisp, but the inside remains slightly soft and doughy, which adds another dimension to the dish. If desired, however, corn tortillas may be substituted.

FILLING

2 fresh poblano chiles, roasted (page 217)

1 fresh jalapeño chile, roasted (optional)

1 to 2 tablespoons vegetable oil

1 small to medium white onion, peeled and chopped (about 1 cup)

3 cloves garlic, peeled and minced

3 or 4 ripe plum tomatoes, diced

½ pound fresh, frozen, or drained and well-rinsed canned *huitlacoche* (*cuitlacoche*) or ½ pound fresh mushrooms, coarsely chopped

Salt to taste

2 to 3 tablespoons chopped fresh cilantro or epazote

1¼ cups shredded Chihuahua or Monterey Jack cheese

DOUGH

2 cups *masa harina*

½ teaspoon salt

1 to 1⅓ cups lukewarm water

Peel, seed, and chop the roasted chiles.

Heat the oil in a large skillet over medium heat. Add the onion and cook, stirring frequently, until lightly browned on the edges, about 5 minutes. Add the garlic and cook for about 2 minutes. Add the tomatoes and increase the heat to medium-high. Cook, stirring occasionally, until most of the juices have evaporated, about 5 minutes. Add the chiles and the *huitlacoche*. Cook over medium heat, stirring often, until the mixture is quite thick, about 10 minutes. Season with salt and stir in the cilantro. Just before you are ready to use the filling, gently fold in the cheese.

Preheat the oven to 225°F.

In a mixing bowl, combine the *masa harina* and salt. Gradually mix in enough lukewarm water to make a moist, pliable dough. Roll the dough into 12 to 14 golf ball–size

balls. Cover with a clean damp kitchen towel so the dough won't dry out.

Using your hands, flatten one ball at a time into a 6-inch tortilla (page 51). Place 2 tablespoons of the filling to one side of the middle of the tortilla. Fold the tortilla in half, like a turnover, and press the edges together to seal in the filling. Continue to make quesadillas until all of the dough and filling are used.

Lightly grease a large well-seasoned griddle or nonstick skillet and place it over medium-high heat. Press down on each quesadilla with a spatula to flatten it, and place it on the griddle. Cook the quesadillas, a few at a time, until browned on both sides and hollow-sounding when tapped, about 3 minutes per side. As they are cooked, transfer the quesadillas to a baking sheet and keep warm in the oven.

THE AZTEC

EMPANADAS DE AMARILLO
CHICKEN EMPANADAS WITH YELLOW MOLE

MAKES 12 TO 14 EMPANADAS

Empanadas de Amarillo, small fresh corn tortillas filled with shredded poultry or meat, yellow mole, and crumbled cheese, are a typical street food in Oaxaca. They were a favorite snack of Beverly's sister-in-law, Dale Black, when she lived there. Dale's favorite recipe for these mildly fiery little turnovers is found in *Tradiciones Gastronomicas Oaxaquenas*, by Ana Maria Guzman de Vasquez Colmenares. This recipe is adapted from hers.

If you like, you can serve the empanadas with additional warm, thinned *Mole Amarillo* (page 97) or with *Ahuaca-mulli* (page 92).

4 cups chicken broth

4 cloves garlic, peeled

1 white onion, peeled and quartered

2 large skinless, boneless chicken breasts

One recipe *Mole Amarillo* (yellow mole sauce, page 97)

2 cups fresh *masa* or *masa harina*

2 tablespoons lard, preferably home-rendered (page 217), or solid vegetable shortening, melted and cooled

1 cup shredded Oaxacan string cheese or shredded mozzarella cheese

¼ cup shredded *hoja santa* leaves, or 12 to 14 small sprigs cilantro and 12 to 14 small sprigs fennel tops

Pour the chicken broth into a large saucepan, add the garlic and onion, and bring to a boil over medium-high heat. Add the chicken and reduce the heat to medium-low. Simmer until the chicken is cooked through, 20 to 30 minutes. When the chicken is cool enough to handle, remove it from the broth and shred it. Reserve about ½ cup of the broth.

Place the mole in a medium saucepan and warm it over low heat, stirring occasionally. If it seems very thick, thin it to a good spreading consistency with a little of the reserved broth.

In a large mixing bowl combine the fresh *masa* with the lard and enough lukewarm water to make a moist but malleable dough. If using *masa harina*, mix it with the lard and 1 to 1⅓ cups lukewarm water to make a moist but not too sticky dough. Cover the dough with a clean damp kitchen towel so it doesn't dry out.

Preheat the oven to 300°F.

Make the empanadas one at a time. Heat a griddle or a small nonstick skillet over medium-high heat. Form a golf ball–size ball of dough into a tortilla, following the directions on page 51. When a few drops of water sprinkled on the griddle jump and dance, place the tortilla on the griddle and cook it for 20 seconds. Then turn the tortilla over and quickly spread 1½ tablespoons of the mole, 2 tablespoons of the chicken, 1 tablespoon of the cheese, and a few shreds of *hoja santa* leaves (or 1 sprig cilantro and 1 sprig fennel) on one side. Fold the tortilla over the filling to make a turnover, pressing down gently around the edges with the tines of a fork to enclose the filling. Cook for about 1 minute on each side, until lightly browned.

Place the empanada on a baking sheet and keep it warm in the oven. Repeat until all the empanadas are cooked. Serve hot.

MOLES

A CORNERSTONE OF MEXICAN CUISINE

Moles (from the Nahuatl word *mulli*, meaning "sauce") are combinations of ground chiles, nuts, seeds, herbs, and spices. They are the cornerstone of Mexican cuisine and form the basis for many wonderful sauces and stews.

The places most known for their moles are the central Mexican state of Puebla, with its sophisticated sweet, hot, and savory mole poblano, and Oaxaca, often called "the Land of Seven Moles." Located in the middle of the southern highlands, the state of Oaxaca is considered to have some of the best moles and the most authentic Indian cooking in Mexico. The most famous Oaxacan moles are the *amarillo* (yellow), *coloradito* (red), and *negro* (black), but there are many others.

Like the *recado* vendors in Yucatecan markets, mole merchants in Puebla and Oaxaca offer pre-ground pastes and powders prepared according to their own special recipes. You may also request that a mole be made and ground following your particular family recipe—although, especially in Oaxaca, the vendors may scowl disapprovingly at the inclusion of some ingredients and the proportions of others.

Most modern Mexican cooks buy mole pastes fresh at the market on the day they plan to use them, and are able to put a sauce together quickly by adding only the onion, tomatoes, and other moist ingredients. Unfortunately, freshly prepared moles are not readily available in the United States, but with a mortar and pestle, or a small electric spice mill or coffee grinder, a heavy-duty electric blender, and a sturdy medium-mesh sieve, it is possible to make a respectable mole with only a reasonable amount of effort.

Of all the Oaxacan moles, the tart and subtly hot *amarillo* is one of the most versatile—and it is also one of the least complicated to make. The sauce gets its name from the red-orange *guajillo* and yellow *costeño amarillo* chiles that give it its characteristic golden-orange color. *Guajillo* chiles are becoming available in many stores across the Unites States that carry dried chiles. *Costeño amarillo* chiles are more unusual, but available through mail order (see Sources). If only *guajillos* are available in your area, make the recipe with 10 to 12 *guajillos*. The sauce will have a good flavor, but its color will not be golden. Dried chiles will keep for up to 1 year.

8 dried *costeño amarillo* chiles

**3 dried *guajillo* chiles
or 3 or 4 *chilcostle* chiles**

**5 large tomatillos, with papery
husks**

1 medium tomato, not too ripe

4 large cloves garlic, unpeeled

1 small white onion, unpeeled

6 black peppercorns

**4 whole cloves, or 1/8 teaspoon
ground cloves**

1/2 teaspoon salt, or to taste

**2 tablespoons lard, preferably home-
rendered (page 217), or vegetable
oil**

**1 tablespoon *masa harina*, or 2 table-
spoons fresh *masa***

**1/2 cup chicken broth, meat broth, or
water**

Preheat a griddle or a heavy skillet over medium heat.

Rinse the chiles thoroughly under cold running water. Remove and discard the stems. Slit the chiles down one side and remove the seeds. Open up the chiles and place them on the hot griddle; toast just until the rinsing water has evaporated. Transfer the chiles to a small saucepan, add enough water to cover and bring to a boil over medium-high heat. Cover and remove from the heat. Allow the chiles to soak for about 20 minutes, until softened.

Meanwhile, roast the tomatillos, tomato, garlic, and onion on the griddle, turning them with tongs, until lightly charred on all sides. As they are done, transfer them to a bowl to catch the juices. Set aside until they are cool enough to handle, then remove the husks from the tomatillos and peel the garlic cloves and onion.

In a spice mill or coffee grinder, grind the peppercorns together with the cloves.

Using a slotted spoon, transfer the chiles to a blender or food processor. Add the roasted vegetables and their juices, and the pepper-clove mixture. Pulse on and off until pureed. Press the puree through a medium-mesh sieve into a bowl. Season to taste with salt.

Melt the lard in a large saucepan over medium heat. When it is hot, add the puree. Reduce the heat to low, cover, and simmer for about 10 minutes, stirring occasionally.

Combine the *masa harina* and the broth in a small bowl. Whisk the mixture into the puree and cook, stirring, over low heat until the sauce is smooth and slightly thickened, about 10 minutes. When cooled, cover and refrigerate for up to 1 week or freeze for up to 1 month.

SALSA VERDE
TOMATILLO SALSA

Tomatillos, also called husk tomatoes, were first cultivated in Mexico. They are not actually a tomato but a variety of *Physalis*, a member of the same family as Cape gooseberries. When ripe, the fruit turns from pale green to yellow. Tomatillos range from about ½ inch to almost 2 inches in diameter and vary in acidity.

Salsa Verde is among the most versatile of Mexican sauces. There are several different ways to make it. Some recipes call for simply boiling and then pureeing the tomatillos. We like the method preferred by cooks in Michoacán, who roast the tomatillos and other ingredients first on a hot *comal*, or griddle. It is a little more work, but it gives the sauce a rounder, less acidic flavor. This is a great sauce to serve with enchiladas or tamales, or to spoon over grilled slices of Oaxacan cheese.

12 to 14 fresh tomatillos, papery husks removed

3 to 6 fresh serrano chiles or 1 or 2 fresh jalapeño chiles, stemmed, seeded if desired

1 white onion, peeled and quartered

4 cloves garlic, peeled

⅓ cup chopped fresh cilantro leaves and stems

1 tablespoon lard, preferably home-rendered (page 217), or vegetable oil

1½ cups water, vegetable broth, or chicken broth

Salt to taste

Preheat a griddle or a large heavy skillet over medium-high heat.

Rinse the tomatillos thoroughly and pat them dry. Place the tomatillos, chiles, onion, and garlic on the hot griddle and roast, turning two or three times with tongs, until browned in spots. Transfer the vegetables to a food processor, add the cilantro, and pulse on and off until pureed.

Heat the oil in a large saucepan over medium heat. Carefully pour in the puree and cook, stirring, until the mixture turns a darker shade of green, about 5 minutes. Stir in the water and add salt to taste. Reduce the heat to low and simmer, stirring occasionally, for 30 minutes. Serve warm. When cooled, cover and refrigerate for up to 1 week.

Of the more than 100 different Mexican chiles, the *guajillo* (little gourd) is one of the most useful. *Guajillos* are usually sold dried. The milder ones are about 5 inches long and 1 to 1½ inches wide. When dried, they are a deep burgundy color, and their flavor is mellow, slightly fruity, with a touch of smokiness. There is also a slightly smaller, thinner, and more pointed variety that is quite hot. Because of their tough skin, *guajillos* require longer soaking than some other varieties.

Look for *guajillos* in supermarkets and specialty food stores; they are becoming much easier to find in the United States. If they are not available in your area, check Sources in the Appendix.

Salsa de Guajillo is extremely versatile. It is wonderful as a filling or sauce for tamales and is also great served over grilled meat or fish.

---

6 to 8 dried *guajillo* chiles

6 to 7 ripe plum tomatoes

⅔ cup chopped white onion

3 cloves garlic, peeled and minced

1½ tablespoons lard, preferably home-rendered (page 217), or vegetable oil

Salt, to taste

Preheat a griddle or a heavy skillet over medium heat.

Rinse the chiles under cold running water. Remove and discard the stems. Slit the chiles down one side and remove the seeds. Open up the chiles, and place them on the hot griddle; toast just until the rinsing water has evaporated. Transfer the chiles to a large saucepan. Add the plum tomatoes and enough water to cover, and bring to a boil over medium-high heat. Cover and remove from the heat. Allow the chiles and tomatoes to soak for about 20 minutes, until the chiles have softened and the tomato skins have split.

Using a slotted spoon, transfer the chiles and tomatoes to a blender. Add the onion and garlic, and puree. Press the puree through a medium-mesh sieve into a bowl.

Melt the lard in a large saucepan over medium heat. When it is hot, carefully add the puree (it may spatter). Reduce the heat to low, cover, and cook, stirring occasionally, for 10 minutes. Season the sauce to taste with salt, and serve warm.

When cooled, the sauce may be tightly covered and stored in the refrigerator for up to 1 week or in the freezer for up to 1 month.

TLATLOYOS
OVAL TORTILLAS FILLED WITH BEAN PUREE

MAKES 8 OR 9 TLATLOYOS

As you enter the food markets of Mexico City, you will see Indian women from the countryside with small portable wood- or charcoal-burning stoves making fresh *tlatloyos* (pronounced *clack-o-yos*), stuffed oval tortillas made with white, blue, or red tinted corn dough. The white ones usually have a black bean filling, the blue are filled with white bean puree, with a stripe of the white filling left showing in the middle, and the red are most often filled with cheese or pureed pork cracklings.

At one of the most popular food stands in the city's huge and colorful Jamaica Market, the cooks were making a larger version of *tlatloyos* called *memelitas*. They fried them in a little lard or oil and topped them with *Salsa de Guajillo* (page 99), a whole grilled chicken breast, and a whole grilled nopal cactus paddle. An interesting presentation and a hearty and tasty meal!

1 quart chicken broth or water

1 small white onion, peeled and quartered

4 cloves garlic, peeled

Salt to taste

1 pound chicken breast, boneless or bone-in

1 recipe tortilla dough (page 51)

2 cups *Tsah Bi Bu'ul* (black bean puree, page 46) or one 15-ounce can refried black beans

1 to 3 tablespoons lard, preferably home-rendered (page 217), or vegetable oil

1 cup *Salsa de Guajillo* (red chile and tomato sauce, page 99) or *Salsa Verde* (tomatillo salsa, page 98)

1 cup shredded lettuce

1 cup crumbled *queso fresco*, goat cheese, or feta cheese

½ cup créme fraîche or sour cream

Pour the broth into a large saucepan, add the onion, garlic, and salt if desired, and bring to a boil over medium-high heat. Add the chicken, reduce the heat to low, and simmer until the chicken is cooked, 20 to 30 minutes. If time permits, allow the chicken to cool in the broth. Remove the chicken from the broth and shred it.

Form ¼ cup portions of the dough into 8 or 9 balls. Cover with a clean damp towel to keep dough from drying out. Following the instructions on page 51, form tortillas about 6 inches in diameter. Spread a rounded tablespoon of bean puree down the middle of each tortilla, and fold in the sides to cover the filling. Use your hands to mold the tortilla into an oval shape with pointed ends. Cook the *tlatloyos* on a moderately hot, well-seasoned *comal* or griddle for about 5 minutes on each side, until thoroughly cooked.

Preheat the oven to 300°F.

Melt 1 to 2 tablespoons of the lard in a large skillet over medium heat. When it is hot, add the *tlatloyos* and fry, turning once, until crisp and heated through. Keep the *tlatloyos* warm in the oven on a baking dish lined with paper towels while cooking the rest. Add more lard as needed.

Serve topped with the salsa, lettuce, chicken, cheese, and créme fraîche.

VARIATIONS: *Tlatloyos* may be made using blue corn *masa* or *masa harina,* following the instructions on page 51. To make red dough, add 1 to 2 tablespoons *Salsa de Guajillo* (page 99) to white tortilla dough. To make white bean puree, puree one 15-ounce can Great Northern beans and season to taste with minced fresh or pureed dried chiles, crumbled avocado leaves or minced cilantro, and salt and pepper.

THE AZTEC

RIGHT: *Tlatloyos* served with a variety of toppings accompanied by *Ahuaca-mulli* (page 92).

CHILAQUILES DE CHILE GUAJILLO
CHILAQUILES WITH GUAJILLO CHILE SAUCE

Fearing the anger of the gods of rain and maize, the Aztec never wasted tortillas and other corn products. Leftover tortillas were added to casseroles or ground into crumbs to use as a thickener for sauces. If they were moldy or too stale for human consumption, they were fed to the animals.

One delicious way to use day-old tortillas is to mix them into a casserole with a chile-based sauce. This dish, *chilaquiles* (or "broken-up old sombreros"), is as popular with modern Mexican cooks as it was in the time of the Aztec. This version of the dish is typical of the cooking of Oaxaca. Serve chilaquiles for a hearty breakfast or brunch.

2 or 3 dried *guajillo* chiles, stems removed, toasted (page 217)

1 large ripe tomato, roasted (page 217)

1 small head garlic, unpeeled, roasted (page 217)

4 tablespoons lard, preferably home-rendered (page 217), or vegetable oil

1 cup chicken broth or water

1 sprig fresh epazote, or 2 or 3 sprigs fresh cilantro

Salt to taste

10 day-old corn tortillas, cut into 2- to 3-inch-wide strips

1½ cups crumbled *queso blanco*, grated mozzarella, or grated Monterey Jack cheese

1 small red onion, thinly sliced into rings and soaked in cold water for 30 minutes, or 1 cup *Cebollas Encurtidas* (pickled onions, page 49), well drained

1 to 2 tablespoons minced fresh cilantro, for garnish

Bring a saucepan of water to a boil, add the toasted chiles, and set aside for about 30 minutes or until softened. Seed them, if desired, and chop coarsely. Place the chiles in a blender or food processor, add the tomato and garlic, and pulse on and off until pureed. Press the puree through a medium-mesh sieve into a bowl; set aside.

Heat 2 tablespoons of the lard in a saucepan or skillet. Add the chile puree and sauté for 2 to 3 minutes. Stir in the chicken broth. Add the epazote. Bring to a boil over medium-high heat, then reduce the heat to medium-low and simmer gently, stirring often, for about 5 minutes. Season to taste with salt.

In another large skillet, heat the remaining 2 tablespoons lard over medium heat. Add the tortilla strips and fry until golden, 1 to 2 minutes. Add the chile sauce and stir gently. Cover, and simmer until the tortillas have soaked up most of the liquid, about 10 minutes. Sprinkle with the cheese, and garnish with the onion slices and cilantro.

NOTE: The fried tortilla pieces may also be transferred to a shallow baking dish, mixed with the sauce, and sprinkled with the cheese. Cover and bake in a preheated 350°F oven for about 20 minutes, until hot.

ENCHILADAS VERDES
CHICKEN ENCHILADAS WITH GREEN SAUCE

SERVES
4 TO 6

Beverly and her sister-in-law, Dale Black, have pursued the perfect *Enchilada Verde* from simple restaurants in Oaxaca to the elegant eateries of Mexico City to the Silver Cities of Taxco, Guanajuato, and Queretaro. We have tasted several delicious renditions of this dish, but from our point of view, the one that surpasses them all is this simple, modest version served at one of the local gathering places around the Zócalo in Cuernavaca. Serve the enchiladas with black beans or with *Tsah Bi Bu'ul* (page 46).

1 quart chicken broth or water

1 small white onion, peeled and quartered

4 cloves garlic, peeled

Salt to taste

1 pound chicken breast, boneless or bone-in

¼ cup vegetable oil

12 (6- to 8-inch) fresh corn tortillas, homemade (pages 51–52), or packaged

1 recipe *Salsa Verde* (tomatillo salsa, page 98), made with chicken broth

1 cup crème fraîche

2 cups shredded Oaxaca, mozzarella, or Monterey Jack cheese

Pour the broth into a large saucepan, add the onion, garlic, and salt if desired, and bring to a boil over medium-high heat. Add the chicken, reduce the heat to low, and simmer until the chicken is cooked, 20 to 30 minutes. If time permits, allow the chicken to cool in the broth; the chicken will be more moist. Remove the chicken from the broth and shred it.

Preheat the oven to 350°F. Grease 4 to 6 individual shallow baking dishes.

Heat the oil in a small skillet. Using tongs, dip the tortillas in the hot oil to soften them. Then place them on paper towels to drain. Place 3 to 4 tablespoons of the chicken on one side of each tortilla, and roll up the tortilla like a tube, leaving the ends open. Place 2 or 3 enchiladas in each baking dish, and top with the *Salsa Verde*. Drizzle with the crème fraîche, and sprinkle with the cheese. Bake for 15 to 20 minutes, until the cheese has melted. Serve hot.

TAMALES DE CENIZA
ASH TAMALES MADE WITH CHEESE AND CHILES

MAKES ABOUT 12 TAMALES

The states of Michoacán and Guanajuato, located west and north of Mexico City, produce many good tamales. Among the region's specialties are *tamales de ceniza,* or ash tamales, so called because they are made with corn that has been nixtamalized using wood ashes instead of ground limestone. The corn is then finely ground, which gives the dough a dense but tender texture. These tamales are usually small and are not formed around a filling. They do, however, sometimes have cheese and other ingredients mixed into the dough.

A typical ash tamale from the city of Patzcuaro, Michoacán, is the *corunda,* which gets its name from its triangular shape. *Corundas* are traditionally wrapped in fresh corn leaves, folded as you would fold a flag into a triangle, with the end tucked into the last fold to make a neat package. In neighboring Guanajuato, similar tamales are shaped into round or square packages and may be wrapped in either corn leaves or husks.

The recipe that follows is adapted from a couple of memorable ash tamales we have eaten, using some helpful ideas from author and Mexican cooking aficionado Nancy Zaslavsky. Though the thought of triangular-shaped tamales wrapped in corn leaves is intriguing and they are fun to make if you have a source, the square version wrapped in fresh or dried husks may be more practical for most cooks. Serve these delicious and unusual tamales as a first course or a snack, topped with *Salsa Verde* (page 98).

35 fresh corn leaves, or 20 fresh or dried corn husks

1 cup *masa harina*

1 cup chicken broth, heated

½ cup lard, preferably home-rendered (page 217), or solid vegetable shortening, cut into small pieces

½ teaspoon salt

½ teaspoon baking powder dissolved in 2 tablespoons cool water

¼ cup *panella* or whole-milk ricotta

2 tablespoons grated *queso anejo* or Romano cheese

1 or 2 fresh serrano or jalapeño chiles, seeded and minced

2 tablespoons minced fresh cilantro (optional)

1 recipe *Salsa Verde* (tomatillo salsa, page 98)

Rinse the fresh corn leaves or husks thoroughly, and allow them to soak in hot water while you prepare the dough. If you are using dried husks, rinse them well, place them in a pot of hot water, and bring to a boil over high heat. Remove from the heat, and allow the husks to soak until softened, about 1 hour.

Place the *masa harina* in the bowl of an electric mixer. While beating at low speed, gradually add the hot chicken broth. Increase the speed to high and beat for 5 minutes. Gradually add the lard and then the salt, continuing to beat until the dough is soft and light, about 10 minutes. Add the dissolved baking powder, the cheeses, chiles, and cilantro, and continue to beat the dough until it is fluffy, 6 to 8 minutes.

If you are making *corundas*, dry the corn leaves with a clean kitchen towel and cut them in half lengthwise, removing the central rib. Place 2 tablespoons of the dough at wide end of a leaf, and fold it up as you would a flag, forming a triangle and tucking in the point. If you are making square tamales,

THE AZTEC

wipe the excess moisture off a fresh or dried husk and place it, concave side up, on a work surface with the point facing away from you. Place about 2 tablespoons of the dough in the middle of the husk. Fold up the bottom to cover the dough, then fold in both long sides, and finally fold down the pointed end to make a neat square package. Tie the tamale in the middle with a string made from a strip of husk (page 219). Repeat, using all the dough.

Line the basket of a small to medium-size steamer with a single layer of damp corn leaves or husks. Arrange the tamales in the basket, standing them upright so they are leaning against each other with the last folded side toward the outside. Top with another layer of damp leaves and a damp kitchen towel. Fill the bottom of the steamer with boiling water, making sure that it does not touch the tamales. Cover tightly and steam the tamales over medium-high heat until the dough separates easily from the wrapper, about 1 hour. (Add more water to the steamer as needed.) Serve warm, topped with *Salsa Verde*.

NOTE: Drop a coin in the steamer water. When you no longer hear the coin rattling, it is time to add more hot water.

TAMALES EN HOJA DE MAIZ
RED OR GREEN CHICKEN TAMALES IN CORN HUSKS

Tehuatepec, in the state of Oaxaca, is known for its strong-minded women and its good food. Thirty years ago, Amelia Woolrich, a Tehuatepec native living in Mexico City, started a specialty tamale business in the basement of her home. With her talent as a cook and her sound business acumen, the business thrived and grew. It is still going strong today. Her daughter, Beatrice Ramirez Woolrich, a talented cook in her own right, works with her mother and also teaches and is involved in other food-related projects.

Amelia and Beatrice's tamales are so wonderfully light, moist, and flavorful that we were determined to include them here. When we made the tamales together in Mexico, they came out beautifully; but the first attempt to re-create them at home was a disaster. They were light, all right, but dry as a bone. At Beatrice's suggestion, we consulted the award-winning cookbooks of Rick Bayless, the Chicago-based chef and authority on Mexican cooking. The recipe that follows is Amelia and Beatrice's, adapted using the guidelines suggested by Bayless in his *Authentic Mexican: Regional Cooking from the Heart of Mexico*. It can be halved successfully.

One 8-ounce package dried
    corn husks

1 whole chicken breast

4 cups chicken broth

⅓ white onion, peeled

2 to 4 cloves garlic, peeled

1⅓ cups quick-cooking (not
    instant) grits

1½ cups *masa harina*

1 cup lard, preferably home-
    rendered (page 217), or solid
    vegetable shortening, chilled

2 teaspoons baking powder

1 teaspoon salt

1 recipe *Salsa Verde* (tomatillo salsa,
    page 98) or *Salsa de Guajillo* (red
    chile and tomato sauce, page 99)

Rinse the corn husks under hot running water. Place them in a pot with enough water to cover, bring to a boil, then remove from the heat. Cover, and allow to sit for 1 hour to soften.

Meanwhile, place the chicken breast in a saucepan and add chicken broth to cover. Add the onion and garlic and bring to a simmer. Simmer until the chicken is cooked through, about 20 minutes. If time permits, let the chicken cool in the broth; the chicken will be more moist. Then remove the chicken, reserving the broth, and shred the meat. Set aside.

Return 2½ cups of the broth to a boil. Pulverize the grits, ⅓ cup at a time, in a spice mill or coffee grinder until finely ground. Transfer to a mixing bowl, stir in the boiling broth, and let stand for 10 minutes. Then add the *masa harina* and knead to make a soft, moist dough. Cover, and allow the dough to cool to room temperature.

Using a heavy-duty electric mixer, beat the lard in a large bowl until it is fluffy and forms stiff peaks, about 1 minute. Add 1½ cups of half of the reserved dough and beat until well blended. Continuing to beat, add the lukewarm broth

(continued on page 108)

LEFT: *Tamales en Hoja de Maiz,* made with *Salsa de Guajillo* (top) and *Salsa Verde* (bottom). The open-ended tamale wrap makes a neater presentation when placed open-side-down in the serving basket.

and the remaining dough, alternating, until the dough has the consistency of a medium-thick cake batter. Sprinkle in the baking powder and salt. Continue to beat for 1 minute, or until a small piece of dough floats when dropped into a bowl of cold water.

Remove a corn husk from the water and pat it dry. Place the corn husk on the work surface in front of you, concave side up. Spread 2 to 3 tablespoons of the dough in an oval shape at the wide end of the husk. Place some shredded chicken on the dough, and press it in slightly. Top with about 1 tablespoon red or green salsa. Wrap according to the instructions for an open-ended wrap (page 222). Repeat with the remaining husks and filling.

Line a steamer basket with damp torn or leftover corn husks. Place the tamales in the basket, standing upright, wide end up, so they are leaning against each other with the folded side to the outside. Cover with any remaining husks and a clean damp kitchen towel. Fill the bottom of the steamer with boiling water, making sure it does not touch the tamales. Cover tightly and steam for about 1 hour, until the dough easily separates from the husk and the tamales hold their shape. Serve the tamales topped with *Salsa Verde* or *Salsa de Guajillo*.

NOTE: Drop a coin in the steamer water. When you no longer hear the coin rattling, it is time to add more hot water.

Tamale-Making Tips from Amelia and Beatrice

- Always use top-quality ingredients.

- Be in a good mood.

- Make the tamales with calmness and love and out of earshot of crying children.

- Test your dough for lightness by dropping a small piece in a bowl of cold water. If it doesn't float, keep beating.

- Place a coin in the water in the bottom of the steamer. If it stops dancing, add water.

- When placing the tamales in the steamer, it helps to bless them, crossing your fingers to form a cross. Then light a candle and pray to San Pascual, the patron saint of cooks.

SOPA DE CHIPILIN CON BOLITAS
CORN SOUP WITH GREENS AND *MASA* DUMPLINGS

SERVES 6

The Zoque people of Chiapas live and cook much as they did when this region was part of the power-ful Aztec Empire. Much of their diet is still based on the Mesoamerican "holy trinity" of corn, beans, and squash. In spring and summer, *chilipin*, a wild green with a flavor somewhere between watercress and spinach, is gathered and used to make a delicious traditional soup. The basic recipe hasn't changed much since pre-Columbian times, but today the dumplings include crumbled fresh white cheese and the soup is sometimes topped with more cheese and a drizzle of heavy cream.

DUMPLINGS

- 1 cup *masa harina*
- ¾ to 1 cup warm water
- ¼ teaspoon salt
- ¼ cup lard, preferably home-rendered (page 217), or solid vegetable shortening
- ½ cup crumbled *queso fresco* or feta cheese

SOUP

- 6 cups chicken broth or water
- 5 or 6 scallions (white and tender green parts), thinly sliced
- 2 cups fresh corn kernels (3 to 4 ears)
- 1 to 3 fresh *serrano* chiles, seeds and ribs removed if desired
- Salt to taste
- 1 cup firmly packed *chilipin* (see headnote) or watercress leaves and tender stems, chopped
- 2 tablespoons *masa harina* dissolved in ¼ cup water

GARNISH

- 1 cup firmly packed *chilipin* or water-cress leaves, coarsely chopped
- ½ cup crumbled *queso fresco* or feta cheese
- ½ cup heavy cream

In a large mixing bowl combine the *masa harina*, ¾ cup of the warm water, and the salt. Mix with a fork until the dough comes together. Knead the dough until it is smooth and no longer sticky. Cover the bowl with a towel and allow it to rest at room temperature for 1 hour.

Using a whisk or an electric mixer, beat the lard until it is light and fluffy. To the dough, add the remaining warm water, the lard, and the cheese, and knead until smooth. Roll the dough into walnut-size balls, cover with a damp towel, and set aside.

Pour the broth into a soup pot and add the scallions, corn, chile, and salt. Bring to a boil over medium-high heat. Reduce the heat to low and simmer for 20 minutes.

Stir in the *chilipin* and the dissolved *masa harina*. Return to a boil, then reduce the heat to low. Drop the dumplings into the barely simmering soup and cook for another 20 min-utes. If the soup seems too thick, add a little water. Garnish each serving with some of the fresh *chilipin*, cheese, and cream.

THE AZTEC

110

SOPA DE TORTILLA
TORTILLA SOUP

In *America's First Cuisines,* Sophie Coe writes that "the Aztec man paid a forfeit if he spilled a bit of maize gruel and the Aztec woman breathed on the maize as she put it into the pot so it would not fear the fire, and picked up the grains of maize scattered on the flour for fear the grains should complain to their lord and she would starve." So sacred was corn that wasting a tortilla or other corn product would have been sacrilege. This respect and thriftiness resulted in many wonderful dishes including *Sopa de Tortilla.* This simple soup combines day-old tortillas with chiles, meat broth, and whatever vegetables are at hand to make a wonderful first course. If you add shredded poached chicken or cooked beef, it is a meal in itself.

8 dried pasilla or *guajillo* chiles

1 dried ancho chile

5 tablespoons lard, preferably home-rendered (page 217), or vegetable oil

1 medium white onion, peeled and sliced

2 cloves garlic, peeled

6 large ripe plum tomatoes, or one 14½-ounce can diced tomatoes, undrained

2 sprigs fresh epazote or cilantro

3 quarts chicken or beef broth, heated

Lard, preferably home-rendered, and/or vegetable oil, for deep frying

12 corn or flour tortillas, cut into thin strips and air-dried overnight

Salt to taste

1 cup crumbled *queso fresco* or feta cheese

2 ripe Hass avocados, peeled, pitted, and diced

¾ cup crème fraîche, or ½ cup sour cream thinned with 2 tablespoons half-and-half

3 to 4 tablespoons chopped fresh cilantro

Rinse the chiles thoroughly under cold running water. Pat them dry, and remove the stems and seeds. Melt 2 tablespoons of the lard in a large skillet over medium heat. When the lard is hot, add the pasilla chiles and sauté for a few seconds on each side, stirring constantly, until they begin to soften slightly and release their fragrance. Remove with a slotted spoon and drain on paper towels. Add the ancho chile to the skillet and sauté briefly; remove and drain. Be careful not to burn the chiles or they will taste bitter.

Using kitchen scissors, cut 3 pasillas into thin strips and reserve for garnish. Place remaining chiles in a bowl and add enough boiling water to cover. Soak the chiles for 15 to 20 minutes, then drain and discard the soaking liquid. While the chiles are soaking, add another tablespoon of lard to the skillet and sauté the onion and garlic over medium heat for 8 to 10 minutes, until lightly browned.

In a blender or food processor combine the soaked chiles with the tomatoes, onion, and garlic. Pulse on and off until pureed. Press the puree through a medium-mesh sieve into a

bowl. Melt the remaining 3 tablespoons lard in a soup pot over medium heat. When the lard is hot, carefully add the puree (it may splatter). Fry the puree, stirring occasionally, until it begins to thicken and the fat rises to the surface, about 10 minutes. Add the epazote and half of the pasilla chile strips. Then stir in the hot broth. Simmer the soup over low to medium-low heat for 30 minutes, stirring occasionally.

Meanwhile, heat lard melted to a depth of 1 inch in a deep skillet over medium heat. The lard is hot enough when it reaches 375°F on a deep-frying thermometer or a tortilla strip lowered into the fat turns golden brown in about 1 minute. Fry the tortilla strips in batches. As they turn crisp and golden, remove them with a slotted spoon and set them aside on crumpled paper towels to drain. If desired, sprinkle the strips lightly with salt.

Taste the soup and add salt if needed. Divide the tortilla strips among individual soup bowls. Ladle in the soup, and garnish each serving with the reserved chile strips, the cheese, avocado, crème fraîche, and cilantro.

SOPA DE FRIJOLES ESTILO PATZCUARO
PATZCUARO-STYLE BEAN SOUP

Tzintzuntzan, the last great capital of the Tarascan Kingdom, overlooked beautiful Lake Patzcuaro in Michoacán, western Mexico. The Tarascans, whose language is apparently unrelated to any other in the hemisphere, managed to defend their borders against the Aztec and never came under their domination. They did, however, share similar basic culinary traditions. This soothing but spicy bean soup is typical of the area around Lake Patzcuaro.

2 cups (about 12 ounces) dried bayo or pinto beans, cooked (see Note, page 113); or four 15-ounce cans pinto beans, undrained

6 dried pasilla chiles or 3 dried ancho chiles, rinsed in cold water, stems and seeds removed

3 tablespoons lard, preferably home-rendered (page 217), or vegetable oil

4 plum tomatoes, roasted (page 217)

4 cloves garlic, roasted (page 217) and peeled

1 small to medium white onion, roasted (page 217), peeled, and quartered

1 quart chicken broth, heated

Salt and freshly ground black pepper to taste

12 corn or flour tortillas, cut into thin strips and air-dried overnight

Lard, preferably home-rendered, and/or vegetable oil, for deep-frying

1 cup crème fraîche, or ¾ cup sour cream thinned with 3 tablespoons half-and-half

1 cup crumbled *queso fresco* or feta cheese

2 ripe Hass avocado, peeled, pitted, and sliced

2 to 3 tablespoons chopped fresh cilantro

In a blender or food processor puree the beans and their liquid. Press the puree through a medium-mesh sieve into a bowl, and set aside.

Pat the chiles dry with paper towels. Melt 1 tablespoon of the lard in a large skillet over medium heat. When it is hot, add the chiles and sauté until they begin to soften and release their aroma, a few seconds on each side. Be careful not to burn the chiles, or they will taste bitter. Reserve 2 pasillas or 1 ancho, and with kitchen scissors cut the remaining chiles into thin strips for garnish.

Without washing the blender, add the fried whole chiles and the roasted tomatoes, garlic, and onion. Pulse on and off until pureed.

Melt the remaining 2 tablespoons lard in a soup pot over medium heat. When it is hot, carefully add the puree (it may splatter). Cook over low heat, stirring occasionally, until the mixture thickens, about 15 minutes. Stir in the bean puree and the hot chicken broth. Simmer over low to medium-low heat, stirring occasionally, until the soup is hot and the flavors have blended, 20 to 30 minutes. Season to taste with salt and pepper.

Meanwhile, heat lard melted to a depth of 1 inch in a large deep skillet over medium heat. The lard is hot enough when it reaches 375°F on a deep-frying thermometer or a tortilla strip lowered into the fat turns golden brown in about 1 minute. Fry the tortilla strips in batches. As they turn crisp and golden, remove them with a slotted spoon and set them aside on crumpled paper towels to drain.

Ladle the soup into individual bowls and garnish each serving with the tortilla and chile strips, crème fraîche, cheese, avocado, and cilantro.

SOPA DE FRIJOLES Y TORTILLAS

OAXACAN BLACK BEAN AND TORTILLA SOUP

Archaeologists and ethnobotanists have found evidence that wild beans were being gathered in Oaxaca as early as 8750 B.C. Black beans, particularly the large plump variety known locally as *ayocotes*, are served as part of most meals in Oaxaca. This simple but very tasty black bean soup is a meal in itself.

One 16-ounce package dried black beans, cooked (see Note), or 8 cups canned black beans, drained

6 tablespoons lard, preferably home-rendered (page 217), or vegetable oil

1 small white onion, chopped finely (about 1 cup)

3 to 4 cups water

6 corn tortillas, cut into triangles or strips

3 or 4 dried Mexican avocado leaves (see Sources), lightly toasted on a griddle and crumbled, or ¼ cup minced fresh cilantro plus 2 tablespoons minced fresh fennel tops

Salt to taste

1 cup crumbled *queso fresco* or feta cheese

Place the beans in a blender and pulse on and off until they are partially pureed but still have some texture.

Heat 2 tablespoons of the lard in a soup pot or a large saucepan over medium heat. Add the onion and sauté for 2 to 3 minutes, until slightly softened. Add the bean puree and 3 to 4 cups water depending on the thickness of the puree. Bring to a simmer, then reduce the heat to low and cook, stirring, for 10 to 15 minutes.

Meanwhile, heat the remaining 4 tablespoons lard in a small skillet. When it is hot, add the tortilla pieces a few at a time and fry until golden, 1 to 2 minutes. Remove them with a slotted spoon and set them aside to drain on crumpled paper towels.

Stir the avocado leaves into the soup, and season to taste with salt. Spoon the soup into individual bowls, with the cheese and tortilla pieces, and serve.

NOTE: To cook the beans, first pick over them to remove any debris. Then rinse them under cold running water until the water remains clear. Place the beans in a large heavy nonreactive pot, and add enough soft or distilled water to cover them by about 5 inches. Soak the beans overnight. (Or if you are in a hurry, bring the beans and water to a boil and simmer them for 10 minutes; cover, turn off the heat, and allow to soak for 1 hour.) At higher altitudes, it may take beans 1 to 3 hours longer to cook.

Place the pot over medium-high heat and bring to a boil. Add to the beans: 1 head garlic, roasted and left whole; 1 white onion, roasted, peeled, and halved; 1 jalapeño chile, roasted, if desired; and 15 fresh epazote leaves or 1 teaspoon dried (optional). Cover and reduce the heat to a steady simmer. While the beans are cooking, gently stir them every 20 minutes or so, and check to make sure the water is at least 1½ to 2 inches above them. (If you need to add more water, add boiling water.) Cook until the beans are nearly tender, about 2 hours.

SOPA DE ELOTE
SWEET CORN SOUP

In the great pre-Hispanic corn cultures of the Americas, the appearance of the season's first tender ears of corn was greeted with rejoicing and thanksgiving ceremonies. The young corn was roasted in the husk and eaten off the cob or made into delicate fresh corn tamales, a naturally sweet-tasting fresh *atole*, or a soup. *Sopa de Elote*, traditionally made in Puebla at this time of year, combines the young corn with onions, chiles, and tomatoes. Though it is best made with freshly picked corn, frozen corn kernels also make a good soup.

3 tablespoons butter or corn oil

½ cup chopped white onion

2 fresh poblano chiles, roasted (page 217), peeled, seeds and ribs removed, cut into thin strips

1 clove garlic, peeled and minced

6 cups fresh corn kernels (8 to 9 ears), or one 16-ounce package frozen corn kernels

1 large ripe tomato, or 4 ripe plum tomatoes, diced

6 cups chicken broth

1 to 2 tablespoons chopped fresh cilantro or parsley

Salt and freshly ground black pepper

Vegetable oil for deep-frying

4 to 6 corn tortillas, cut into small strips

1 cup crumbled *queso fresco*, or crumbled feta, or 1 cup sour cream

Melt the butter in a large saucepan over medium heat. Add the onion and sauté until slightly softened, 1 to 2 minutes. Add the chile strips, garlic, and 2 cups of the corn kernels. Cook, stirring often, for 3 to 4 minutes. Remove from the heat and set aside.

In a blender or food processor puree the 4 remaining cups of corn kernels together with the tomato and 1½ cups of the chicken broth. Press the puree through a coarse-mesh sieve into the saucepan.

Add the remaining 4½ cups chicken broth, half of the cilantro, and salt and pepper to taste. Bring the soup to a boil, then reduce the heat to low and simmer, stirring occasionally, for 10 to 15 minutes, until the flavors are well blended.

Meanwhile, pour the oil to a depth of 1 inch in a skillet and heat. Fry the tortilla strips until they are crisp and golden, about 1 minute. Remove them with a slotted spoon and set them aside. Drain them on crumpled paper towels.

Ladle the soup into individual bowls and top each serving with the cheese, tortilla strips, and cilantro.

THE AZTEC

RIGHT: *Sopa de Elote* is brightened with a garnish of chile, tortilla strips, and fresh cilantro.

CHILEATOLE

MASA-THICKENED CORN, CHILE, AND HERB SOUP

Corn was the most important food for the Aztec—and for all the other great native cultures of Mesoamerica. Much of it was consumed in liquid or semiliquid form as a beverage, soup, or porridge called *atolli* (or *atole*). To prepare *atolli*, nixtamalized corn is ground into a flour dough similar to that used to make tortillas and tamales. The *masa* is then thinned with cool water or broth, flavored to taste, simmered, and served either hot or cold. There are many different versions of *atolli*, both sweet and savory.

While visiting the great Jamaica Market in Mexico City with our friend Lila Lomeli, we met a vendor of Lila's acquaintance who specializes in making *chileatole*, a fresh chile- and herb-flavored *atolli*. From a large cauldron, he ladled this nourishing soup-drink into disposable cups. Golden kernels of fresh corn floated in a creamy celadon-colored liquid, rich with the earthy flavor of *masa*, fragrant with herbs, and warm with chile. From bowls of chopped tomatoes, cilantro, chiles, onion, and *queso fresco*, we selected toppings for our *chileatole* and stood chatting, savoring every nourishing drop. Though the recipe here, like the one we ate that day, is purely vegetarian, *chileatole* is also delicious when made with chicken broth and supplemented with shredded poached chicken breast.

4 ears fresh corn, or 2 cups frozen corn kernels

8 cups water

¾ cup fresh *masa* or *masa harina*

1 cup firmly packed fresh baby spinach leaves, well washed

3 or 4 tomatillos, papery husks removed, rinsed

1 to 2 fresh serrano or jalapeño chiles, stems removed, seeded if desired

6 to 8 sprigs fresh cilantro

4 to 6 sprigs fresh epazote (optional)

2 fresh *hoja santa* leaves, stem and center rib removed, or ½ cup chopped fresh fennel bulb and tops

½ white onion, peeled and coarsely chopped (about 1 cup)

1½ teaspoons salt, or to taste

1 tomato, chopped, for garnish (optional)

1 white onion, chopped, for garnish (optional)

2 serrano chiles or 2 jalapeño chiles, chopped, for garnish (optional)

½ cup crumbled *queso fresco* or feta, for garnish (optional)

Chopped fresh cilantro, for garnish (optional)

Using a sharp chef's knife, cut the corn kernels off of the cobs. Bring 5 cups of the water to a boil in a large saucepan, add the corn, and cook over high heat for 5 minutes.

Dissolve the fresh *masa* or *masa harina* in the remaining 3 cups water. It should have the consistency of heavy cream. Stir the *masa* mixture into the corn. Reduce the heat to medium-low and simmer, stirring often, for 15 minutes.

In a blender or food processor combine the spinach, tomatillos, chiles, cilantro, epazote (if using), *hoja santa*, and the

onion. Puree, adding a little water to help liquefy the mixture if necessary. Add the puree to the corn and season with the salt. Simmer over medium-low heat, stirring often, for about 10 minutes. If the *chileatole* seems too thick, add more water; if it seems thin, simmer it a little longer.

Ladle the *chileatole* into bowls or mugs and sprinkle with any of the garnishes as desired.

Fresh corn, cooked on or off of the cob, is a favorite snack in Mexico. At the huge Jamaica Market in Mexico City, there are several stands devoted to selling corn. The boiled or grilled whole ears are threaded onto sharp sticks and eaten as North Americans would eat a corn dog at the county fair. The boiled ears are generally spread with mayonnaise, then rolled in grated cheese. The grilled ones are served sprinkled with lime juice and ground red chile.

Esquites, fresh corn kernels that have been cut off the cob, are simmered with onion, green chiles, and epazote, then served in paper cups with plastic spoons. Today they are usually cooked in butter, but recipes dating back to Aztec times call for cooking the corn in *pulque,* an alcoholic beverage made from the maguey cactus. *Esquites* makes a great side dish with grilled poultry or meat, and is also good served over rice as a vegetarian main course.

5 to 6 ears fresh corn, or 3 cups
    frozen corn kernels

4 tablespoons butter

1 tablespoon corn oil

1½ cups diced white onion

1 to 2 fresh serrano or jalapeño
    chiles, stems removed, seeded if
    desired, minced

½ cup finely chopped fresh epazote
    or cilantro

Salt to taste

Fresh cilantro sprigs, for garnish

Using a sharp chef's knife, cut the corn kernels off the cobs. Melt the butter with the oil in a large skillet over medium heat. When the butter turns clear and the foam begins to subside, add the onion and chiles and sauté until softened, about 5 minutes. Stir in the corn, epazote, and salt. Cover, and cook over low heat until the corn is tender, 10 to 15 minutes. Serve garnished with cilantro.

NOPALITOS A LA MEXICANA
SAUTÉED CACTUS MEXICAN-STYLE

Cactus has been important as a food in Mexico since pre-Hispanic times. Both the fruit (*tunas*) and the leaves (*nopalitos*) are eaten. After being carefully dethorned, cactus leaves (or paddles) may be grilled whole or sliced and boiled. Recent discoveries indicate that they are not only delicious but also may be helpful in combating diabetes.

This recipe for sautéed *nopalitos* was given to us by Josefina Carrillo Luna, who lives in Mexico City but is originally from the neighboring state of Michoacán. Serve this as a side dish, a filling for tacos, or as part of a salad (see Variation).

6 fresh nopal cactus paddles, spines removed (see Note), well rinsed

1 to 2 tablespoons corn oil

1 small white onion, peeled and chopped (about 1 cup)

6 to 8 ripe plum tomatoes, diced (2½ to 3 cups)

2 or 3 fresh serrano chiles or 1 or 2 jalapeño chiles, seeded if desired, minced

Freshly ground black pepper to taste

Salt

⅓ cup chopped fresh cilantro

Bring a large saucepan of lightly salted water to a boil.

Stack up the cleaned paddles and slice them crosswise into thin strips. Place the strips in the boiling water and cook until crisp-tender, 15 to 20 minutes. Rinse well under cold running water, and drain thoroughly.

Heat the oil in a large skillet over medium-high heat. Add the onion and sauté until translucent, 3 to 5 minutes. Add the cactus strips, tomatoes, and chiles. Sauté until hot, 2 to 3 minutes. Season with salt and pepper. Add the cilantro, toss, and serve.

VARIATION: Josefina also likes to prepare this dish as part of a salad. In that case, the ingredients remain the same but the tomatoes and chiles are not cooked. Though they are not as good as the fresh ones, canned *nopalitos* in vinegar are acceptable for a salad. Arrange the tossed salad ingredients on a bed of baby greens, drizzle with a light vinaigrette dressing, and sprinkle with crumbled goat cheese or *queso fresco*.

NOTE: When selecting fresh cactus paddles, look for ones that are firm, not shriveled or wrinkled, and about 8 inches long. Even if they have been dethorned, it is best to wear gloves when handling the paddles. With a sharp knife or vegetable peeler, trim off the edge that outlines the paddle, including the blunt end where it was attached to the plant. Scrape off any stickers that remain, and use the tip of the knife to dig out any that are imbedded. Rinse the paddles well under cold running water.

THE AZTEC

RIGHT: *Nopalitos a la Mexicana* can be used as a tortilla filling or as the basis for a salad.

HUEVOS OAXAQUEÑOS
EGGS OAXACA-STYLE

Though we've always enjoyed *Huevos Oaxaqueños* when visiting Oaxaca, the idea of adding water to a cooked egg dish and then allowing it to simmer for 10 or even 20 minutes sounded terrible. Surely it would toughen the eggs and should be done only as a last resort—to hold them if the brunch guests were late, perhaps. After testing the recipe with and with out the extra water and simmering, however, we found that the traditional Oaxacan technique produces lighter, fluffier eggs. There is always something new to learn!

Serve these with hot tortillas and *Tsah Bi Bu'ul* (page 46).

3 to 4 fresh serrano or jalapeño chiles, roasted (page 217)

3 medium to large ripe tomatoes, roasted (page 217)

1 small white onion, peeled and quartered

2 cloves garlic, peeled

1 to 2 tablespoons vegetable oil

Salt and freshly ground black pepper to taste

½ cup diced cooked nopal cactus paddles or canned *nopalitos* in water, well drained (optional)

8 large eggs, lightly beaten together with 1 tablespoon water

2 tablespoons butter

¼ cup water

1 tablespoon chopped fresh cilantro

Remove the stems and seeds from the roasted chiles. Place the chiles, tomatoes, onion, and garlic in a blender or food processor and puree. Press the puree through a medium-mesh sieve into a bowl.

Heat the oil in a skillet or saucepan over medium-high heat. Add the puree and fry, stirring frequently, for about 5 minutes. Season with salt and pepper, and set aside. (This sauce may be made in advance and kept in the refrigerator for 1 to 2 days; reheat it before adding it to the omelet.) Add the cactus (if using) to the sauce.

Season the eggs with ½ teaspoon salt and with pepper to taste. Melt the butter in a large nonstick or well-seasoned skillet over medium heat. Pour in the eggs and stir with a wooden spatula, gathering the edges in toward the middle; then allow the eggs to set like a soft omelet. Pour the sauce around the edges of the omelet, and using the spatula, cut in toward the center so that the sauce is distributed throughout. Pour ¼ cup water around the outside edge. Cover the pan and allow the eggs to simmer over low heat for 10 to 15 minutes. Stir gently, garnish with the cilantro, and serve.

RAJAS DE CHILE POBLANO CON HUEVO
EGGS SCRAMBLED WITH CHILES AND ONION

The term *rajas* means "strips" in Spanish. Among the most common *rajas* used in Mexican cooking are those made from roasted poblano chiles. Poblanos are usually dark green in color and look like small, slightly smashed bell peppers. They are becoming increasingly available in supermarkets across the United States, which is great because they are versatile and delicious. Because of their size and moderate heat, they are a good choice both for *rajas* and for *chiles rellenos*.

Serve the eggs with a basket of hot corn tortillas.

1 to 2 tablespoons butter

1 tablespoon vegetable oil

1 or 2 fresh poblano chiles, roasted (page 217), peeled, seeded, and cut into strips

1 small white onion, peeled and thinly sliced (about 1 cup)

8 large eggs, beaten together with 1 tablespoon water

Salt and freshly ground black pepper to taste

Melt the butter with the oil in a large nonstick or well-seasoned skillet over medium heat. When the foam begins to subside and the butter turns clear, add the chile strips and the onion. Sauté until the onion has softened and its edges begin to turn golden, about 5 minutes. Add the eggs and cook, stirring constantly with a wooden spoon or spatula, until the eggs are softly scrambled, 2 to 3 minutes. Season to taste with salt and pepper, and serve immediately.

CHILPACHOLE
VERACRUZ-STYLE SHRIMP STEW

Since pre-Hispanic times, tiny briny-tasting dried shrimp have been crushed or ground to use as a seasoning in sauces like the one for this shrimp sauté from the state of Veracruz. The flavors of the fresh and dried shrimp combine with the hot and smoky *chipotle* chiles to make *Chilpachole* an unusual and memorable dish. Dried shrimp are sold in the Mexican or Asian spice sections of many supermarkets in the United States.

Serve the shrimp and sauce over fried corn tortillas or hot fluffy rice.

1½ pounds fresh jumbo shrimp (16 to 20 per pound)

1 tablespoon dried shrimp

½ cup vegetable oil

1 small head garlic, unpeeled

2 cups hot water

2 dried ancho chiles

1 dried chipotle chile or canned chipotle chile in adobo sauce

1 small onion, peeled and sliced

2 ripe tomatoes, roasted (page 217)

3 tablespoons chopped fresh epazote or cilantro

Salt to taste

Rinse the fresh shrimp. Shell and devein them, reserving the shells. Set the shrimp and the shells aside.

Rinse the dried shrimp, and drain well. Place a lightly oiled skillet over low heat, add the dried shrimp, and cook, stirring constantly, until dry and crisp, about 2 minutes. Remove them with a slotted spoon and allow them to cool slightly. Then, using an electric spice mill, coffee grinder, or blender, grind the shrimp to make a powder. (This can also be done the traditional way, with a mortar and pestle.) Set aside.

Heat 2 tablespoons of the oil in a large skillet. Add the reserved shrimp shells and sauté until red, 2 to 3 minutes. Using a slotted spoon, transfer the shells to a blender, add the garlic and hot water, and liquefy. Strain and set the liquid aside, discarding the solids.

Stem, seed, and remove the ribs from the dried chiles; rinse

thoroughly. In a dry or lightly oiled skillet over medium heat, lightly toast the chiles a few seconds on each side, just until the rinsing water has evaporated. Set aside.

In the same skillet fry the onion in 2 to 3 tablespoons of the oil until it turns golden, 3 to 4 minutes. Remove the onion with a slotted spoon and set aside; leave the remaining oil in the skillet.

Place the toasted dried chiles, and (if using), the seeded canned chipotle chile with a coat of its adobo sauce, in a clean blender container. Add the onion and tomatoes and puree. Add the puree to the oil in the skillet, and fry for 1 to 2 minutes. Stir in the ground dried shrimp and the reserved shrimp liquid. Bring to a boil, reduce the heat to medium-low, and cook until the liquid is reduced by about one-third, 8 to 10 minutes. Add the fresh shrimp and the epazote, and simmer until the shrimp turn pink, 5 to 7 minutes. Season to taste with salt, and serve.

TORTAS DE CAMARON
DRIED-SHRIMP FRITTERS

SERVES 4

Salting and sun-drying boiled shrimp was a pre-Hispanic method of preserving them for later use and for transport to distant areas. Though these days frozen shrimp are available year-round, cooks throughout Mexico continue to use dried shrimp in certain sauces and other dishes because of their distinctive concentrated flavor. Tiny dried shrimp are available in 1-ounce packages and are found in the Mexican or Asian spice sections of many supermarkets. They are also available through mail order (see Sources).

Tortas de Camaron are traditionally served at Easter and Christmas. These delicate little fritters have a slightly briny flavor that is like "essence of shrimp." They stand up well to the smoky, fruity heat of the *Salsa de Guajillo* and are complemented by the crunchy and slightly tart cactus. Serve a basket of warm corn tortillas alongside.

This recipe was given to us by Josefina Carrillo Luna. *Tortas de Camaron* are a specialty of her mother-in-law, Irene Diego, who lives in Toluca, in the state of Michoacán.

3 or 4 fresh nopal cactus paddles (about ½ pound), spines removed (see Note, page 118), well rinsed

4 tablespoons vegetable oil

2 ounces small dried shrimp

2 tablespoons *masa harina*

2 eggs, at room temperature

1 recipe *Salsa de Guajillo* (red chile and tomato sauce, page 99)

Bring a large saucepan of lightly salted water to boil.

Stack up the cleaned cactus paddles and slice them crosswise into thin strips. Place the strips in the boiling water and cook until crisp-tender, 15 to 20 minutes. Rinse them well under cold running water, drain thoroughly, and set aside.

Oil a large nonstick or well-seasoned skillet with about 2 teaspoons of the oil and place over medium heat. Add the dried shrimp and cook, stirring constantly, until crisp and lightly toasted, 2 to 3 minutes. Remove them with a slotted spoon and allow to cool slightly. Using an electric spice mill, coffee grinder, or blender, grind the shrimp to make a powder. (This can also be done the traditional way, with a mortar and pestle.) Combine the ground shrimp with the *masa harina* and set aside.

Warm a deep medium-size mixing bowl slightly. Add the eggs and beat with an electric mixer until very thick, fluffy, and lemon-colored, about 5 minutes. Gently but thoroughly fold the shrimp mixture into the eggs.

Line a baking sheet with paper towels and set aside.

Add the remaining oil to the skillet and place over medium-high heat. Spoon rounded tablespoons of the egg mixture into the hot oil and cook, turning once, until browned on both sides, 1 to 2 minutes. As they are cooked, transfer the shrimp fritters to the baking sheet to drain. You should have about twelve 2-inch fritters.

Pour off all but a thin film of oil from the skillet, and add the *Salsa de Guajillo* and the cactus strips. Bring to a simmer over medium heat. Return the shrimp fritters to the pan and simmer until heated through, about 5 minutes. Serve immediately.

THE AZTEC

123

PESCADO EN TAMAL
FISH WRAPPED IN CORN HUSKS

With their capital, Tenochtitlan, located in the middle of a great lake, the Aztec ate a variety of small fresh fish and other lake creatures. Wrapping a fish in corn husks before grilling or steaming was the ancient equivalent of wrapping it in aluminum foil. The advantage of the husks is that they impart their own special flavor to the food—and they are biodegradable.

10 large dried corn husks

3 dried *guajillo* chiles

4 small whole trout or other whole fish (½ to ¾ pounds each), cleaned

Juice of 1 lemon

Juice of 1 lime

4 cloves garlic, peeled and sliced paper-thin

Salt to taste

1 lemon, thinly sliced

4 fresh sprigs cilantro

1½ tablespoons corn oil, if grilling the fish

1 recipe *Salsa de Guajillo* (red chile and tomato sauce, page 99)

Bring a large pot of water to a boil. Rinse the corn husks well in hot water, add them to the boiling water, and set aside until pliable, about 1 hour.

Meanwhile, place the chiles in a saucepan, add enough water to cover and bring to a boil. Remove from the heat and allow to soak for 20 minutes. Then stem, seed, and remove the ribs from the chiles, and cut them into strips.

Rinse the trout well under cold running water and pat dry. Place them in a nonreactive baking dish or bowl and add the lemon juice, lime juice, chile strips, garlic, and salt. Set aside to marinate at room temperature for about 15 minutes.

Place a few chile strips, a couple of halved lemon slices, a couple of garlic slices, and a sprig of cilantro inside the body cavity of the each fish. Drain the corn husks and pat them dry. Place 2 corn husks in front of you, concave side up, with their wide ends overlapping by about 2 inches and the points turned out—forming a shape like a canoe. Place the

fish in the husks and spoon in some of the marinade. Wrap the fish in the husks and tie the package at each end with strips of husk (page 219) or kitchen string. Wrap the remaining fish in the same manner.

TO GRILL: Lightly oil the outside of the husks. Grill the trout over a moderately hot fire, turning once, until they feel firm to the touch when you press down gently on the husks, about 20 minutes.

TO STEAM: Place the fish in the top of a steamer over boiling water (make sure they don't touch the boiling water below). Steam for about 30 minutes, or until the fish feels firm when you press down gently on the husks.

Serve the fish "tamales" in their husks. Pass the *Salsa de Guajillo* separately.

L E F T : Corn husks wrap whole fish like a tamale, imparting a special flavor to the fish when cooked.

HUACHINANGO EN MOLE VERDE
RED SNAPPER FILLETS IN GREEN MOLE SAUCE

SERVES 6

The green mole recipe that follows is adapted from the wonderful one served at Restaurante El Bajio in Mexico City. Carmen Ramirez, the owner, specializes in the cooking of her native Veracruz. Her green mole is typical of Xalapa (Jalapa), the state capital. Unlike versions from other regions that often contain pumpkin seeds and tomatillos, Xalapan *mole verde* is mostly fresh herbs and, of course, the traditional jalapeños. When we ate at the restaurant, we had chicken in green mole, which was delicious, but Carmen also likes to serve the sauce with the fresh fish for which Veracruz is famous. It would be wonderful with sautéed shrimp, too.

GREEN MOLE

10 small to medium-size romaine lettuce leaves, coarsely chopped

½ cup firmly packed fresh cilantro leaves

4 to 6 sprigs fresh epazote (optional)

4 fresh *hoja santa* leaves, central rib and stem removed, coarsely chopped, or ½ cup chopped fresh fennel bulb and tops

2 fresh jalapeño chiles, stems removed, seeded if desired

2½ to 3 cups chicken broth or water

3 tablespoons corn or vegetable oil

1 small to medium-size white onion, peeled and chopped (about 1¼ cups)

4 cloves garlic, peeled and chopped

Salt and freshly ground black pepper to taste

1 chayote, pitted, peeled, and diced

⅓ cup sliced fresh green beans (1-inch pieces)

1 small to medium-size zucchini, ends trimmed, scrubbed and diced

Six 5- to 6-ounce boneless, skinless red snapper fillets or other firm fish fillets

1 or 2 limes, thinly sliced

Place the romaine leaves, cilantro, epazote (if using), *hoja santa,* and chiles in a blender or food processor. Add 1½ cups of the broth, and pulse on and off until pureed.

Heat 2 tablespoons of the oil in a sauté pan or large skillet over medium heat. Add the onion and garlic and sauté until translucent, about 5 minutes. Add the herb puree and cook over medium-low heat, stirring occasionally, for 15 minutes.

Press as much of the mole as possible through a medium-mesh sieve into a bowl. Discard any solids that remain in the strainer, and return the mole to the pan. Season to taste with salt and pepper. Stir in the remaining 1 to 1½ cups broth and bring the mole to a simmer over medium heat. The sauce should be thick enough to coat the back of a spoon.

Add the chayote, beans, and zucchini, and simmer over medium-low heat, stirring occasionally, until the sauce has reduced slightly and the vegetables are crisp-tender, 20 to 30 minutes.

Meanwhile, brush both the snapper fillets and the rack of a barbeque or a stove-top grill lightly with the remaining oil. Prepare a fire in a barbeque, or preheat stove-top grill or broiler to medium-hot. (If using a broiler, line a broiler pan with aluminum foil and brush it with oil.) Season the fish lightly with salt and pepper. Grill or broil the fillets for 3 to 5 minutes per side, depending on their thickness. Transfer the fillets to a serving platter, surrounding them with lime slices, and top with the mole.

THE AZTEC

126

LOMO DE PUERCO EN CACAHUETE
PORK LOIN IN PEANUT AND RED CHILE SAUCE

SERVES 6 TO 8

This outstanding and uncomplicated recipe was given to us by Josefina Carrillo Luna, who learned how to make it from a friend from the state of Veracruz. It is a variation on the dishes enriched with pumpkin and squash seeds that have been made in Mexico for thousands of years. The combination of *guajillo* chiles and peanuts gives the sauce a beautiful red-orange color, subtle heat, and wonderful flavor.

1 boneless pork loin roast (about 3 pounds)

Salt and freshly ground black pepper to taste

5 tablespoons peanut or vegetable oil

1 white onion, peeled and halved

3 or 4 large cloves garlic, peeled

1 bay leaf

1 chicken bouillon cube (optional)

14 to 16 dried *guajillo* chiles, rinsed, seeded, and roasted (page 217)

1 cup blanched raw or dry-roasted peanuts, skins removed

1 tablespoon minced fresh cilantro or parsley (optional)

Pat the roast dry with paper towels, and season it all over with salt and pepper. Heat 2 tablespoons of the oil in a Dutch oven over medium-high heat. Add the roast and, turning it with tongs, brown it on all sides, 15 minutes. Pour in enough water to cover the pork by 1 inch. Add one half of the onion, 2 or 3 cloves garlic, the bay leaf, and the bouillon cube (if using). Bring to a simmer over medium-high heat, then reduce heat to medium-low and cover the pan, leaving the lid ajar to allow some of the liquid to evaporate. Simmer gently for about 45 minutes, until the pork is just done and the broth is reduced to about 5 cups. (If you are preparing the pork in advance, allow it to cool in the broth.) Transfer the roast to a cutting board. Strain and reserve the broth, discarding the onion, bay leaf, and garlic.

Meanwhile, place the roasted chiles in a saucepan, add water to cover, and bring to a boil over high heat. Remove from the heat, cover, and allow the chiles to soak for 20 to 30 minutes, until softened.

Heat 1 tablespoon of the oil in a skillet over medium heat. Add the peanuts and sauté until just golden, 1 to 2 minutes. Watch carefully so they don't burn. Using a slotted spoon, remove the peanuts to a bowl and set aside.

Drain the chiles and transfer them to a blender or food processor. Add the remaining onion and the garlic clove, and pour in 1½ cups of the broth from the reserved pork roast. Pulse on and off until pureed. Press the puree through a medium-mesh sieve into a bowl. Return the puree to the blender and add the peanuts. Pulse on and off until pureed.

Heat the remaining 2 tablespoons oil in a clean, dry Dutch oven over medium-high heat. Carefully add the chile-peanut mixture (it may splatter) and fry for about 5 minutes, stirring frequently.

Stir in 1½ to 2 cups of the reserved broth and reduce the heat to medium-low. Taste the sauce, and add salt or pepper if needed. Slice the pork roast and, holding the slices together so that the roast retains its basic shape, place it in the sauce along with any meat juices that escaped when you sliced it. Cover the pan and simmer the pork gently in the sauce for about 20 minutes to allow the flavors to blend. If the sauce begins to look too thick, stir in a little additional broth or water. Sprinkle with cilantro (if using) before serving.

PIPIÁN ROJO DE PATO
DUCK IN RED CHILE AND PUMPKIN-SEED SAUCE

Pipiánes, elegant green or red chile sauces thickened and enriched with ground pumpkin or squash seeds, have been a mainstay of Mexican cuisine since pre-Hispanic times. Though *pipiánes* are delicious, they can be delicate. If cooked over high heat or stirred too vigorously, the sauce may separate, which doesn't affect the flavor but does mar the appearance of the dish. Our friend Yolanda Ramos Galicia, a respected anthropologist and cooking teacher from Tlaxcala, makes wonderful *pipiánes* and moles. She advises her students to stir both sauces very gently, and to always use a wooden spoon or spatula: "Pull the spoon slowly along the bottom of the pan from the outer edges in toward the middle." If, in spite of your best efforts, the sauce still turns lumpy, it will usually smooth out if pressed through a medium-mesh sieve and then returned to the pot. Many chile-based sauces in Tlaxcala and Puebla contain anise seed; in other areas *hoja santa*, which also has an aniselike flavor, is used. Yolanda tells us that the anise seeds are thought to make the chile more digestible. We find that anise is also a very complementary flavor and especially good with duck. Serve the duck and sauce with a basket of hot corn tortillas or over rice.

One 5½- to 6-pound duck	8 cups water	1 cup plus 2 tablespoons hulled raw pumpkin seeds (*pepitas*)
¼ teaspoon anise seeds	8 dried *guajillo* chiles, stems removed, rinsed and seeded	8 cloves garlic, unpeeled
4 to 6 black peppercorns	2 dried ancho chiles, stems removed, rinsed and seeded	Fresh fennel or anise tops, for garnish
Salt to taste	Boiling water	
1 white onion, peeled and sliced		

Remove the giblets, neck, and visible fat from the body cavity of the duck and set aside. Rinse the duck inside and out under cold running water, and pat it dry with paper towels. With a sharp knife, cut the duck into 8 serving pieces (see Note, page 130).

Place the anise seeds and peppercorns in a spice mill or pepper grinder, and grind. Season the duck pieces with the anise-pepper mixture, and sprinkle with salt to taste. Set aside.

In a large saucepan combine the duck back, neck, wing tips, and giblets (except the liver) with half of the onion, the 8 cups water, and 1 teaspoon salt. Bring to a simmer over medium-high heat, then reduce the heat to low and simmer until the liquid is reduced to about 5 cups, about 30 minutes. Strain the broth into a large measuring cup or bowl, and set aside. Discard the solids.

Meanwhile, place a piece of duck fat in a sauté pan or Dutch oven. Cook over medium heat until enough of the fat is rendered to cover the bottom of the pan. Remove the unrendered portion and set it aside. Place the seasoned duck pieces in the pan, skin side down, and cook, turning two or three times with tongs, until golden brown, about 30 minutes. Remove the duck pieces and set aside.

(continued on page 130)

LEFT: The delicate sauce of *Pipián Rojo de Pato* benefits from gentle stirring with a wooden spoon during cooking.

While the duck is cooking, arrange the damp chiles on a preheated griddle or skillet over low heat and toast, turning them with tongs, until the moisture evaporates and they puff slightly, about 1 minute. Do not burn the chiles or they will be bitter. Place the toasted chiles in a bowl, add boiling water to cover, and allow the chiles to soak for about 20 minutes, until softened.

Pour off all but about 3 tablespoons fat from the pan and reserve. Add the pumpkin seeds to the pan and cook, stirring, over medium-low heat until they have all popped and turned golden, about 5 minutes. Remove the seeds with a slotted spoon and set aside. Add the remaining onion and the garlic, and sauté until golden, 4 to 5 minutes. Using a slotted spoon, transfer the chiles, all but 1 tablespoon of the pumpkin seeds, and the onion and garlic to a blender or food processor. Add 1 cup of the duck broth and pulse on and off until the mixture is liquefied.

Press the puree through a medium-mesh sieve into a bowl. Return 1 to 2 tablespoons rendered fat to the pan, and place it over medium heat. When the fat is hot, stir in the pumpkin-seed mixture and cook for 5 minutes, stirring gently by pulling a wooden spoon slowly from the outer edges of the pan toward the center. Gradually stir in the remaining 4 cups broth. Return the duck pieces to the pan. Cover and simmer over medium-low heat, stirring gently from time to time, for 20 to 30 minutes, until the duck is tender and cooked through. Garnish with the fennel and a sprinkling of the reserved toasted pumpkin seeds, and serve.

NOTE: To cut a duck into serving pieces, use poultry shears to cut through the joint where the thigh joins the body, and remove the legs. Sever the joint between the thigh and the drumstick, and separate them. Next, separate the breast and wings from the back by cutting along both sides of the back parallel to the backbone. Remove the breast and split it down the middle. Cut off the bony wing tips, if they are still attached. Cut each breast half diagonally into 2 serving pieces, one of which has the wing attached. Reserve the back, wing tips, and giblets, except for the liver, for stock; save the fat to render for frying.

GUAJALOTE EN "COLORADITO"

TURKEY IN REDDISH MOLE

The Spanish arriving in the New World were served the elaborate chile-based sauces that the Aztec called *molli*. After the Conquest, as Old World ingredients like cloves, almonds, and sesame seeds were introduced, talented cooks incorporated them into their recipes, and over the years *molli* became *mole*.

Mole Coloradito, popularly called *"Coloradito,"* is one of the seven classic moles of Oaxaca. It is a wonderful sauce for turkey or chicken and is also delicious with beef. Our version is adapted from one published in *Tradiciones Gastronomicas Oaxaqueñas*, by Ana Maria Guzman de Vasquez Colmenares. Although it has quite a few ingredients, it is not difficult to make and is worth the effort. The sauce may be made in advance and refrigerated, tightly covered, for 5 to 6 days or frozen for up to 1 month.

Serve this dish with rice and/or a basket of hot tortillas.

1 half turkey breast (3 to 4 pounds), or one 3½- to 4-pound chicken

2 cloves garlic, peeled

½ medium white onion, peeled

salt to taste

6 dried *guajillo* chiles, seeded and toasted

3 dried ancho chiles and 3 dried pasilla chiles, or 6 dried ancho chiles, seeded and toasted

⅓ cup sesame seeds, lightly toasted

6 black peppercorns

4 whole cloves

One 2-inch piece cinnamon stick, preferably Mexican cinnamon

¼ teaspoon dried oregano, preferably Mexican oregano

6 large ripe plum tomatoes, roasted (page 217)

4 cloves garlic, roasted (page 217) and peeled

½ medium white onion, roasted (page 217) and peeled

¼ cup raisins

¼ cup lard, preferably home-rendered (page 217), or vegetable oil

1½ ounces (½ tablet) Mexican, bitter-sweet, or semi-sweet chocolate

2 large red potatoes, boiled until crisp-tender, peeled, and diced

Place the turkey breast in a Dutch oven and add enough water to cover. Add the raw garlic, raw onion, and 2 teaspoons salt. Bring to a gentle boil over medium-high heat. Reduce the heat to low and simmer until the turkey is cooked through, about 1 hour. If time permits, allow the turkey to cool in the broth. Remove the turkey from the broth. Discard the skin and bones, and shred the meat. Strain the broth, and set the meat and broth aside.

Meanwhile, place the chiles in a saucepan, add water to cover, and bring to a boil over high heat. Then remove the pan from the heat, cover, and allow the chiles to soak for 20 to 30 minutes, until softened.

Place the sesame seeds, peppercorns, cloves, cinnamon, and oregano in a spice grinder, or small coffee grinder, and grind to a powder.

Drain the chiles and place them in a blender or food processor. Add the roasted tomatoes, roasted garlic, roasted onion, raisins, and sesame mixture. Pulse on and off until pureed. Press the puree through a medium-mesh sieve into a bowl.

Melt the lard in a Dutch oven or large sauté pan over medium heat. When the lard is hot, carefully add the puree (it may splatter). Cook, stirring, for 5 minutes, then reduce the heat to low and stir in 2 cups of the turkey broth. Simmer, covered, stirring frequently, for 20 minutes. Add the chocolate and stir until melted and well blended, about 5 minutes. Add the turkey and the potatoes. Simmer, uncovered, over low heat, stirring gently from time to time, until the flavors have blended, about 30 minutes. If the sauce seems thick, add a little more turkey broth. Season with salt if needed, and serve.

AMARILLO DE VENADO
VENISON IN YELLOW MOLE SAUCE

SERVES 6

In his *Historia Verdadera de la Conquista de la Nueva Espana,* Bernal Diaz del Castillo, a soldier in Cortès's army, described the abundant wild game served at banquets in the court of Motecuhzoma: "Every day they cooked for him hens, turkeys, pheasants, partridges, quails, venison, wild pigs, marsh birds, pigeons, hares and rabbits and many kinds of birds and things that are reared in these lands." Like the Maya, the Aztec worshipped the sun, and gold- and red-colored foods and sauces pleased them and showed respect for the gods. Though the recipe that follows has changed little since those days, it would be as at home in a trendy New York restaurant as it was in the palace of the great Aztec emperor.

Pass a basket of hot corn tortillas when you serve the stew.

2 pounds tender venison or beef, cubed (loin or tenderloin)

3 tablespoons corn or vegetable oil

2½ cups *Mole Amarillo* (yellow mole sauce, page 97)

2 cups venison broth, beef broth, or water

½ pound fresh green beans, cut into 1-inch lengths

1 chayote, peeled, seeded, and diced

1 small to medium-size zucchini, scrubbed, trimmed, and diced

2 large red potatoes, peeled and diced

Salt and freshly ground black pepper to taste

2 to 3 tablespoons chopped fresh cilantro

Pat the venison dry with paper towels. Heat the oil in a Dutch oven over medium-high heat. When the oil is hot, add the venison and brown the cubes lightly on all sides, 6 to 8 minutes. Do not allow the pieces to touch, or they won't brown properly; if necessary, brown the meat in two batches.

Meanwhile, combine the mole and the broth in a large saucepan. Cook, stirring, until hot. Add the mole mixture to the browned venison, and stir well to loosen and incorpo-

rate any browned pan juices. Reduce the heat to low, cover, and simmer until the venison is tender, 20 to 25 minutes.

Stir in the beans, chayote, zucchini, and potatoes, and continue to simmer, covered, for 15 minutes or until the vegetables are tender. Season to taste with salt and pepper, sprinkle with the cilantro, and serve.

THE AZTEC

132

GORDITAS DE QUESO Y PILONCILLO

CHEESE AND BROWN SUGAR *GORDITAS*

Makes 12 gorditas

There are many different versions of *gorditas* (the word translates to "little fat ones")—these delicious little *masa* patties may be thick and substantial or thin-shelled and puffy, and either sweet or savory. We like this sweet version, from Christina Olvera, who is originally from Puebla. She serves her light, puffy *gorditas* for breakfast with a cup of coffee or *Champurrado* (page 138).

Piloncillos, the Mexican brown sugar cones used in this recipe, are very hard. Don't attempt to chop them in a food processor or you may break the blade. First use a hammer to crush them; then transfer the chunks to a spice grinder, food processor, or blender.

1½ cups *masa harina*

1 cup whole-milk ricotta

½ cup crushed and ground *piloncillos* (Mexican brown sugar cones), or ½ cup firmly packed dark brown sugar

½ teaspoon ground cinnamon

Pinch of salt

2 to 4 tablespoons lukewarm water

Vegetable oil for deep-frying

⅓ cup confectioners' sugar mixed with ½ teaspoon ground cinnamon

Jam or honey (optional)

Place the *masa harina* in a large mixing bowl. Add the ricotta, *piloncillos,* cinnamon, and salt, and mix well. Gradually knead in enough of the lukewarm water to make a moist and pliable but not sticky dough. Divide the dough into 12 golf ball–size balls. Cover with a clean damp kitchen towel, or with plastic wrap, so the dough won't dry out.

Place a well-seasoned or nonstick griddle or skillet over high heat. Using a tortilla press or your hands, form the dough into 5-inch tortillas (page 51). After you form each tortilla, lightly toast it on the hot griddle for about 30 seconds on each side.

Preheat the oven to its lowest setting. Line 2 baking sheets with several layers of paper towels.

When all the tortillas have been toasted, heat ¾ inch of oil in a large heavy pot over medium-high heat. When a cube of bread dropped in the oil turns golden brown in about 1 minute, the oil is the right temperature. Fry the tortillas, one at a time, in the hot oil. When they puff, gently turn them over and lightly fry the other side. Use a slotted spoon to transfer each *gordita* to a baking sheet to drain. Place 1 baking sheet in the oven to keep the *gorditas* warm until all are cooked. Sprinkle them with the cinnamon-sugar and serve immediately. If desired, the *gorditas* may be split and spread with jam or drizzled with honey.

ALEGRÍAS
PUFFED AMARANTH AND HONEY ROUNDS

MAKES ABOUT 45 ROUNDS OR 20 SQUARES

Alegrías (which means "joys" in Spanish) are a Mexican sweet with a long and interesting history. Amaranth is extremely nutritious, high in both protein and lysine. It was an important crop for the Aztec, who celebrated the harvest each year by binding the puffed seeds together with honey or human blood, shaping them into the forms of gods, and eating them. The Spanish found the practice distasteful—and a mockery of the Christian communion. Consequently they forbade the cultivation and consumption of amaranth on pain of death. Fortunately they were not successful in completely suppressing this valuable crop, and puffed amaranth and honey confections are still popular. These days, however, *alegrías* are usually shaped into rounds, squares, or bars and are eaten as a nutritious snack.

We were anxious to include a recipe for *alegrías* in this book but were concerned that puffed amaranth might not be available in the United States. However, it may be available at your local health-food store (where it is often sold as a breakfast cereal). Thanks to the help of the staff at the Frontera Grill, Rick Bayless's outstanding restaurant in Chicago, we also were able to find mail-order sources for this interesting product (see Sources).

1 cup honey

1 cup water

2 teaspoons fresh lime juice

1 teaspoon pure vanilla extract (optional)

4 to 5 cups puffed amaranth

½ cup large raisins (optional)

½ cup whole, shelled almonds (optional)

Combine the honey, water, and lime juice in a large skillet. Place over medium heat and cook, stirring, for 20 to 30 minutes, until the syrup thickens and a few drops form a firm ball when dropped into cold water. A candy thermometer should register about 245°F. Remove the skillet from the heat, and add the vanilla, 4 cups of the amaranth, and the raisins (if using). Using a large wooden spoon, stir until the amaranth and the raisins are lightly coated with the syrup. If the mixture seems heavy and sticky, stir in ½ to 1 cup of the remaining amaranth.

TO MAKE ROUNDS: Butter or oil a mini-muffin pan. Fill the cups with the amaranth mixture and press it down firmly with lightly buttered fingers. Do not refrigerate, but let the mixture cool just enough to set, and then unmold. Repeat until all of the mixture has been used.

TO MAKE SQUARES OR BARS: Press the hot amaranth mixture evenly to a buttered or oiled 9 x 12-inch shallow baking pan. While the mixture is still hot, press almonds decoratively into the top if desired. Do not refrigerate, but let the mixture cool just enough to set. Then, using a lightly buttered sharp knife, cut the mixture into 2-inch squares.

THE AZTEC

DULCE DE CACAHUETE CON MIEL

AZTEC PEANUT BRITTLE

At the entrance to the food markets and subway stations of Mexico City, there are often vendors selling *Dulce de Cacahuete* and other traditional Mexican sweets. Most of these confections were originally made with honey, but as sugar became more available and less expensive than honey, the recipes changed. This one combines *piloncillos,* the unrefined brown sugar cones first introduced by the Spanish, with honey. This very tasty brittle is mostly peanuts bound with just enough syrup to hold them together. It is usually sold in round patties. As a variation, substitute hulled toasted pumpkin seeds (*pepitas*) for the peanuts.

5 ounces *piloncillos* (Mexican brown sugar cones), or ⅔ cup firmly packed dark brown sugar

1¼ cups water

2 tablespoons honey

1 teaspoon fresh lime juice

1½ cups unsalted peanuts, blanched or dry-roasted, lightly toasted

1 tablespoon butter or mild vegetable oil, plus additional for the baking sheet

Butter a baking sheet and set it aside. Place the *piloncillos,* water, honey, and lime juice in a large heavy skillet. Cover, and cook over medium heat, stirring occasionally, until the sugar is completely dissolved, 10 to 15 minutes. Uncover and boil over medium-high heat, stirring occasionally, for about 20 minutes, until the syrup is reduced and thickened and a drop forms a firm ball when dropped into cold water. A candy thermometer should register 245°F to 250°F. Remove from the heat and add the peanuts. Stir until the nuts are thoroughly coated with the syrup.

Using a large buttered spoon, drop the nut mixture by spoonfuls onto the baking sheet. Flatten them into 2½-inch patties. When the candies are fairly firm but still warm, loosen them with a spatula and turn them over. When completely cool, the candies are ready to eat. Wrapped individually in plastic wrap and stored in a cool dry place, they will keep for several weeks.

TUNAS Y PIÑA AZTECA
PRICKLY PEARS AND PINEAPPLE TOSSED WITH MESCAL AND HONEY

SERVES 6

In *America's First Cuisines,* anthropologist and food historian Sophie Coe tells about the Aztec use of both cactus fruit and pineapple. Citing Bernardino de Sahagún, who described thirteen different varieties of *tunas* (fruit) eaten by the Aztec, Coe tells us that "some were sweet, some were sour, some could be eaten raw, and some needed cooking." Pineapple originated in the hot, humid regions of Paraguay and Brazil, but "by the time of the conquest, it was known in the West Indies, Mexico and the Maya area as well as South America."

Modern Mexican cooks often combine the beautiful scarlet-fleshed *tunas* of the nopal cactus with golden pineapple and toss them with honey and mescal or tequila. It is a colorful, delicious, and easy dessert that is deeply rooted in the pre-Columbian past.

1 large ripe pineapple	**⅓ cup honey**	**⅓ cup mescal or tequila**
6 fresh prickly pears		

Peel and core the pineapple, and cut the fruit into large bite-size chunks. You should have about 7 cups. Reserve 2 cups of chunks and any juice. Place the remaining chunks in a glass or pottery serving bowl.

With a sharp knife, trim the ends off the prickly pears. Make a cut through the skin down the length of each pear, then peel off the skin. Cut the prickly pears into quarters and add them to the pineapple in the bowl.

Place the reserved pineapple and any juice, the honey, and mescal in a blender or food processor. Pulse on and off until pureed. Pour this sauce over the pineapple and prickly pears, and allow to macerate for 30 minutes, refrigerated, before serving. Toss gently, and serve.

RIGHT: A selection of Aztec sweets includes *Tunas y Piña Azteca, Alegrías* (page 134), and *Dulce de Cacahuete con Miel* (page 135).

CHAMPURRADO
MASA-THICKENED HOT CHOCOLATE

SERVES 4

In her fascinating and passionately written book *The Food and Life of Oaxaca: Traditional Recipes from Mexico's Heart,* restaurateur and author Zarela Martinez describes *champurrado* as being "like a cup of hot chocolate combined with breakfast porridge." This wonderfully soothing and sustaining drink combines two of the most important pre-Columbian ingredients, corn *masa* and chocolate. The earliest versions would have been made with water and sweetened with honey, but today, even in very traditional Oaxaca, the recipe usually calls for sugar-sweetened Mexican chocolate and often also includes milk. Serve *champurrado* for breakfast or as an afternoon pick-me-up, alone or accompanied by *Gorditas de Queso y Piloncillo* (page 133).

⅓ cup fresh *masa* or *masa harina*

5 cups cold water or 3 cups water plus 2 cups milk

¼ teaspoon salt (optional)

Two 3-ounce tablets Mexican chocolate

In a mixing bowl combine the fresh *masa* or *masa harina* with 1 cup of the water, stirring until smooth. In a medium saucepan combine the *masa* mixture, the remaining 4 cups water, and the salt (if using). Bring to a boil over medium heat, stirring constantly. Reduce the heat to low and simmer, stirring occasionally, until the mixture is thickened to the consistency of thin cooked cereal, 15 to 20 minutes.

Add the chocolate and continue to stir until melted and thoroughly combined. Remove the pan from the heat and beat with a traditional wooden *molinillo* or a handheld electric mixer, a whisk, or an egg beater until a thick froth forms on top.

Pour into mugs and spoon some of the foam on top.

ATOLLI DE MAIZ AZUL OTOMI
OTOMI-STYLE BLUE CORN BEVERAGE

SERVES
4 TO 6

Our friend Yolanda Ramos Galicia, an anthropologist and cook from Tlaxcala, suggested that we include this very typical *atolli* (or *atole*) from the Otomi, a prominent tribe whose villages lie, as Yolanda puts it, "*en las faldas de la Malinche*" (in the skirts of the Malinche), the volcano named for Cortès's interpreter and lover that dominates the Tlaxcalan landscape. The fiercely independent Otomi were skilled bowmen and on occasion acted as mercenaries for the Aztec, though they lived in the rival state of Tlazcallan (modern Tlaxcala).

Otomi cooks often flavor and perfume their strikingly deep purple *atolli* with both canela (Mexican cinnamon) and orange leaves. Since it is difficult to find orange leaves that have not been sprayed with pesticides, we have substituted orange-flower water. The blue corn flour labeled "for *atole*" sold in the United States does not have the vivid color of the Tlaxcalan flour, but the taste is similar.

⅓ cup blue corn flour

5 cups cold water, or 3 cups water and 2 cups milk

Two 3-inch pieces cinnamon, preferably Mexican cinnamon

⅓ to ½ cup honey or sugar, to taste

¼ teaspoon salt

½ teaspoon orange-flower water (optional)

In a small bowl combine the blue corn flour with 1 cup of the water. Transfer the corn mixture to a large saucepan and stir in the remaining 4 cups water, the cinnamon, honey, and salt. Cook over medium heat, stirring frequently, until the *atolli* thickens to the texture of a light porridge, 25 to 30 minutes. Stir in the orange-flower water (if using) and pour the *atolli* through a medium-mesh sieve into a pitcher. Serve hot.

THE AZTEC

139

the inca

chapter
three

The Culinary Fantasy of the Andes

JACK WEATHERFORD

The cuisine of the Andes offers some of the most diverse yet least known foods on the planet. Small village markets offer candy-striped potatoes, tubers with the flavor of butterscotch, blackberries the size of plums, beans that explode like popcorn, and fruits that taste like ice cream. Even the crops we all know—potatoes, beans, corn, and chiles—come in sizes, flavors, and colors unique to this region.

The agricultural civilizations of the Andes developed largely in isolation over many thousands of years. They shared a few crops, such as corn and beans, with Mesoamerica, but most of the great variety of fruits, beans, roots, and tubers of the Andes were known nowhere else in the world prior to the arrival of the Spanish in the sixteenth century.

Civilization in the Andes stretches back many thousands of years and reached a cultural climax under the Inca, who ruled the empire that they called Tawantinsuyo—the empire of the four directions. Whereas many of the world's most influential civilizations built their capital cities around great fortresses for defense or arenas for public games, the Inca world centered on a garden. So important was food and agriculture in this empire that all four directions converged on a magical garden of silver and gold located at the heart of the capital city of Cuzco, which means "navel" in the native Quechua language. Within Cuzco the spiritual and political center was the royal garden, in which all the stalks of corn, fruits, and leaves were made of gold and silver. Even insects made of precious metals rested among the leaves. The Inca emperor tended this garden in a series of rituals as a way of ensuring the fertility of the land in his kingdom.

The uniqueness of Andean cuisine derives from its very special environmental mix. The Andes consist of a long sequence of mountains and valleys bordered by jungle on the interior and desert along the coast. Some of the world's highest peaks separate green, lush jungle from the dry scrub area. As one ascends the mountain peaks, the growing conditions change radically within a few hundred feet. In this landscape of varying altitudes, temperatures, and moisture, a mosaic of ecological niches and micro-zones produce a great variety of plants. The Inca fully exploited this variety, and most farm families cultivated fields at many different altitudes. In fact, the variety of foods produced in the Andes at the time of Inca rule probably exceeded the variety of any other geographic zone of comparable size on the planet.

In addition to their skill at farming, the Inca were great engineers. By the sixteenth century they had built the most expansive road system in the world. The main road ran the length of the empire: more than three thousand miles through the Andes from modern Quito, Ecuador, past Santiago, Chile. Another two thousand miles of major arteries connected it to surrounding areas, such as Argentina and Colombia, and linked up with many thousands of miles of local roads.

Constructed from stone, the road passed through the valleys and up the sides of the mountains. It crossed deserts and wound around glaciers. It spanned some of the steepest gorges in the world by means of cable bridges woven from natural fibers. Called Capac Nan, the Beautiful Road, it had curbs and gutters to drain rain into ditches, reinforced walls to protect it from falling rocks, and adobe walls to protect it from blowing sand in the deserts.

In a time when most of the world's people ate only what grew within a few miles of their home, the Inca in the mountains could enjoy fresh fish and fruits brought up from the coast, and the people in the coastal plain could eat the vegetables of the mountains. A peasant in the Inca empire probably had a more varied diet than did the royal families of France or England of that era.

Along the Capac Nan, the Inca built a series of stations, called *tambos*, which provided rest facilities for travelers and large warehouses of foods and other goods for the army. (In order to move as quickly as possible, the Inca army did not carry food supplies when it was on the march.) To keep the warehouses stocked at all times, the Inca developed sophisticated methods of preservation. They preserved llama and other types of meat by air-curing it in areas with very low humidity. This cured meat was known as *charqui*, and is familiar to us today as jerky. To preserve starchy foods, such as potatoes and other tubers, the Inca developed a freeze-drying technology, alternately freezing the potatoes and then thawing them and pressing out the moisture.

The Spaniards who conquered South America wanted gold and silver and showed little interest in agriculture. They initially ignored the Andean crops, and in some cases outlawed the foods so that the farmers would cultivate the wheat, grapes, olives, and other foods preferred by the conquerors.

The Andean foods that were brought back to Europe were greeted with suspicion. The potato seemed as strange to Europeans three hundred years ago as amaranth and quinoa seem to us today. Many Europeans avoided the potato for a variety of superstitious reasons: it grew under the ground (the realm of the devil), it had such a twisted form they feared it caused leprosy, it was not mentioned in the Bible, it generated from its own tuber, unlike European crops, which grew from seed. In time, however, with pressure from the enlightened monarchs of the eighteenth century, such as Frederick William of Prussia and Catherine the Great of Russia, peasants switched from grains to potatoes. Once they adopted the more productive and nutritious potato, their diets improved immediately and life expectancy increased.

On the other hand, the natives of the Andes quickly adopted the new foods that came in from Africa, Asia, and Europe. They easily incorporated the meat from the goats, sheep, pigs, cows, and chickens introduced by the Spaniards. They also added new crops, such as rice and bananas, and learned to prepare new foods, such as bread and cheese.

Today the people of the Andes still enjoy some of the most varied crops and foods of any people in the world. Although potatoes, corn, sweet potatoes, avocados, peanuts, pineapples, tomatoes, beans, squash, and chiles are familiar to us all, other culinary treasures, like quinoa, amaranth, yuca root, and cherimoya, have only recently been introduced to North American markets—and still others remain unknown outside of Peru and Bolivia.

Distribution of these once exotic foods and information about how to prepare them has improved dramatically in the last few years. These days it is not uncommon to find a variety of fresh chiles, cilantro, Jerusalem artichokes, and gold- or purple-fleshed potatoes even in small-town supermarkets. If this trend continues, one day dishes such as *Torrejas de Quinoa* (crisp savory quinoa pancakes, page 203) or *Ají de Pollo* (chicken in a spicy golden chile and peanut sauce, page 187) will be as "American" to us as another old Inca favorite—corn on the cob.

CHILES IN INCA CUISINE

As for the Maya and the Aztec, for the Inca fasting meant eating without salt or chiles. These two seasonings were considered so basic that an old Quechua saying goes, "Am I your salt or chile that you always have me in your mouth and speak ill of me?"

There are four important varieties of chiles in Andean cooking. (They are sold in Latin American grocery stores in the United States in several forms—fresh, dried whole, ground, or pureed in jars. Many also are available by mail order; see Sources.) The term *ají* appears to be used generically for chiles in the Andean region. *Ajíes* have distinctive flavors, but after experimenting with other chiles, we we have suggested some possible substitutions within the recipes themselves and on page 223. Note that the chiles below are listed from the most hot to mild.

AJÍ ROCOTO (OR *LOCOTO*)

A very hot green, yellow, or red chile with a rounded shape somewhat like a bell pepper. There are several varieties of different sizes. *Rocotos* are sold fresh or dried and ground. Minced or ground *rocoto* is used in ceviches and salsas; large *rocotos* are often stuffed and baked, after first being halved, seeded, and blanched in *five* changes of sugared water to diminish their heat.

AJÍ AMARILLO OR ROJO

A hot, slender, pointed chile—3 to 5 inches long—available in yellow (*amarillo*) and red (*rojo*). These chiles are sold fresh, dried whole, dried and ground into powder, and pureed in a jar.

AJÍ MIRASOL

A medium-hot, yellow-red chile, 3 to 5 inches long and 1 to 1½ inches wide, tapering to a point. It may be found fresh, but is most often sold dried, either whole or ground into powder.

AJÍ PANCA

A mild, reddish-brown chile, 3 to 5 inches long and 1 to 1½ inches wide. It is usually sold dried, or ground into powder.

PASTA DE AJÍ
ANDEAN-STYLE CHILE PASTE

Chile pastes, made with fresh or dried chiles, are used in soups, stews, and sauces. Many Andean cooks keep containers of different *ají* pastes on hand in the refrigerator or freezer.

1 to 3 fresh or dried *ají rocoto* or 6 fresh or dried *ají amarillo* or rojo, ají mirasol, or ají panca

3 to 4 tablespoons mild salad oil (canola or corn) or water

½ teaspoon salt, or to taste

If you are using fresh chiles, peel them (if desired), seed them, and remove the ribs. You may either blanch the chiles in boiling water or roast them for easier peeling. Coarsely chop the fresh chiles. Combine the chopped chiles, oil, and salt in a blender, and puree. If you have chosen not to peel the chiles, press the mixture through a medium-mesh sieve into a bowl for a smoother paste.

If you are using dried chiles, soak them in hot water to cover for 30 minutes. Then drain, peel (if desired), seed them, and remove the ribs. Coarsely chop the reconstituted chiles. Combine the chopped chiles, oil, and salt in a blender, and puree. If you have chosen not to peel the chiles, press the mixture through a medium-mesh sieve into a bowl for a smoother paste.

The paste may be stored in a tightly covered container in the refrigerator for 1 week, or in the freezer for several months.

NOTES: If none of these chiles, or their substitutes, is available, we suggest using Asian chile-garlic sauce, which you can find in jars in the specialty food section of most supermarkets, as a substitute for the red or yellow *ají* paste or sauce. The sauce contains garlic, so you may want to reduce the amount of garlic called for in the recipe. Some brands are very hot, so proceed with caution.

The commercially available ground *ají* powder—such as ground *ají mirasol*—is convenient, but it tends to be hotter than the paste because the chiles are often ground with the seeds and ribs intact. If a recipe calls for 3 tablespoons of *ají* paste, substitute 1½ to 3 teaspoons powder, depending on the heat of the particular chile.

SALSA DE AJÍ AMARILLO
PERUVIAN YELLOW CHILE SAUCE

MAKES ABOUT ½ CUP

This simple sauce is almost always available on Peruvian tables, so that anyone with a taste for fire may stir it into their soup or stew. Our friends Cecilia Bedia de Ustua and Felicita PasaPera Villegos, who live in Lima, taught us how to make it. While not blistering hot, its taste is definitely authoritative! Similar sauces may be made with *ajíes rojo, ajíes mirasol,* or other chiles.

4 tablespoons *Pasta de Ají Amarillo* (chile paste, page 147), or Asian chile-garlic sauce (see Note, page 147)

2 tablespoons finely chopped red onion

1 to 2 tablespoons corn oil or extra-virgin olive oil

2 tablespoons fresh lime juice

Salt to taste

1 teaspoon minced fresh cilantro

1 teaspoon minced fresh mint

1 teaspoon minced fresh parsley

In a small bowl whisk together the *Pasta de Ají,* onion, and oil. Add the lime juice and season to taste with salt. Stir in the herbs. Let the sauce sit for at least 15 minutes to allow the flavors to blend. It may be covered and stored in the refrigerator for 1 to 2 days, but it is best when eaten within a few hours of preparation.

LLAJUA
BOLIVIAN-STYLE SALSA

MAKES ABOUT 1 CUP

Antonio Paredes-Candia, a spritely octogenarian with a flowing white mane and a dashing black cape, is considered one of Bolivia's greatest food historians. When we met with Don Antonio in La Paz, he shared with us this recipe for *Llajua,* the most typical Bolivian table sauce.

1 large tomato, peeled, seeded, and chopped

1 small fresh green *ají rocoto,* or 1 jalapeño chile, seeded and deveined, and minced

1 to 3 sprigs of Italian parsley, chopped

1 to 3 springs of *huacatay* (see Sources) or tarragon, chopped

1 to 2 springs of mint, chopped

Salt to taste

Using a mortar and pestle or a blender, grind together the tomato, *ají,* and herbs to form a fairly smooth sauce. Season to taste with salt. If the sauce seems too thick, stir in a little cold water. Let sit for at least 15 minutes to allow the flavors to blend. *Llajua* may be covered and stored in the refrigerator for 1 to 2 days.

SALSA DE MANÍ
ECUADORIAN SPICY PEANUT SAUCE

Peanuts were first domesticated in Bolivia around A.D. 500, and from there they spread throughout South America and around the world. They are used as either a garnish or a thickener in many Andean dishes and are also made into a drink called *chicha de maní.*

Ecuadorians serve this peanut sauce with *Llapingachos* (page 202), but it is also great with grilled meat or chicken. It may seem like extra trouble to sauté and strain the annatto seeds, but you'll see that they turn the sauce a lovely terra-cotta color.

1 tablespoon annatto (*achiote*) seeds (optional)

2 tablespoons lard, preferably home-rendered (page 217), or peanut oil

1 tablespoon *Pasta de Ají Amarillo* (chile paste, page 147), or ½ to 1 teaspoon ground *ají amarillo* chile powder or Asian chile-garlic sauce (see Note, page 147)

1 cup finely chopped onion

1 clove garlic, peeled and minced

2 cups chopped fresh or canned tomatoes with their juice

½ cup pure, unsweetened peanut butter (available in health- or natural-food stores)

1 tablespoon fresh lime juice

Salt to taste

2 tablespoons chopped fresh cilantro or parsley

Combine the annatto seeds and the lard (if using) in a heavy-bottomed saucepan over medium-low heat. Stir, pressing on the seeds with a wooden spatula, for 3 to 4 minutes, until the lard has melted and turned a rich orange color. Strain the lard into a bowl and discard the seeds.

Return the lard to the saucepan and add the chile, onion, and garlic. Cook over medium heat, stirring often, until the onion begins to soften, 3 to 4 minutes. Add the tomatoes.

Cook for 3 to 4 minutes, stirring and crushing the tomatoes with the spatula. Add the peanut butter and reduce the heat to medium-low. Simmer the sauce, stirring constantly, until the peanut butter is thoroughly incorporated and the sauce has turned a beautiful orange-red color, 3 to 4 minutes. Stir in the lime juice and season to taste with salt. Then stir in the cilantro. Serve warm.

CEVICHE DE CAMARONES
ECUADORIAN SHRIMP CEVICHE

Though *ceviche*, *seviche*, or *cebiche*—as it is written in different locales—is popular along the Pacific coast from Mexico to Chile, most aficionados agree that the best is still found in its land of origin, Peru and Ecuador, the heart of what was once the great Inca empire.

Ecuador is a fascinating country with a large Quechua-speaking population and cooking traditions strongly rooted in the pre-Columbian past. Ecuadorian *ceviches* are usually made with the juice of bitter Seville oranges and are often garnished with popcorn and *cancha*, toasted corn kernels similar to corn nuts. This sounds odd, but the combination of textures and flavors is intriguing and delicious.

This recipe is an adaptation of a dish served at La Longita, a *cevicheria* in the Ecuadorian coastal city of Salinas. Douglas Rodriguez, chef-owner of the restaurants Chicama and Pipa in New York City, tasted this shrimp ceviche in Ecuador and declared it outstanding. We agree with him and thank chef Rodriguez for sharing the recipe with us.

1 pound jumbo shrimp (16 to 20 per pound)

1 large ripe firm tomato, or 2 or 3 ripe plum tomatoes

1 small white onion

2 fresh jalapeño chiles or *ajíes amarillos*

1 red bell pepper

½ cup bitter (Seville) orange juice, or ¼ cup sweet orange juice combined with ¼ cup lime juice

1 tablespoon sugar

Salt to taste

Hot sauce to taste (optional)

½ cup chopped red onion

¼ cup chopped fresh cilantro

½ cup freshly made unsalted popcorn

½ cup *cancha* (toasted corn kernels) or corn nuts

Bring a large saucepan of water to a boil.

While the water is heating, peel the shrimp, leaving the last segment of the tail shell attached. Devein and rinse them. Fill a large bowl with ice water, and set it aside. Drop the shrimp into the boiling water, remove the pot from the heat, and blanch the shrimp for 1½ minutes. Using a metal strainer, immediately remove the shrimp from the water and transfer them to the ice water bath to cool thoroughly. Drain the shrimp well and place them in a nonreactive mixing bowl.

Cut the tomato and onion in half. Preheat a well-seasoned griddle or heavy skillet over medium-high heat. Place the tomato and onion halves, the chiles, and the bell pepper on the griddle and roast for 6 to 8 minutes, turning with tongs,

until lightly browned on all sides. Seed and chop the tomato, and peel and chop the onion. Place the chiles and the bell pepper in a closed paper bag for a few minutes to steam. Then, using a small sharp knife, peel them and remove and discard the stems, ribs, and seeds.

Place the tomato, onion, chiles, bell pepper, orange juice, and sugar in a blender or food processor and puree until smooth. Season to taste with salt and hot sauce. Pour the marinade over the shrimp, and toss to combine. Cover and refrigerate for at least 1 hour or up to 8 hours.

Just before serving, toss the ceviche with the red onion and cilantro. Transfer the mixture to individual plates, sprinkle with the popcorn and *cancha,* and serve.

RIGHT: *Ceviche de Camarones* is garnished with popcorn and *cancha*, toasted corn kernels.

CEVICHE DE LENGUADO
PERUVIAN SOLE CEVICHE

While doing research in Peru, we had lunch with friends at Las Brujas de Caliche, one of a handful of restaurants in Lima dedicated to serving *Nueva Cocina Andina* (New Andean Cuisine). Among the dishes we sampled was a delicious sole ceviche marinated in the juice of an acidic, tart native fruit called *tumbo*. It is now thought that *tumbo* may have been used to prepare ceviche long before citrus fruits were introduced by the Spanish in the sixteenth century. As *tumba* is not available outside Peru, this recipe substitutes a combination of lime and orange juices.

1½ **pounds skinless sole, flounder, or tilapia fillets**

1 **clove garlic, peeled**

1 **tablespoon coarse salt**

1 **teaspoon ground *ají rojo* or other medium-hot ground red chile**

¾ **cup fresh lime juice**

¼ **cup fresh bitter (Seville) orange juice or sweet orange juice**

1 or 2 **fresh *ají amarillo*, or jalapeño or serrano chiles, seeded and minced**

1 **small red onion, peeled and thinly sliced**

2 to 3 **tablespoons extra-virgin olive oil (optional)**

4 to 6 **Boston lettuce leaves, rinsed and dried**

1 **ear fresh corn, boiled and cut into 6 to 8 slices**

1 **sweet potato, boiled, peeled, and cut into 6 to 8 slices**

8 to 12 **Alfonso or Kalamata olives**

1½ **tablespoons chopped fresh cilantro**

Wipe the fish fillets with a damp cloth and cut them on the diagonal into ¼ x 4-inch strips. Set aside in a nonreactive bowl.

Using a mortar and pestle, grind the garlic, salt, and ají rojo into a smooth paste. Combine the paste with the lime and orange juices, and mix thoroughly. Pour the marinade over the strips of fish. Cover and marinate, refrigerated, for 1 hour.

Remove the fish from the refrigerator, add the fresh chiles, onion, and oil (if using), and mix gently. Allow the ceviche to sit for 5 to 10 minutes at room temperature before serving.

Arrange the lettuce leaves on small serving plates. Using a slotted spoon, place a portion of ceviche on the lettuce. Garnish each plate with corn slices, sweet potato slices, and olives. Sprinkle with the cilantro, and serve.

NOTE: To get the maximum amount of juice from oranges and limes, soak them in hot water before squeezing.

CEBICHE CALIENTE DE PESCADO

PERUVIAN HOT FISH CEVICHE

SERVES
2 TO 3

This is a surprising and tasty way to use leftover *Cebiche de Lengado.* We like it so much that we now marinate extra fish fillets so there will be some left over. For this hot ceviche, leave the fillets in larger pieces instead of slicing them into thin strips. Serve this with *Salsa de Ají Amarillo* (page 148).

1 egg, beaten

1 cup dry bread crumbs

½ teaspoon ground *ají rojo* or *amarillo* or cayenne pepper

Salt and freshly ground black pepper to taste

1 pound sole, flounder, or other fish, marinated as for *Cebiche de Lenguado* (opposite)

Vegetable oil for frying

1 sweet potato, boiled, peeled, and sliced

1 ear fresh corn, boiled and cut into ½-inch slices

Place the egg in a shallow bowl. Combine the bread crumbs, *ají,* and salt and pepper in another shallow bowl.

Remove the fish from the marinade. Dip the fillets in the egg, then in the bread crumb mixture, coating them thoroughly.

Fill a large deep skillet with oil to a depth of 1 inch, and place it over medium-high heat. When a cube of bread dropped into the oil turns golden brown in 1 minute, the temperature is right for frying. Slide the fish fillets into the hot oil and fry until golden, about 1 minute. Drain the fish on paper towels, and then arrange them on a platter along with the slices of sweet potato and corn. Serve hot.

CEBICHE DE ALMEJAS A LA BRASA
GRILLED CLAM CEVICHE

Clam ceviche is popular in Peru. *Almejas*, a Pacific clam about the size of the littlenecks and small cherrystones available in the United States, are often sold at ceviche stands in the market *en vaso*, in a glass—these days a disposable plastic container. To stretch the clams, the vendors slice them wafer-thin and combine them with chopped onion, salt, fiery ground *rocoto* chile, cilantro, parsley, and freshly squeezed *limón*. The ceviche is tossed with *mote* (boiled corn that is similar to hominy) and *cancha* (toasted corn kernels).

Small, tender littleneck clams on the half shell make a pretty and delicate ceviche. In this interesting labor-saving Peruvian version, the clams are placed on the grill for a few minutes so that they open easily. If you use a wood fire, it will give them a subtle smoky flavor that is a nice complement to the citrus marinade.

36 fresh unshucked littleneck or small cherrystone clams

1 gallon cold water

¼ cup plus ½ teaspoon coarse salt (preferably sea salt)

1 tablespoon cornmeal or all-purpose flour

3 small to medium-size potatoes (1 white, 1 purple, and 1 gold)

½ cup fresh lemon juice (2 large lemons)

¼ cup fresh lime juice (1 to 2 limes)

1 to 3 teaspoons seeded, minced *ají rocoto*, or ½ to 1 seeded, minced habanero chile or 1 or 2 seeded, minced jalapeño chiles

1 small red onion, peeled and thinly sliced lengthwise

2 to 3 tablespoons chopped fresh cilantro, dill, or fennel tops

2 ripe tomatoes, diced

3 to 4 tablespoons extra-virgin olive oil (optional)

Bibb or Boston lettuce leaves

As soon as you purchase the clams, place them in a pan of cold water and scrub them with a vegetable brush. If necessary, change the water two or three times, until no hint of sand or grit remains. Then soak the scrubbed clams for about 2 hours in the gallon of cold water combined with ¼ cup of the salt and the cornmeal (to help clean the sand and grit out of the clams' digestive tracts).

Meanwhile, place the potatoes in a saucepan of lightly salted cold water. Bring to a boil over high heat. Reduce the heat to medium and boil gently for 20 to 30 minutes, until the potatoes are tender when pierced with a knife. Drain, and, when cool, peel and dice the potatoes. Set aside.

Drain the clams thoroughly. So they won't fall through the bars of the grill, arrange them in a single layer in a large grill basket, or poke small holes in a sheet of heavy-duty aluminum foil and place it over the grill. (A stovetop grill pan also works well.) Grill the clams for 5 to 7 minutes, turning the shells once after 2 minutes. As their shells open, transfer the clams to a nonreactive bowl, trying not to spill the juices. With a small knife, loosen each clam from its top shell. Remove the top shell, leaving the clams on the bottom shell. When all of the clams have been transferred to the bowl, add the lemon and lime juices, *ají rocoto*, onion, half of the cilantro, and ½ teaspoon salt. Cover the bowl and marinate the clams, refrigerated, for 1½ to 2 hours. Stir occasionally to make sure all the clams are thoroughly coated.

Add the potatoes and tomatoes to the clams. Toss gently and let stand at room temperature for 5 to 10 minutes. Drizzle with the oil (if using) and toss again. Adjust seasoning, adding more salt if needed. Sprinkle with the remaining cilantro, and serve on small plates lined with the lettuce leaves.

LEFT: Multicolored potatoes add to the presentation of *Cebiche de Almejas a la Brasa*.

CEBICHE DE ATÚN
PERUVIAN CANNED TUNA CEVICHE

Much of the tuna consumed worldwide is caught and canned along the Pacific coast of Peru and Chile. This quick, easy, and flavorful ceviche is adapted from a recipe of the late Jorge Stanbury Aguirre, one of Peru's most beloved and respected cooking authorities. It makes an unusual last-minute appetizer or snack and will appeal even to those who are not ceviche aficionados. For a light lunch, serve it with crusty French or Italian rolls.

One 6-ounce can solid white tuna in water

1 fresh jalapeño chile, seeded and minced

1 small red onion, peeled and finely chopped

1 ripe tomato, diced

1 tablespoon chopped fresh cilantro

Salt and freshly ground black pepper, to taste

¼ cup fresh lime juice (1 to 2 limes)

2 to 3 tablespoons extra-virgin olive oil

Fresh cilantro sprigs, for garnish

Drain the tuna and invert it onto a small platter. Sprinkle the chile and onion over the tuna and allow it to stand for a few minutes. Then add the tomato, chopped cilantro, and salt and pepper to taste, and gently mix together. Sprinkle the lime juice over all, and drizzle with the oil. Garnish with sprigs of cilantro and serve.

CEBICHE DE PATO
DUCK CEVICHE

Peru is a land of many ceviches, both raw and cooked. Braised duck ceviche is a specialty of the *cebicherias* in the ancient city of Huacho, on the Pacific coast north of Lima. Some cooks marinate the duck and then simmer it in the marinade. Others remove the duck pieces from the marinade and brown them lightly in rendered duck fat or oil before simmering. We prefer the latter technique because it gives the skin a golden color and seals in the juices.

One 5-pound Long Island duckling

½ cup cold water

2 to 3 tablespoons *Pasta de Ají Mirasol* (chile paste, page 147) or 1½ to 3 teaspoons Asian chile-garlic sauce (see Note, page 147)

⅓ cup fresh lime juice (about 2 limes)

1 clove garlic, peeled and crushed

1 teaspoon ground cumin

Salt to taste

1⅔ cups fresh orange juice (3 to 4 oranges)

1 red onion, peeled and thinly sliced

1 yellow onion, peeled and thinly sliced

1 small stick cinnamon, preferably Mexican cinnamon

1 to 2 tablespoons chopped fresh cilantro or flat-leaf parsley

1 pound yuca root, peeled, boiled, cored, and diced or 1 sweet potato, boiled, peeled, and diced

Remove the giblets and excess fat from the body cavity of the duck and set aside. Rinse the duck inside and out under cold running water and pat dry. Using a sharp knife, cut the duck into 8 serving pieces (see Note, page 130). Remove the skin from the breast and thigh pieces and set aside. Discard the back, wing tips, and giblets, except for the liver, or set them aside for making stock. Place the other pieces and the liver in a nonreactive bowl and set aside.

Cut the reserved skin into narrow strips. Place the skin and any reserved duck fat in a small saucepan with the cold water. Cook over low heat for 10 to 12 minutes, stirring occasionally, until the water evaporates, the fat is rendered, and the strips of skin are crisp and golden. Pour the fat through a strainer into a bowl. Drain the cracklings on paper towels and reserve both the cracklings and the fat.

In a small bowl combine the *Pasta de Ají*, lime juice, garlic, cumin, and 1 teaspoon salt. Blend well and rub this mixture over the duck pieces. Add the orange juice, red and yellow onions, and the cinnamon stick. Cover and marinate, refrigerated, for at least 2 hours or overnight.

Remove the duck pieces from the marinade, pat dry with paper towels, and set aside. Pour the marinade through a strainer into a bowl. Discard the cinnamon stick and reserve both the drained onion and the strained marinade.

Place ¼ cup of the rendered duck fat in a Dutch oven over medium-high heat. Sauté the marinated duck liver for about 1 minute on each side; remove and set aside. Add the duck pieces and cook, turning them with tongs, until they are seared and golden on all sides, 6 to 8 minutes. Remove the duck pieces and set aside. Add half of the drained onion to the Dutch oven and sauté until slightly softened, about 1 minute. Return the duck pieces, but not the liver, to the pan. Stir in the reserved marinade and bring to a boil. Reduce the heat to low, cover, and simmer until the duck is tender, 30 to 40 minutes. Add the remaining marinated onion, stir, and cook for 1 minute more.

Remove from the heat and allow the duck to cool slightly. Taste, and add more salt if needed. Thinly slice the sautéed duck liver. Transfer the ceviche to a serving dish, and sprinkle with the reserved cracklings, sliced liver, and cilantro. Garnish with the yuca, and serve warm or at room temperature.

TAMALES DE QUINOA
QUINOA TAMALES WITH PORK FILLING

SERVES
6 TO 8

MAKES ABOUT 15 TAMALES

Quinoa (pronounced *keen-wa* or *kee-noo-ah*) was a sacred food for the Inca, who called it *chesiya mama*, the "mother grain." Each year the Inca emperor, using a golden spade, planted the first quinoa seeds of the season, and at the solstice, priests bearing golden vessels filled with quinoa seeds made offerings to *Inti,* the Sun.

Quinoa seeds are rich in protein, high in fiber, and a good source of lysine, calcium, phosphorus, and vitamins B and E. Before they are eaten, the seeds must be processed to remove their bitter coating. After washing or dry-polishing, the ready-to-cook seeds are white or beige in color. In this recipe the versatile seeds are turned into a wonderfully nutty-tasting tamale dough that complements the subtle spiciness of the pork filling. Serve the tamales alone or topped with *Salsa de Ají Amarillo* (page 148).

2⅓ cups (1 pound) uncooked quinoa

8 cups water

2 or 3 dried *ají amarillo* or other dried medium-hot yellow or red chiles

1 cup boiling water

½ cup lard, preferably home-rendered (page 217), solid vegetable short-ening, or rendered bacon fat

2 cloves garlic, peeled and crushed

½ teaspoon annatto (*achiote*) seeds (optional)

1 cup finely chopped white or yellow onion

½ teaspoon ground cumin

¼ teaspoon freshly ground black pepper

2 to 3 teaspoons salt

10 ounces lean boneless pork loin, cut into ½-inch cubes

2 cups water

One 16-ounce package frozen banana leaves, thawed, or one 8-ounce package dried corn husks

25 to 35 unsalted, dry-roasted peanuts

12 to 15 Kalamata olives, pitted and halved

Place the quinoa in a sieve and rinse it well under cold running water. Rub it between your hands while you rinse it, to remove any bitter residue. Drain it, place it in a large saucepan, and add 8 cups water. Bring to a boil over high heat, stirring occasionally, then reduce the heat to low and simmer, uncovered, for about 10 minutes, or until the quinoa is barely tender. Do not overcook it. Pour the quinoa through a strainer and drain it well. Transfer to a food processor, and process with two or three quick on-off pulses. Place the quinoa in a bowl and set aside.

Seed the dried chiles and place them in a small bowl with the boiling water. Allow the chiles to soak for about 30 minutes, until softened. Drain, reserving the soaking water, and finely chop the chiles. Set the chiles and the soaking water aside.

In a Dutch oven or a large deep skillet, heat the lard, garlic, and annatto seeds over low heat. Stir, pressing on the garlic and annatto seeds until the lard melts and turns a bright red-orange color and the garlic releases its flavor. Remove the garlic and the seeds with a slotted spoon, and discard. Add the onion, cumin, pepper, reserved chiles, 1 teaspoon of the salt, and the diced pork to the pan. Sauté over medium-high heat until the pork is lightly browned, 4 to 6 minutes. Add the reserved chile soaking water and continue cooking over medium heat until the pork is cooked through and all of the liquid has evaporated, 10 to 15 minutes. Remove the pork with a slotted spoon and set it aside. Add the cooked quinoa and 2 cups water. Simmer over low heat, stirring constantly and scraping the bottom of the pan, until the quinoa has absorbed all of the liquid. Check the seasoning and add 1 to 2 teaspoons salt, to taste.

Rinse the thawed banana leaves thoroughly in hot water and wipe off any mold. With scissors, cut along the sides of the tough center rib and remove it. Cut the leaves into 12 x 15-inch pieces. Then, before using, soak the leaves in hot water, or roll them up and steam them for about 20 minutes, until softened. (Dried corn husks should be thoroughly rinsed with hot water and soaked in hot water for at least 30 minutes before using.)

Place a banana leaf on the work surface in front of you with the smoother side up and the grain running from left to right. If there are holes in the leaf, patch with another banana leaf.

Spoon 3 tablespoons of the quinoa mixture onto the middle of a banana leaf, about 3 inches from the near edge. Flatten the quinoa into a 4 x 3-inch rectangle. Place 2 to 3 pieces of meat, 2 peanuts, and 1 olive in the middle of the rectangle. Cover the filling with about 3 more tablespoons of the quinoa mixture. Lift the near edge of the leaf up over the tamale to enclose it. Then roll the tamale away from you until you reach the other side of the leaf. Fold the ends in toward the center and tie the tamale securely with banana-leaf string or kitchen string. Repeat until all of the leaves, quinoa, and filling are used. (If you are using corn husks, use 3 per tamale as in the canoe wrap demonstrated on pages 220–221.)

Arrange the tamales in the top of a steamer over boiling water. Steam for 1 hour, or until they feel fairly firm to the touch. Check occasionally and add more boiling water to the bottom of the steamer if needed. (If you don't have a steamer, improvise by placing the tamales on a rack in a roasting pan. Fill the bottom of the pan with boiling water, being careful not to let it touch the tamales, and cover it tightly with aluminum foil. Steam in a preheated 350°F oven for 1 hour.) Let the tamales rest for about 10 minutes before serving. Open them carefully to avoid being burned by the steam.

NOTE: Drop a coin in the steamer water. When you no longer hear the coin rattling, it is time to add more hot water.

TAMALES CUZQUEÑOS
CUZCO-STYLE PORK TAMALES

MAKES 8 TO 12 TAMALES

In the Quechua language, *cuzco* means "navel," and indeed it was the center of the Inca empire. Today this lovely colonial city, which is built over temples of much greater antiquity, remains the center of native Andean culture and spirituality. Even the food in Cuzco is special. The mild but haunting flavor of *ají panca* permeates these tamales and gives them a rosy hue. Like Cuzco itself, their aroma draws you close, and their substance nourishes both body and soul. Serve them with *Salsa de Ají Amarillo* (page 148).

2 cloves garlic, peeled and minced

2 tablespoons ground *ají panca* or sweet paprika

1 to 1½ teaspoons ground *ají rojo* or cayenne pepper

2 teaspoons ground cumin

1 teaspoon salt

¼ teaspoon freshly ground black pepper

1½ pounds boneless pork tenderloin

½ cup lard, preferably home-rendered (page 217), rendered bacon fat, or solid vegetable shortening

2 cups chicken broth

6 cups cooked *mote* or four 16-ounce cans white hominy, rinsed and thoroughly drained

2 eggs

1 teaspoon baking powder

3 tablespoons Pisco or light rum

One 8-ounce package dried corn husks

2 hard-cooked eggs, chopped

In a small bowl combine the garlic, *ají panca, ají rojo,* cumin, salt, and pepper. Stir well. Rub half the seasoning mixture over the pork, and reserve the rest.

Melt 2 tablespoons of the lard in a large skillet over medium-high heat. Place the pork in the skillet and sear it, turning with tongs, until it is browned on all sides, 8 to 10 minutes. Add the remaining seasoning mixture and sauté for 1 minute. Add the chicken broth and reduce the heat to low. Simmer, covered, until the pork is just cooked through, 15 to 20 minutes.

Remove the pork and set it aside. Turn the heat to medium-high and boil the broth, uncovered, until it is reduced to about ¾ cup. Remove it from the heat and reserve.

When the pork is cool enough to handle, slice it about ¼ inch thick and return the slices and any juices to the skillet.

In a heavy-duty mixer, mix the *mote,* and add the remaining 6 tablespoons lard, the eggs, baking powder, Pisco, and ¼ cup of the broth from the skillet. Transfer the mixture to a large mixing bowl and knead it until it forms a smooth, moist dough. Set aside.

Prepare the corn husks and ribbons for making the canoe wrap as described on pages 220–221.

Place 2 large corn husks on a work surface with the wide ends overlapping and the pointed ends facing in opposite directions. Place a third husk in the center. Spoon 3 tablespoons of the dough onto the middle husk. Press 1 or 2 slices of pork and 1 to 2 teaspoons of the chopped egg into the center of the dough. Cover with another 3 tablespoons of dough, making sure that the filling is totally enclosed. Bring one of the long sides of the husks up over the filling, then bring up the other side. Fold both pointed ends toward the middle to form a neat rectangular package. Slip a corn husk ribbon under the tamale and tie it securely in the middle. Repeat this process until all the husks, dough, and filling are used up.

Arrange the tamales in the top of a steamer over boiling water. Steam for 60 to 70 minutes, or until they feel fairly firm to the touch. Check occasionally and add more boiling water to the bottom of the steamer if needed. (If you don't have a steamer, improvise by placing the tamales on a rack in a roasting pan. Fill the bottom of the pan with boiling water, being careful not to let it touch the tamales, and cover it tightly with aluminum foil. Steam in a preheated 350°F oven for 60 to 70 minutes.) Let the tamales rest for about 20 minutes before serving. Open them carefully to avoid being burned by the steam.

NOTE: Drop a coin in the steamer water. When you no longer hear the coin rattling, it is time to add more hot water.

JAUNES

YUCA AND RICE TAMALES WITH CHICKEN FILLING

MAKES 12 JAUNES

Yuca, also called *cassava* or *manioc*, is an important food in the tropics of Central and South America. This woody-looking root is native to the Amazon and has been cultivated along the coast of Peru since about 2000 B.C. If desired, *jaunes* may be topped with any of the salsas in this chapter.

FILLING

4 cups well-seasoned chicken broth

1 large white or yellow onion, chopped (about 1½ cups)

2 to 3 tablespoons *Pasta de Ají Amarillo* (chile paste, page 147), or 1 to 3 teaspoons *ají amarillo* or 2 to 3 teaspoons Asian chile-garlic sauce (see Note, page 147)

2 teaspoons ground turmeric

1½ pounds boneless, skinless chicken breasts

¼ cup lard, preferably home-rendered (page 217), or solid vegetable shortening

1 ripe tomato, peeled and diced (1 cup)

2 cloves garlic, peeled and minced

¼ cup golden raisins

¼ cup capers, drained

DOUGH

2 pounds yuca root

1 tablespoon salt

½ cup uncooked rice

1 egg

One 16-ounce package frozen banana leaves, thawed, or one 8-ounce package dried corn husks

½ cup unsalted, dry-roasted peanuts (optional)

Combine the chicken broth, half of the chopped onion, 2 tablespoons *Pasta de Ají*, and the turmeric in a large saucepan. Bring to a boil over medium-high heat. Add the chicken breasts and reduce the heat to medium-low. Simmer, uncovered, until the chicken is barely cooked through, about 15 minutes. Remove the chicken and dice or shred it into bite-size pieces. When it has cooled slightly, pour the broth, with the onion, into a blender or food processor, and puree. Set the chicken and the broth mixture aside.

Melt the lard in a large skillet over medium heat. Add the remaining onion, the chicken, tomato, and garlic. Sauté until the onion is translucent, 8 to 10 minutes. Stir in the reserved broth mixture, the raisins, and the capers, and simmer for 10 minutes. Pour the mixture through a colander placed over a large bowl. Transfer the drained chicken and vegetables to a separate bowl, adding a few tablespoons of the broth to keep them moist. Pour the remaining broth into a large measuring cup; you should have 2 cups (if not, add water). The chicken and broth may be prepared ahead to this point; cover and refrigerate for 1 to 2 days. (Do not skim the fat from the broth.)

Scrub the yuca with a vegetable brush under cold running water. Cut it into pieces 4 to 5 inches long. With a sharp paring knife, cut a slit through the skin down the length of each piece of yuca. With the point of the knife, loosen the skin and peel it off in one piece, like the bark on a tree. If you will not be cooking the yuca immediately, place it in a bowl of cold water so it won't discolor.

Bring a large pot of water to a boil. Add the salt and the peeled yuca, and cook until it is tender when pierced with a knife, about 20 minutes. Drain and, when they are cool enough to handle, slice the pieces lengthwise, pulling out and discarding the tougher woody core and reserving the tender outer flesh.

Meanwhile, in another saucepan over medium-high heat, bring the reserved 2 cups chicken broth to a boil. Stir in the rice, cover, and reduce the heat to low. Simmer the rice for 25 to 30 minutes, until very tender.

Mash the yuca or put it through a ricer or food mill. Combine it thoroughly with the cooked rice. Add the egg

(continued on page 163)

and mix thoroughly to make the dough. Taste, and add additional *Pasta de Ají* if desired.

Rinse the thawed banana leaves thoroughly in hot water and wipe off any mold. With scissors, cut along the sides of the tough center rib and remove it. Cut the leaves into 12 x 15-inch pieces. Then, before using, soak the leaves in hot water, or roll them up and steam them for about 20 minutes, until softened.

Place ¼ cup of the dough in the center of a banana leaf. Pat or spread the dough out to form a round about 6 inches in diameter. Press lightly in the middle to make a well. Place 3 rounded tablespoons of the reserved chicken filling in the well.

Add 2 or 3 peanuts (if using). Pull up the sides of the leaf, and using a strip of banana leaf or kitchen string, tie the *jaune* like a beggar's purse. If a split develops in the leaf, place the wrapped tamale on another leaf and double-wrap to prevent leaking. (If you are using corn husks, rinse them thoroughly with hot water and soak them in hot water for at least 30 minutes before using. Form the *jaunes* following the instructions for the canoe wrap on pages 220–221.)

Arrange the tamales in the top of a steamer over boiling water. Steam for 50 to 60 minutes, or until they feel slightly firm to the touch. Check occasionally and add more boiling water to the bottom of the steamer if needed. (If you don't have a steamer, improvise by placing the tamales on a rack in a roasting pan. Fill the bottom of the pan with boiling water, being careful not to let it touch the tamales, and cover it tightly with aluminum foil. Steam in a preheated 350°F oven for 50 to 60 minutes.) Let the tamales rest for about 10 minutes before serving. Open them carefully to avoid being burned by the steam.

NOTE: Drop a coin in the steamer water. When you no longer hear the coin rattling, it is time to add more hot water

LEFT: *Jaunes*, shown both closed and open, served with *Salsa de Maní* (page 149) on the side.

SALTEÑAS
BOLIVIAN MEAT EMPANADAS

MAKES ABOUT 25 SALTEÑAS

Salteñas, the spicy beef Bolivian version of empanadas, are usually eaten as a midmorning snack and are always accompanied by a cold drink, perhaps a glass of beer or a bottled soft drink, but never by coffee or tea.

In our research in La Paz, we were accompanied by Raul Garron Claure—a man who knows his *salteñas.* After comparing the wares of several different establishments we declared the Palacio de la Empanada the best in town. Raul also taught us how to eat a *salteña* so the juicy filling doesn't end up on the front of one's shirt: experts nibble off one end of the pastry and suck out the filling or, more delicately, use a small spoon to eat it.

Prepare both the dough and the filling at least 2 to 3 hours before assembling the *salteñas.*

DOUGH

6 cups all-purpose flour

1 tablespoon sugar

1 teaspoon salt

6 tablespoons lard, preferably home-rendered (page 217), or solid vegetable shortening, chilled

2 egg yolks

½ cup milk

1½ cups lukewarm water

FILLING

3 tablespoons lard, preferably home-rendered, or solid vegetable shortening

1½ cups chopped white onion

½ cup finely chopped scallions (white and tender green parts)

2 to 3 tablespoons *Pasta de Ají Rojo* (chile paste, page 147), or 2 to 3 teaspoons ground *ají rojo* or other medium-hot red chile, or 2 to 3 teaspoons Asian chile-garlic sauce (see Note, page 147)

1 teaspoon ground cumin

1 teaspoon dried oregano (preferably Mexican oregano)

1 tablespoon sugar

1 pound top round or boneless top sirloin beef, cut into very small pieces

¾ teaspoon Worcestershire sauce or vinegar

Salt and freshly ground black pepper to taste

½ cup canned beef consommé with gelatin, or 1½ tablespoons unflavored gelatin dissolved in ½ cup cold water

2 tablespoons finely minced fresh parsley

½ cup raisins

1 cup diced red, white, or yellow boiling potatoes, boiled until just tender

1 cup fresh or frozen peas, blanched and well drained

2 hard-cooked eggs, chopped

12 Kalamata olives, pitted and halved

EGG WASH

2 eggs

¼ cup milk

Prepare the dough: In a large mixing bowl combine the flour, sugar, and salt. Using a pastry blender or two knives, cut the lard into the flour until the mixture resembles small peas. In a measuring cup or small bowl, beat together the egg yolks, milk, and 1 cup lukewarm water. Make a well in the flour mixture and add the liquid. Mix with a fork until the dough comes together, adding more water as needed. Knead the dough for 2 to 3 minutes on a lightly floured surface until

smooth and uniformly combined. Wrap it in plastic wrap or a clean damp kitchen towel, and refrigerate for 2 to 3 hours or overnight.

Prepare the filling: Melt the lard in a large sauté pan or deep skillet over medium-high heat. Add the onion, scallions, *Pasta de Ají,* cumin, and oregano, and sauté until the onion begins to soften, 2 to 3 minutes. Stir in the sugar. Add the beef and continue to cook, stirring, until meat loses its pink color. Add the Worcestershire sauce and taste for salt and pepper. Remove from the heat and allow to cool. Then stir in the consommé, parsley, raisins, and potatoes. Cover and refrigerate until lukewarm.

When you are ready to assemble the salteñas, stir the peas into the beef mixture. (You will add the egg and olives as you assemble the salteñas.)

Assemble the *salteñas:* Preheat the oven to 500°F.

Divide the dough into about 25 portions and roll them into golf ball–size balls. Keep them covered with a damp towel.

Prepare the egg wash by whisking the eggs and milk together in a small bowl.

On a lightly floured surface roll a ball of dough out to form a 4-inch round. Place 1 heaping tablespoon of the beef filling in the center of the round, and add a bit of chopped egg and a piece of olive. LIghtly brush the edges of the dough with egg wash, lift up the sides, and seal them to make a ropelike seam along the top. Repeat with the remaining balls of dough and the filling. Arrange the completed *salteñas* on a lightly floured baking sheet, and brush with the remaining egg wash.

Place the baking sheet in the oven and immediately lower the oven temperature to 425°F. Bake the *salteñas* until the crust is a rich golden brown, 15 to 20 minutes. Serve warm, straight from the oven.

In Bolivia, the spirits of the dead are coaxed into visiting the living during a three-day ceremony centered on *Taque Santun Arupa* (*Todos Santos* or All Saints' Day). Every family puts *t'ant'a wawas*— small figures made of bread to represent family members who have passed away—on a commemorative altar in the house. Llamas and horses, suns and moons, and ladders to heaven are other popular shapes.

Some Andean bakers give their bread a distinctive flavor by boiling the water to be used for the dough with chamomile, mint, and a sprinkling of anise seed—you could use one or two herbal tea bags.

The information about the traditional Bolivian observance of *Taque Santun Arupa* and most of the *T'ant'a Wawas* in the photograph were shared with us by our friends Marty de Montaño and José Moñtano. This recipe is adapted from their own.

1 package dry yeast, or 1 tablespoon bulk yeast

3 teaspoons sugar

1 cup lukewarm water, flavored or plain (see Headnote), or more as needed

2 cups white bread flour

1 cup quinoa flour (available at health-food stores; also see Sources) or whole-wheat flour

1 teaspoon salt

1 egg, beaten

6 tablespoons lard, preferably home-rendered (page 217), or solid vegetable shortening, melted and cooled to lukewarm

Whole cloves or raisins and slivered almonds, for decorating

¼ teaspoon annatto (*achiote*) seeds (optional)

EGG WASH

1 egg

2 tablespoons water

In a small bowl dissolve the yeast and 1 teaspoon of the sugar in 1 cup lukewarm water. Place the bread flour in a large mixing bowl. When the yeast begins to bubble, make a well in the center of the flour and pour in the yeast mixture. Gradually mix the flour into the yeast until well combined. Cover with a slightly damp clean kitchen towel and allow the dough to rise in a warm place until it has doubled in volume, about 1 hour.

Punch down the dough and add the quinoa flour, the remaining 2 teaspoons sugar, the salt, egg, and 4 tablespoons of the melted lard. Mix well. If the dough seems dry, gradually add just enough lukewarm water, 1 tablespoon at a time, to obtain a soft, smooth dough. Knead the dough for 5 to 10 minutes on a lightly floured surface until it becomes elastic and no longer sticks to your hands. Place it in a clean bowl, cover it with a clean damp kitchen towel, and allow it to rise until doubled in volume, about 20 minutes.

Punch down the dough and divide it into 6 to 8 pieces, depending on the size of the figures you want to make. Shape the dough into the forms you choose, using cloves or raisins for eyes, and perhaps a slivered almond for the mouth. Place the loaves on a lightly greased baking sheet, cover with a damp cloth, and allow to rise until doubled in size, about 20 minutes.

(continued on page 168)

RIGHT: *T'ant'a wawas* are formed into a variety of figures and shapes. Note the rosy tint created with annatto-seed tinted lard.

Meanwhile, preheat the oven to 400°F.

If you like, mix the annatto seeds with the remaining 2 tablespoons lard. Place the mixture in a small saucepan over medium-low heat and melt, pressing on the seeds with a wooden spoon until they tint the lard. Strain and brush the tinted lard on the figures' faces to color them. Prepare the egg wash by whisking the egg and water together in a small bowl, and brush it lightly over the *t'an'ta wawas*—but not over the faces if you have tinted them with the lard.

Bake for about 20 minutes, or until the crust is golden brown. Transfer the *t'an'ta wawas* to a wire rack and allow to cool.

NOTE: This dough may also be divided in half and baked in 2 lightly greased 4 x 8-inch loaf pans. It is wonderful toasted for breakfast.

PUKACAPAS
BOLIVIAN CHEESE PASTRIES

Pukacapas, which means "red tops" or "red capes" in Quechua, are the savory cheese-filled pastries traditionally served during Carnival in Bolivia. When they stop to rest, the colorfully costumed bands of celebrants feast on platters piled high with hot fragrant *pukacapas*. Thus fortified, they have the strength to keep on dancing.

DOUGH

**1 package dry yeast, or
1 tablespoon bulk yeast**

1½ cups lukewarm water

1 teaspoon salt

1 teaspoon sugar

**6 tablespoons lard, preferably
home-rendered (page 217), or
solid vegetable shortening,
melted**

2 to 3 cups white bread flour

FILLING

1 cup diced fresh mozzarella cheese

1 cup crumbled feta cheese

**1 cup finely chopped onion, rinsed
under hot water and well drained**

**1 tablespoon minced fresh
huacataya (see Sources) or
dried tarragon**

**Salt and freshly ground black
pepper, to taste**

**3 to 4 tablespoons heavy cream,
evaporated milk, or whole milk**

**1 to 2 teaspoons ground *aji rojo* or
other medium-hot red chile**

Prepare the dough: In a large bowl dissolve the yeast in the lukewarm water. When the yeast begins to bubble, add the salt, sugar, 4 tablespoons of the melted lard, and the flour. Mix well. On a lightly floured surface, knead the dough until it comes together, 5 to 10 minutes. Shape the dough into a round and place it on a floured board. Cover the dough with a slightly damp clean kitchen towel and allow it to rest in a warm place until it has doubled in volume, 45 minutes to 1 hour.

Prepare the filling: In a mixing bowl toss together the cheeses, onion, huacataya, and salt and pepper to taste.

Punch down the dough and roll it out on a lightly floured surface to a thickness of ¼ inch. Using a 3-inch biscuit cutter, cut out 30 rounds. Place 1 tablespoon of the filling on half of the rounds. Lightly brush the edges with cream, and place the remaining rounds on top. Press down around the edges with the tines of a fork to seal them.

Lightly grease a baking sheet or line it with baking parchment, and arrange the pastries on the sheet. Mix the *aji* with the remaining 2 tablespoons melted lard, and brush the mixture over the tops of the pastries. Cover the sheet with a kitchen towel and allow the pastries to rise for 15 to 20 minutes (see Note).

Meanwhile, preheat the oven to 375°F.

Bake the *pukacapas* until the crusts are golden brown and the tops are rosy, 15 to 20 minutes. Serve warm.

NOTE: If you want, you can skip the final rising before baking the *pukacapas*. They won't be quite as light, but they will still be delicious.

CHAIRO PACEÑO
BOLIVIAN MEAT AND VEGETABLE SOUP

Chairo, a hearty, nourishing meat and vegetable soup, is a specialty of La Paz. It is customarily served as a first course for Saturday lunch. Though today many people make it with beef, purists would say that authentic *chairo* must be made with *chalona*—a special *charqui* made of llama, alpaca, or mutton, dried in the strong sun and intense cold of the altiplano.

If you like, serve a small bowl of *Llajua* (page 148) alongside.

1 pound lean beef (or lamb) stew meat, cut into bite-size pieces

¼ pound *Charqui* (jerky, page 194) or peppery seasoned beef jerky, chopped

8 cups beef broth or water, or a combination

2 tablespoons corn oil

1 cup finely chopped white onion

1 to 2 tablespoons *Pasta de Ají, Mirasol,* or *Amarillo* or *Rojo* (chile paste, page 147), or 1½ to 3 teaspoons Asian chile-garlic sauce (see Note, page 147)

1 ripe tomato, peeled, seeded, and diced

¼ cup plus 1 teaspoon minced fresh Italian parsley

½ teaspoon ground cumin

½ teaspoon dried oregano (preferably Mexican oregano)

4 cups diced red, yellow, or white potatoes (2 to 3 potatoes)

1 cup *chuño* (freeze-dried potatoes), well rinsed and chopped (optional; see Sources)

1 cup diced carrots

½ cup fresh or frozen lima beans

½ cup fresh or frozen peas

1 cup precooked *mote* or canned hominy

½ cup cooked wheat (see Note) or cooked rice

Salt to taste

1 teaspoon minced fresh cilantro

1 teaspoon minced fresh oregano (preferably Mexican oregano)

1 teaspoon minced fresh mint

Place the beef and *Charqui* in a large soup pot, add the broth, and bring to a simmer over high heat. Cover, reduce the heat to low, and simmer gently until the meats are tender, about 1½ hours.

Heat the oil in a skillet. Add the onion and *Pasta de Ají,* and sauté over medium heat for 1 to 2 minutes, until softened. Stir in the tomato, ¼ cup of the parsley, cumin, and dried oregano, and continue to cook, stirring, for about 1 minute.

Add the onion mixture to the soup and stir in the potatoes, *chuño* (if using), carrots, and lima beans. Simmer the soup for 15 minutes. Stir in the peas, *mote,* and wheat and con-

tinue to cook until the peas are tender and all of the ingredients are heated through, 8 to 10 minutes.

Add salt to taste and stir in the remaining 1 teaspoon minced parsley along with the cilantro, fresh oregano, and mint.

NOTE: In Bolivia, cooked presoaked whole-grain wheat is sold in the markets. Tabbouleh bulghur is a good substitute. Prepare the tabbouleh following the package instructions, but omit the seasoning packet (¼ cup tabbouleh soaked in ⅓ cup boiling water yields ½ cup cooked).

AGUADITO DE POLLO
PERUVIAN CHICKEN SOUP

Aguaditos are hearty broth-based main-course soups that include both rice and potatoes along with meat and other vegetables. The predominant seasonings are chiles and lots of fragrant fresh cilantro.

This recipe for chicken *aguadito* was given to us by Roman Viscarra, of Pisaq, Peru. We stayed with Roman, a talented Andean musician, his wife, Fielding, and their children, Suni and Tica, at their charming bed-and-breakfast, Hostel Pisaq. Pisaq is located in a breathtakingly lovely mountain valley about an hour's drive from Cuzco.

This valley was a holy place for the ancient Inca and remains so for their descendants. The *Apu*, or guardian spirit, of the town of Pisaq is the condor. If you look closely at Linli, the sacred mountain that dominates the vista, you will notice that the agricultural terraces on one side of the mountain form the shape of a giant condor. This has been so for many hundreds of years. It remains a mystery how the Inca, without benefit of aerial photography, had the perspective to produce these huge images. Today their descendants maintain and farm the ancient terraces while the great bird keeps its vigil over the people of Pisaq.

¾ cup fresh cilantro leaves and stems, plus ½ cup chopped fresh cilantro

¼ cup water

1 to 2 tablespoons mild vegetable oil such as corn or canola

1 chicken, cut into 8 serving pieces

Salt and freshly ground black pepper to taste

1 yellow onion, peeled and chopped (about 1¼ cups)

2 cloves garlic, peeled and minced

1 to 3 teaspoons *Pasta de Ají Rojo* (chile paste, page 147) or Asian chile-garlic sauce (see Note, page 147)

4 to 6 yellow, purple, or red potatoes (or a combination), peeled and halved

¼ cup uncooked rice

1 cup fresh or frozen peas

1 cup fresh or frozen corn kernels

Put the ¾ cup cilantro leaves and stems in a blender, add the water, and liquefy. Set aside.

Heat the oil in a soup pot over medium heat. Pat the chicken pieces dry with paper towels, and season with salt and pepper. Add the chicken to the pot and cook, turning the pieces with tongs, until lightly browned, 6 to 8 minutes. Remove the chicken and set aside.

Add the onion, garlic, and *Pasta de Ají* to the pot and sauté until the onion begins to soften, 1 to 2 minutes. Return the chicken to the pot, add water to cover, and bring to a sim-mer. Add the potatoes and rice, and stir in the liquefied cilantro. Cook until the chicken, potatoes, and rice are tender, 30 to 40 minutes.

Skim off any fat from the top of the soup. Stir in the peas and corn, and cook until just tender, 8 to 10 minutes. Just before serving, adjust the seasonings and add the ½ cup chopped cilantro. Using tongs, transfer pieces of chicken and potatoes to wide shallow soup bowls. Fill each bowl with broth, and serve.

SOPA WALLAK'HE

PINK TROUT AND POTATO SOUP FROM LAKE TITICACA

The ancestors of the Inca are said to have first emerged from Lake Titicaca. The people who dwell on and around this huge inland lake, located in Bolivia near the Peruvian border, have always lived by fishing. Several years ago, pink-fleshed "golden trout" were introduced into mountain streams that feed the lake and into the lake itself. These handsome fish have thrived and have boosted the local economy, but at the expense of the less showy native fish like *pejerrey*, which have literally been consumed by the new arrivals.

Sopa Wallak'He is the traditional Andean fisherman's soup. Its new incarnation using golden trout would have pleased the Inca, who worshiped the sun and prepared many "golden" foods to honor him. The firm but delicate pink fillets swim through a rainbow of gold, purple, and white potatoes in a clear broth tinted and spiced with *mirasol* chiles. In Bolivia the soup is usually flavored with *k'hoa*, a mint that grows wild on the shores of the great lake. We have found that a combination of mint and cilantro is a good substitute. If you wish, you may do as the Quechua and Aymara people do and add diced cooked *chuño* or *tunta* (freeze-dried or water-cured potatoes) to the soup along with the fresh ones.

3¾ to 4 pounds whole golden trout, arctic char, or coho salmon or 1½ to 2 pounds fillets

2 fresh or dried yellow *mirasol* chiles, or other medium-hot yellow or orange fresh chiles such as *sandia* chiles, or dried chiles such as *costeño amarillo* chiles

6 cups water

2 yellow potatoes (such as Yukon Gold), peeled and quartered

2 white potatoes, peeled and quartered

2 purple potatoes, peeled and quartered

1 yellow onion, peeled and chopped

1 clove garlic, peeled and minced

1 tablespoon chopped fresh mint

1 tablespoon minced fresh cilantro

Clean the fish well, removing the scales but leaving the skin intact. Cut off the heads and rinse them under cold water; set the fish and the heads aside.

Remove the stems, ribs, and seeds from the chiles. If you are using dried chiles, remove the stems, ribs, and seeds, and then soak the chiles in hot water to cover for about 20 minutes. Put the chiles in a blender or food processor, add 2 tablespoons water (or soaking liquid) and puree. Set the chiles aside.

Combine the water and the fish heads in a large saucepan and bring to a boil over high heat. Add the potatoes, onion, garlic, chile puree, and half of the mint and cilantro. Reduce the heat to medium-low and simmer for 15 to 20 minutes,

until the potatoes are almost tender. Remove and discard the fish heads. Add the trout to the broth and continue to simmer for 8 to 10 minutes, until both the fish and the potatoes are cooked. Carefully remove the trout and fillet them. Remove and discard any skin from the fillets. Place 1 or 2 pieces of fish and 2 to 3 pieces of potato in each soup plate. Spoon in the broth, sprinkle with the remaining mint and cilantro, and serve.

NOTE: If you are using fillets, ask your fishmonger for 3 to 4 fish heads to use in the broth. If fish heads are not available, substitute ½ to 1 cup clam juice or one 4½-ounce can of vegetable or chicken broth for an equal amount of water.

THE INCA

RIGHT: *Sopa Wallak'he*, pink trout and potato soup from Lake Titicaca

CHUPE DE CAMARONES
PERUVIAN SHRIMP CHOWDER

The recipe for this exceptional shrimp chowder was given to us by Roman Viscarra, who is a musician and innkeeper in the ancient Peruvian town of Pisaq. Roman's mother, Cleopatra, is a fabulous cook, and this is one of her specialties. It is easy to make and as elegant as the most delicate French bisque. When Peruvians refer to *camarones*, they often mean crayfish, which can also be used here.

1 pound jumbo shrimp (16 to 18 per pound), peeled and deveined, shells reserved

2 tablespoons corn or canola oil

1 white or yellow onion, peeled and chopped

2 or 3 cloves garlic, peeled

2 or 3 fennel stalks and bulbs chopped, feathery tops minced and reserved; or 2 ribs celery, chopped, plus ¼ teaspoon dried fennel seed

1 teaspoon annatto (*achiote*) seeds (optional)

½ teaspoon ground *ají rojo*, or 1 teaspoon ground dried cayenne pepper

1 teaspoon salt

2 cups water

One 12-ounce can evaporated milk

2 potatoes (gold, purple, and/or white), peeled and diced

2 ears fresh corn, or 1½ cups frozen corn kernels

2 tablespoons butter

2 eggs

1 cup diced *queso fresco* or feta cheese

1½ tablespoons minced fresh Italian parsley (if fresh fennel was not used)

Rinse the shrimp; drain them well and set aside. Chop the shells.

Heat the oil in a large saucepan, over medium heat. Add the shrimp shells, onion, garlic, and fennel to the pan and sauté for a few seconds. Stir in the annatto (if using), *ají*, and salt. Cook, stirring, until the onion is softened but not browned 2 to 3 minutes. Add the water and simmer for about 5 minutes. Stir in the evaporated milk. Pour the liquid through a wire strainer into a bowl, pressing on the shells and vegetables to extract the flavor. Discard the vegetables and shells.

Return the liquid to a clean saucepan. Add the potatoes and corn, and simmer over low heat for about 10 minutes, until the vegetables are tender.

Meanwhile, melt the butter in a skillet, and sauté the shrimp over medium-high heat for 1 to 2 minutes, just until they turn pink. Set aside.

Remove the ears of corn from the saucepan and, when they are cool enough to handle, use a sharp chef's knife to cut the corn into rounds about 1 inch thick. Return the corn to the chowder. Add the eggs to the chowder, one at a time, and stir briefly with a fork to form "rags." Stir in the shrimp and immediately remove the pot from the heat. Add the cheese, garnish with the reserved minced fennel tops or parsley, and serve.

CHUPE DE MANI
BOLIVIAN SPICY PEANUT CHOWDER

Peanut chowder is a favorite Bolivian dish. The recipe that follows is adapted from one served to us by Lourdes Peñaloza Ramirez, a young woman from Cochabamba whose skill in the kitchen belies her youth. Since ready-to-cook pasta is widely available, many cooks, including Lourdes, add it to their *chupes*. She also did something we had never seen before: she sautéed the raw macaroni in oil before adding it to the soup. We were skeptical, but it was very good. Other peanut chowders we tasted in Bolivia used diced potatoes and/or rice instead of pasta. Heartier versions include pieces of cooked beef, lamb, or chicken, and other vegetables like diced carrots. In traditional Cochabambina style, Lourdes serves her *Chupe de Mani* with a side dish of hot, crisp french-fried potatoes. For those who like it spicier, she also provides a bowl of *Llajua* (page 148).

¾ **cup raw skinless peanuts, or ½ cup pure, unsweetened creamy peanut butter (available at health- or natural-food stores)**

6 **cups flavorful beef or chicken broth, homemade or reduced-sodium (see Note)**

3 **tablespoons vegetable oil**

1 **red onion, peeled and finely chopped (about 1¼ cups)**

2 **ripe tomatoes, chopped, or one 14 ½-ounce can diced tomatoes with their juice**

1 **teaspoon dried oregano (preferably Mexican oregano)**

½ **teaspoon ground cumin**

1 **cup uncooked penne or other tubular macaroni, or ½ cup uncooked rice**

½ **cup fresh or frozen baby lima beans**

½ **cup fresh or frozen peas**

Salt and freshly ground black pepper to taste

1 **tablespoon minced fresh Italian parsley**

1½ **teaspoons chopped fresh mint leaves (optional)**

If you are using raw peanuts, combine them with 1 cup hot water and set them aside to soak for 15 to 20 minutes.

Pour the broth into a soup pot or a large saucepan, and bring it to a boil over medium heat.

Meanwhile, heat 2 tablespoons of the oil in a large saucepan over medium heat. Add the onion and sauté for 1 minute. Add the tomatoes, oregano, and cumin and sauté until the onion has softened and some of the tomato liquid has evaporated, about 5 minutes.

Add the onion mixture to the broth. In a blender, puree the peanuts with their soaking liquid. When the broth mixture comes to a boil, add the pureed peanuts (or peanut butter, if using) but do not stir until the broth returns to a boil.

Then reduce the heat to medium-low and stir well with a wooden spoon.

In a clean skillet heat the remaining 1 tablespoon oil. Add the pasta and sauté over medium heat for 3 to 4 minutes, until golden. Add the pasta to the soup, and stir in the lima beans. Cook over medium heat, stirring occasionally, for 30 minutes. Add the peas and continue to cook until the pasta, beans, and peas are tender, 20 to 30 minutes. Season the soup with salt and pepper to taste. Sprinkle each serving with the parsley and mint.

NOTE: If you happen to have made homemade beef or chicken broth for this recipe, remove any meat from the bones, dice it, and return it to the strained broth for a heartier dish.

THE INCA

CHUPE DE ZAPALLO
BOLIVIAN SQUASH CHOWDER

At the produce markets in Peru and Bolivia, you might see vendors using a saw to cut pieces from a huge squash that has a tough green hull and vivid chartreuse flesh; *zapallos* are so big (probably 30 to 40 pounds) that they are sold in pieces. Their flavor is somewhere between that of a pumpkin, acorn squash, and butternut squash. They are used in many Andean dishes, including this delicious soup, which is adapted from recipes given to us by two fine Bolivian cooks, Maria Christina Rojas, from La Paz, and Marcia Saavedra de Bakovic, of Cochabamba.

2 to 3 pounds winter squash (New England sweet pie pumpkin, or acorn or butternut squash)

2 to 3 tablespoons vegetable oil

1½ cups chopped red or yellow onion

1 clove garlic, peeled and minced

6 cups chicken broth

1 to 2 tablespoons *Pasta de Ají Mirasol* or *Amarillo* (chile paste, page 147) or 1½ to 3 teaspoons Asian chile-garlic sauce (see Note, page 147)

Salt and freshly ground black pepper to taste

1 or 2 yellow potatoes (such as Yukon Gold), peeled and diced

2 ears fresh or frozen corn

1 cup fresh or frozen peas

1 heaping tablespoon minced fresh Italian parsley

Peel and dice the squash. Heat the oil in a soup pot over medium heat. Add the squash, onion, and garlic. Sauté until the onion begins to soften, 2 to 3 minutes. Add the broth and bring to a boil. Reduce the heat to medium-low, cover, and simmer for 30 minutes. Taste, and add *Pasta de Ají*, salt, and pepper to taste. Transfer the vegetables and broth to a blender or food processor in batches, and puree.

Return the puree to the pot and add the potatoes and corn. Simmer for 10 minutes. Remove the corn and, using a chef's knife, cut the ears into rounds about ½ inch thick. Return the corn to the chowder and stir in the peas. Continue to simmer until the vegetables are tender, 5 to 7 minutes. Serve immediately, garnished with the parsley.

SERVING SUGGESTION: Cut a "lid" off 1 large or 6 small winter squash. Remove the seeds and strings, and season the inside with salt and pepper. (Do not remove any of the flesh.) Place the squash in a shallow roasting pan and add about 1 inch of water to the pan. Cover tightly with aluminum foil and bake until the squash is no longer raw but still holds its shape, 20 to 30 minutes. Serve the *chupe* in the squash "bowl," sprinkled with parsley.

THE INCA

RIGHT Hearty *Chupe de Zapallo* is shown served in "bowls" of winter squash.

CHUPE DE QUINOA
QUINOA AND POTATO CHOWDER

Fasting was a concept familiar to the Inca. During these periods of abstinence, they ate sparingly and denied themselves salt, chiles, and the company of the opposite sex. To break the fast it was customary to eat a *chupe*, a healthful and fortifying soup.

Chupe de Quinoa has been made for hundreds of years, though the canned milk is a modern addition. The soothing combination of quinoa and potatoes, with a zesty dash of red and golden chiles, makes it as popular today as it was in the time of Atahualpa, the emperor who greeted Pizarro.

½ **cup uncooked quinoa**

7 ½ **cups water**

2 **tablespoons mild vegetable oil such as canola**

¼ **cup finely chopped red onion**

1 **clove garlic, peeled and minced**

2 to 3 **tablespoons** *Pasta de Ají Rojo* **(chile paste, page 147), or 1 to 3 teaspoons Asian chile-garlic sauce (see Note, page 147)**

2 **tablespoons** *Pasta de Ají Mirasol* **(chile paste, page 147) or 1 to 2 teaspoons ground** *ají amarillo*

3 to 4 **yellow potatoes (such as Yukon Gold), peeled and quartered**

2 **ears fresh or frozen corn**

2 **cups fresh or frozen baby lima beans**

Salt to taste

½ **cup evaporated milk or half-and-half**

4 **eggs**

8 **ounces crumbled** *queso fresco* **or feta cheese**

1 **tablespoon minced fresh cilantro**

1 **tablespoon minced fresh Italian parsley**

Rinse the quinoa well, rubbing it between your hands under cold running water, and drain. Place it in a saucepan with 3 cups of water, and bring to a boil over high heat. Cover, reduce the heat to low, and cook until tender, 20 to 30 minutes.

Meanwhile, in a deep sauté pan or pot, heat the oil over medium heat. Add the onion and garlic and cook, stirring, for 2 to 3 minutes, until softened and golden. Add the *Pastas de Ají* and continue to cook, stirring, for about 2 minutes. Then add the remaining 4½ cups water and the potatoes, corn, lima beans, and 2 teaspoons salt. Cover and boil gently until the vegetables are tender, 15 to 20 minutes.

Remove the corn and, using a chef's knife, cut the ears into rounds about 1 inch thick. Return the corn to the soup. Stir in the cooked quinoa and the evaporated milk. Break the eggs into the soup one at a time, and stir to break them up slightly as they cook—they should retain some texture. Remove from the heat. Stir in the cheese, and add more salt if needed. Sprinkle with the cilantro and parsley, and serve.

POROTOS GRANADOS
CHILEAN BEAN SOUP

Evidence of bean cultivation in the Andes dates back some 8,000 years. Among the earliest South American varieties are the lima bean and the common white bean. The lima bean is often represented in the painted ceramics and woven tapestries of the ancient Moche culture of Peru (A.D. 100 to 800).

Thick, hearty bean soups are a Chilean specialty and may be made with several different varieties of beans—fresh, dried, frozen, or canned. When available, fresh beans are delicious; precooked dried beans are also fine. We often end up using frozen limas or black-eyed peas because it cuts down on preparation time and because they remain firm when cooked. Canned beans may also be used, as long as they are not mushy. Simply add them, undrained, to the soup during the last 10 minutes of cooking.

Like chowders, *chupes* usually include other diced or whole vegetables, such as potatoes, squash, corn, or peas, which add flavor, color, and texture. This soup would originally have been flavored with an Andean herb such as *huacataya* or *quilquiña*, both species of marigold. Today basil is often used.

One 16-ounce package frozen baby lima beans or black-eyed peas

Salt to taste

¼ cup vegetable oil

3 tablespoons mild ground red chile or sweet paprika

1 teaspoon ground *ají rojo* or cayenne pepper (optional)

2½ cups diced winter squash (acorn or butternut squash)

1 cup chopped white onion

2 cloves garlic, peeled and minced

2 cups chicken broth

2 tablespoons chopped fresh basil

3 ears fresh or frozen corn

6 to 8 sprigs fresh basil, for garnish

Cook the beans in lightly salted water, following the package instructions, until almost tender, 20 to 30 minutes. Drain the beans, reserving 1 cup of the cooking liquid, and set aside.

Meanwhile, heat the oil in a large saucepan over medium heat. Stir in the mild and hot ground chiles and sauté for a few seconds. Add the squash, onion, and garlic. Continue to cook, stirring gently, for about 5 minutes, until the onion is translucent. Add the chicken broth, drained beans, reserved cooking liquid, and chopped basil. Bring to a boil over medium-high heat. Reduce the heat to medium-low, cover, and simmer until the squash and beans are tender, about 20 minutes.

Add the corn and cook for 5 minutes. Remove the corn and cut the ears into rounds about ½ inch thick. Return the corn to the chowder, garnish each portion with a basil sprig, and serve.

PICANTE DE CAMARONES
PERUVIAN SHRIMP IN SPICY CHILE-GARLIC SAUCE

SERVES 4

Residents of the southern Peruvian city of Arequipa often gather with friends on a long sunny afternoon at their favorite *picanteria*. These simple establishments specialize in serving *picantes*—dishes of seafood, fish, meat, or vegetables in fiery sauces made with red and golden chiles and garlic. To extinguish the fire, patrons wash down their *picantes* with cooling glasses of corn beer, called *chicha*. A glass or two of Nájar, a local anisette, clears the palate and allows the Arequipans to keep eating.

- 1 pound large shrimp (21 to 25 per pound), unshelled, heads on if possible
- 4 tablespoons mild salad oil or olive oil, as needed
- 2 cloves garlic, peeled and lightly crushed, but left whole
- 1½ cups chicken broth or water
- 1½ to 2 teaspoons ground *ají amarillo* or 2 to 3 tablespoons *Pasta de Ají Amarillo* or *Mirasol* (chile paste, page 147), or Asian chile-garlic sauce (see Note, page 147)
- 1 to 2 teaspoons medium-hot ground red chile
- 1 teaspoon sweet paprika
- ½ pound yellow potatoes (such as Yukon Gold), boiled, peeled, and diced
- ½ cup Pisco or light rum (optional)
- ½ cup grated Parmesan or Romano cheese
- Salt to taste
- 1 tablespoon minced fresh Italian parsley
- Hot cooked rice
- 2 hard-cooked eggs, sliced

Cut off the heads, and peel and devein the shrimp, leaving the last segment of the tail attached. Set the shrimp shells and heads aside. Heat 2 tablespoons of the oil in a large skillet over medium heat. Add the shrimp and the garlic. Sauté until the shrimp turn pink and the garlic is golden but not burned, 2 to 3 minutes. Remove the shrimp and garlic with a slotted spoon and set aside.

Add the shrimp shells and heads to the skillet and sauté until they turn red. Using a slotted spoon, transfer the shells and heads to a blender or food processor. Add the garlic. Heat 1 cup of the chicken broth in a saucepan, and add the hot broth to the blender. Pulse on and off until the shells are almost liquefied. Press the shell mixture through a strainer into a bowl. Discard the solids and set the liquid aside.

Add the remaining 2 tablespoons oil to the skillet. Stir in the yellow and red ground chiles and the paprika; sauté for 1 minute. Add the potatoes and stir so that they are coated with the chile mixture and don't stick to the pan. Stir in the shrimp liquid and the Pisco, if using. Simmer over medium-high heat, stirring often, until the liquid is reduced by about half, about 5 minutes. Return the shrimp to the skillet.

Stir in the cheese and simmer briefly until just heated through. Season to taste with salt. Sprinkle with the parsley. Serve with the hot rice, and garnish with the egg slices.

THE INCA

180

SUDADO DE PESCADO
AROMATICALLY STEAMED FISH FILLETS

The Humboldt Current flows north along the Pacific coast of Peru and Ecuador and provides the region with some of the most varied and magnificent seafood in the world. Since pre-Columbian times, the coastal peoples of South America have been skillful fishermen, and for centuries they have steamed their catch in pits between layers of seaweed. Today Peruvians prepare *sudados* by steaming the seafood in a stovetop steamer over a broth that is fragrant with herbs and chiles. A dish this simple, flavorful, and elegant will never go out of fashion.

We used a basket steamer as is sold for pasta, with two bottom layers and a basket on top.

1 lemon

2 to 3 pounds salmon, grouper, halibut, or other fish fillets

2 tablespoons mild cooking oil such as corn or canola

Salt and freshly ground black pepper to taste

7 cups cold water

One 2.1-ounce package *kombu* or other dried edible seaweed

1 cup *chicha* (corn beer) or white wine (optional)

1 head garlic, unpeeled, cut in half horizontally

2 or 3 fresh or dried *ají amarillo* or *rojo* chiles

¼ cup coarse salt (preferably sea salt)

1 tablespoon black peppercorns

2 teaspoons fennel seeds

6 to 8 sprigs fresh *huacataya* (see Sources), or a combination of fresh tarragon and fresh mint

3 pounds small new potatoes, scrubbed and halved

3 to 4 tablespoons melted butter (optional)

3 to 4 teaspoons minced fresh *huacataya*, or a combination of minced fresh tarragon and fresh mint

Cut the lemon in half, and slice one of the halves into thin rounds. Set the slices and the unsliced half aside.

Rub the fish with the oil, and season it with salt and pepper.

Pour 3 cups water into a large bowl, and squeeze the lemon half into the water. (Reserve the squeezed-out lemon.) Add the seaweed and allow it to soak for 10 minutes. Drain, and wrap the individual fish fillets in pieces of seaweed. Set aside.

Pour 4 cups water into a steamer and add the *chicha* (if using), the squeezed lemon half, and the garlic, chiles, coarse salt, peppercorns, fennel seeds, and the sprigs of *huacataya*. Bring to a boil over medium-high heat. Lower the heat to medium and simmer for about 10 minutes. Then place the potatoes in the first steamer basket and sprinkle them with salt and pepper. Cover, and steam for 10 minutes. Arrange the seaweed-wrapped fillets in the top basket and steam for 12 to 20 minutes, depending on the thickness of the fillets.

Arrange the fillets (still in their edible wrappers) and the potatoes on a platter or individual plates. Garnish with the lemon slices, and if desired, drizzle the melted butter over the fish and potatoes. Sprinkle with the minced *huacataya* and serve.

OCOPA DE CAMARONES

SHRIMP AND POTATOES IN CHILE-CHEESE SAUCE

SERVES
4 TO 6

Ocopa is a traditional dish from Arequipa, the colonial city in southern Peru that is known for its dazzling white volcanic–brick buildings and for its great food. *Ocopa* always contains potatoes drizzled with a creamy cheese, nuts, and golden chiles, but the sauce has almost as many versions as there are cooks. It may be as thick as a heavy mayonnaise or thin enough to pour. White bread soaked in milk— or, more recently, crumbled animal crackers—are often used in place of the pureed potato to thicken the sauce. When it is available, Peruvians flavor the sauce with *huacataya*, a wild member of the mint family with a slight anise flavor. Though it is not possible to duplicate the elusive flavor of this herb, we have found that fresh tarragon or a combination of tarragon and mint makes a good substitute.

Ocopa with shrimp is an elegant variation on the traditional potato dish. The shells and coral of the shellfish add flavor and a rosy hue to the rich, piquant sauce, and the shrimp's delicate flavor complements the potatoes. Serve this as a first course as the Peruvians do, or as a main course for lunch or a light supper.

Arequipans also eat a lot of freshwater crayfish. If they are available in your area, you may want to substitute them for the shrimp in this recipe.

7 small yellow or red potatoes (about 2 pounds)

Salt

1½ pounds large shrimp (21 to 25 per pound), unpeeled, with heads, if possible

½ cup plus 2 tablespoons salad oil or mild olive oil

1 small red onion, peeled and chopped (½ cup)

2 cloves garlic, peeled and chopped

1 tablespoon ground *ají amarillo* or medium-hot ground red chiles

½ teaspoon sweet paprika (optional)

1 cup crumbled feta cheese (about 4 ounces)

½ cup evaporated milk or half-and-half

¼ cup coarsely chopped walnuts or peanuts, lightly toasted

1½ tablespoons coarsely chopped fresh *huacataya* (see Sources), or a combination of fresh tarragon and fresh mint

1 tablespoon fresh lemon juice

8 to 12 Boston or romaine lettuce leaves

2 hard-cooked eggs, cut into wedges

8 to 12 Kalamata olives (optional)

4 to 6 sprigs fresh *huacataya* or tarragon, for garnish

Place the potatoes in a large saucepan with enough water to cover by 2 inches. Add 1 tablespoon salt and bring to a boil. Boil gently over medium heat until the potatoes are tender when pierced with a knife, 20 to 30 minutes. Drain, and set aside until cool enough to peel. Peel the potatoes and slice them about ½ inch thick.

Meanwhile, bring another pot of lightly salted water to a boil. Drop in the shrimp, and cook until the shells turn bright

red and the flesh looks white, 3 to 6 minutes. Reserving 1 cup of the cooking water, drain the shrimp. Cut off the heads and peel the shrimp. Reserve the heads and shells and any of the red-orange coral from the heads to flavor the sauce.

Heat 2 tablespoons of the oil in a skillet over medium heat. Add the onion, garlic, ground chiles, and paprika, and sauté until the onion is golden around the edges, 2 to 3 minutes. Set aside.

THE INCA

182

Place the shrimp shells, heads, coral, and reserved cooking water in a blender or food processor, and pulse on and off until the shells are almost liquefied. Press the mixture through a metal strainer into a cup, and set aside. Discard the solids.

Rinse out the blender. Place 3 or 4 of the potato slices, the onion mixture, and the cheese in the blender. Add the reserved shrimp liquid and the evaporated milk. Pulse on and off until pureed. With the blender running at full speed, pour in the remaining ½ cup oil in a thin stream. The sauce will thicken like a mayonnaise as the oil is incorporated. It should be creamy but still pourable. Add the nuts and chopped *huacataya,* and pulse on and off to blend. Whisk in the lemon juice and season to taste with salt.

Arrange the remaining sliced potatoes on a platter lined with lettuce leaves, and drizzle with half of the sauce. Arrange the shrimp around the potatoes, and garnish with the eggs, olives, and *huacataya* sprigs. Serve, passing the remaining sauce separately.

SECO DE CHOROS
PERUVIAN RICE WITH MUSSELS

SERVES 6

There are a number of different dishes called *seco* in Peru. The one thing that they seem to have in common is a generous amount of cilantro. Some *secos* are indeed dry, as the Spanish word implies, but others have quite a bit of sauce. Jorgé Stanbury, a musician, cookbook author, and *bon vivant* who collected hundreds of recipes during his travels in Peru, had another explanation for this confusing name. According to Stanbury, "there used to exist several kinds of gourd put to different uses depending on their size. You had small *cojuditos* for drinking *chicha*, and much larger *potos* and *shecos*, which were used to serve food—the gourd used to serve this stew was a *sheco*, which became a *seco*."

3 pounds Pacific mussels (such as New Zealand green lip mussels; see Note)

4 tablespoons olive oil

1 large white onion, peeled and diced (about 2 cups)

2 cloves garlic, peeled and minced

2 to 3 tablespoons *Pasta de Ají Amarillo* or *Mirasol* (chile paste, page 147) or 1 tablespoon ground *ají amarillo* or *mirasol*, or Asian chile-garlic sauce (see Note, page 147)

1 cup light beer

1½ cups uncooked rice

3 cups chicken broth

1 medium-hot dried red chile, seeded and crumbled

1 cup tightly packed fresh cilantro leaves, chopped

½ cup fresh mint leaves, chopped

½ cup fresh or frozen peas

Wash the mussels thoroughly in several changes of cold water, scrubbing with a stiff brush until no trace of mud or sand remains. Set the mussels aside. Do not pull off their stringy beards until right before cooking, as this will cause them to die and spoil.

In a pot that is large enough to hold the mussels, heat the oil over medium heat. Add the onion, garlic, and *Pasta de Ají*, and sauté until the onion begins to turn golden at the edges, about 5 minutes. Add the beer and cook until the liquid is reduced by half, 4 to 5 minutes. Add the rice, chicken broth, and dried chile. Bring to a boil, cover the pot, and cook over medium-low heat until most of the liquid has been absorbed and the rice is tender, about 20 minutes. Stir the rice, scraping the bottom of the pan.

Fold in ¾ cup of the cilantro and all but 2 tablespoons of the mint. Fold in the peas, and add the mussels, burying them in the rice. Cover and steam over medium-low heat, shaking the pan occasionally, until all the shells open, 8 to 12 minutes. Transfer the *seco* to a serving bowl, sprinkle with the remaining cilantro and mint, and serve.

NOTE: When you buy mussels, make sure that the shells are tightly closed. Discard any with open, cracked, or broken shells.

THE INCA

RIGHT: The green lip of Pacific mussels adds color to the presentation of *Seco de Choros*; the ground *ají amarillo* (right) adds the spice.

184

AJÍ DE POLLO

PERUVIAN CHICKEN IN GOLDEN CHILE AND NUT SAUCE

SERVES
6 TO 8

Ají means "hot chile" in the Quechua language and also refers to many different dishes in which chiles are the dominant seasoning. *Ají de Pollo* is a popular special-occasion recipe in Peru. It has very traditional Native American roots combined with some early Spanish colonial influences, such as thickening the sauce with wheat bread. We have enjoyed several delicious *Ajíes de Pollo*, but agree that the recipe given to us by Señora Maria Teresa Montoya de Salcido of the ancient Inca city of Cuzco is exceptional.

Palillo is an Andean herb that give foods a golden color. It is not readily available outside of Peru, but turmeric may be substituted.

6 cups chicken broth

1 yellow onion, peeled and quartered

One ½-inch piece fresh ginger, peeled and sliced

6 to 8 whole cloves

2½ to 3 pounds split chicken breasts

5 or 6 dried *ají mirasol* chiles or 1 to 3 teaspoons ground *ají amarillo* or other medium-hot ground chiles

1 cup fresh orange juice

3 tablespoons fresh lime juice

4 slices white bread, crusts removed

1 cup evaporated milk or half-and-half

¼ cup vegetable oil

3 red or yellow onions, peeled and diced

½ teaspoon *palillo* or turmeric (optional)

6 to 8 small yellow, red-skinned, or purple potatoes, peeled

Salt

1 cup chopped unsalted dry-roasted peanuts or lightly toasted walnuts

3 cups hot cooked rice (optional)

2 hard-cooked eggs, cut into wedges

12 Kalamata olives

2 tablespoons chopped fresh cilantro or Italian parsley

In a Dutch oven combine the chicken broth with the quartered onion, the ginger, and cloves. Bring to a boil over medium-high heat. Add the chicken and reduce the heat to medium-low. Cook the chicken in the barely simmering broth for 20 minutes.

Meanwhile, if you are using dried chiles, remove the stems and seeds and place the chiles in a bowl; add the orange and lime juices and let soak for about 20 minutes to soften. Place the chiles (or the chile powder) and orange and lime juices in a blender or food processor and liquefy. Pour the chile puree into a bowl and set aside. Without washing the blender, place the bread and evaporated milk in the blender and puree. Set aside.

Remove the poached chicken from the broth. Pull the meat from the bones and shred each breast half into 6 to 8 pieces. Pour the broth through a strainer into a bowl, and set aside.

Heat the oil in a large, deep skillet over medium heat. Add the chopped onions and the *palillo* and sauté until the onion is translucent, about 5 minutes. Add the chile puree and continue to cook, stirring, until most of the liquid has evaporated, 8 to 10 minutes. Add the bread mixture and cook, stirring, for a few seconds. Add 2 cups of the broth and continue to cook, stirring occasionally, until the sauce has thickened and a spatula leaves a track on the bottom of the pan, 15 to 20 minutes.

Meanwhile, place the potatoes in a large saucepan and add water to cover. Add 1 tablespoon salt and bring to a boil, then reduce the heat and boil gently until tender, about 15 minutes. Drain, and keep warm.

Add the shredded chicken and 2 more cups of the broth to the sauce. Reduce the heat to low and simmer gently, stirring occasionally, until the sauce has thickened enough to coat the back of a spatula, 10 to 15 minutes. Stir in the nuts. Adjust the seasonings, adding salt to taste. Serve the *ají* with the boiled potatoes and, if desired, with hot rice. Garnish with the eggs and olives. Sprinkle with cilantro.

LEFT: *Ají de Pollo*, with its golden chile sauce, is a classic of Peruvian cuisine.

THE INCA

187

CONEJO AL HORNO
ROAST RABBIT WITH CHILES, GARLIC, AND HERBS

SERVES 4

While walking through the outdoor food market in Pisaq, an ancient Peruvian town that sits in a fertile valley surrounded by mountains, we noticed vendors selling sheaves of barley and stopped to enquire about what people did with it. "Oh," answered the vendor, "it is for feeding the *cuy.*" *Cuy,* the Andean guinea pig, has for perhaps thousands of years been an important meat animal for the indigenous people of the Andes. This sounds strange and unappetizing to many foreigners, especially those of us who have had pet guinea pigs, but the barley-fed *cuy* are clean and taste—dare we say it?—a lot like chicken or rabbit.

In Peru and Bolivia, whole *cuy,* rabbits, or chickens are often rubbed with lemon, ground chiles, garlic, spices, and vinegar made from *chicha,* the traditional corn beer. They are then stuffed with bouquets of fresh herbs and whole chiles and left to marinate before being roasted to a golden brown either in a *pachamanca* (the traditional earth oven) or in the bread oven of the neighborhood bakery.

The essence of the chiles, spices, and herbs permeates the meat and gives it a truly delicious flavor. Andean guinea pig is not readily available, and even rabbit is not to everyone's taste but if you like roast chicken, this is a recipe you should try. Serve it with *Pastel de Papas* (page 201).

Two 1½- to 2-pound rabbits or 2 large Cornish hens

1 lemon, halved

1½ tablespoons *Pasta de Ají Amarillo* or *Mirasol* (chile paste, page 147) or 2 to 4 teaspoons ground *ají amarillo*

2 cloves garlic, peeled

1 teaspoon ground cumin

1 teaspoon salt (preferably coarse or sea salt)

1 tablespoon white balsamic vinegar or rice vinegar

1 bunch fresh *huacataya* (see Sources), or 4 to 6 sprigs each of fresh tarragon, mint, and cilantro

2 whole fresh jalapeño or other small hot chiles (optional)

3 tablespoons butter, melted, or mild salad oil

Rinse the rabbits inside and out under cold running water and pat dry with paper towels. Remove any excess fat from the body cavity (and remove the giblets from hens, if using). Rub the rabbits with the lemon halves and set aside.

Using a mortar and pestle, combine the *Pasta de Ají*, garlic, cumin, 1 teaspoon salt, and the vinegar to a smooth paste. Rub the rabbits inside and out with the mixture. In a small bowl toss the *huacataya* and the jalapeños (if using) with 1 tablespoon of the melted butter. Stuff the body cavities with the mixture. Cover and allow the rabbits to marinate, refrigerated, for 2 to 3 hours.

Preheat the oven to 400°F.

Brush the rabbits generously with the remaining 2 tablespoons melted butter, and place them in a shallow roasting pan. Roast for 15 minutes. Reduce the temperature to 375°F, cover the pan with aluminum foil, and continue to roast for 30 minutes. Uncover the pan and baste the rabbit with the pan juices. Continue to cook, uncovered, until the juices run clear when a thigh is pierced with a knife, 15 to 20 minutes more. Split the rabbits in half, and serve.

BISTEK CON PESKE DE QUINOA
STEAK WITH RELISH AND QUINOA TOSSED WITH CHEESE

Serves 4

Cooked quinoa is tossed with cheese and evaporated milk for a delicious and versatile side dish. In Peru and Bolivia it is usually served with a sautéed or grilled beef or pork fillet, topped with a fresh relish of red onion, tomato, lime juice, salt, and cilantro. *Hierba buena,* an herb in the mint family, usually replaces the cilantro when pork is served; you can approximate its flavor by mixing mint with cilantro.

This recipe was given to us by Roman and Fielding Viscarra. It is a typical meal that they serve at their charming Hostel Pisaq in Pisaq, Peru.

QUINOA

1 cup uncooked quinoa

2 cups water

½ to ¾ cup diced *queso fresco* or shredded mozzarella cheese

½ cup evaporated milk or heavy cream

Salt to taste

RELISH

1 small red onion, peeled and slivered lengthwise

1 large tomato, diced

1 to 2 tablespoons fresh lime juice

Salt to taste

1 to 2 tablespoons minced fresh cilantro, or *hierba buena* (see Sources), or a combination of cilantro and fresh mint if using pork

STEAKS

2 teaspoons minced garlic

½ teaspoon ground cumin

Salt and freshly ground black pepper to taste

4 small boneless beef steaks, or pork tenderloin fillets sliced ½ inch thick

1 to 2 tablespoons olive or canola oil

Place the quinoa in a sieve and rinse it well under cold running water. Rub it between your hands while you rinse it, to remove any bitter residue.

Put the quinoa in a saucepan, add the water, and bring to a boil. (Do not add salt until after the quinoa is cooked, or it won't cook properly.) Cover, reduce the heat to low, and simmer until tender, about 20 minutes.

While the quinoa is cooking, stir all the relish ingredients together in a small bowl, and set aside.

Prepare the steaks: Stir together the garlic, cumin, and salt and pepper. Pound the steaks to an even thickness of about

¼ inch, and rub the seasoning mixture over them. Heat the oil in a large skillet over medium-high heat. Add the steaks and brown them quickly on both sides. Reduce the heat to medium-low and cook for 1 to 3 minutes per side (4 to 6 minutes per side for pork).

Fluff the quinoa with a fork and toss it with the cheese, evaporated milk, and salt to taste. Divide the quinoa among 4 plates, and arrange the steaks on the plates. Top the steaks with the relish, and serve.

HUATÍA
ANDEAN WINTER STEW

For feasts and ceremonial occasions, out of respect for Pachamama (Mother Earth) the Inca cooked foods in an earth oven called a *pachamanca*.

The Quechua-speaking peoples from the mountain pueblos around Lima prepare a wonderful herb and chile–seasoned stew that is cooked underground in a tightly covered clay pot. To prepare this *huatía*, meat and sliced onions are layered in the pot with a marinade of vinegar and spices. A bouquet of fresh herbs and chiles is added. The pot is then sealed and placed in the *pachamanca* to simmer slowly. After several hours, when the meat is meltingly tender and the broth is spicy and fragrant, the *huatía* is ready. It is served accompanied by sweet potatoes that have roasted alongside the stew.

This recipe is adapted from one developed by Isabel Alvarez, a passionate food historian and chef. Her Lima restaurant, El Señorío de Sulco, serves a *huatía* that brings comfort on the coldest Andean evening and a smile to the face of Pachamama.

2 or 3 fresh *ajíes amarillo* or jalapeño chiles, to taste

½ cup white balsamic vinegar or rice vinegar

¼ cup water

2 teaspoons ground cumin

2 tablespoons corn oil

Salt

3 pounds lean lamb or beef stew meat, cut into 3- to 4-inch pieces

3 small to medium-size yellow onions, peeled and quartered

6 sprigs fresh *hierba buena* (see Sources) or mint

6 sprigs fresh *huacataya* (see Sources) or basil (preferably a small-leafed variety)

6 sprigs fresh cilantro

6 sprigs fresh rosemary

6 sprigs fresh Italian parsley

6 sweet potatoes

Sprigs of fresh Italian parsley and cilantro, for garnish (optional)

Seed and coarsely chop one of the chiles. Place it in a food processor with the vinegar, water, cumin, oil, and 1½ teaspoons salt. Puree the mixture.

Place the lamb in a large nonreactive bowl and add the vinegar mixture. Toss, cover, and marinate in the refrigerator for several hours or overnight.

If you are using a clay cooker, soak it in water following the manufacturer's instructions. If you don't have a clay cooker, use a Dutch oven.

Preheat the oven to 350°F.

Place the onions in a single layer in the bottom of the pot. Scatter the fresh herbs on top of the onions. Then add the meat and marinade. Nestle the remaining whole chiles (to taste) on top. Cover and bake, stirring occasionally, until the meat is very tender, 2 to 3 hours.

Meanwhile, peel the sweet potatoes and place them in another clay pot or Dutch oven. Sprinkle them with salt, cover, and bake until tender, about 1 hour. (The potatoes may also be left unpeeled, wrapped tightly in aluminum foil, and baked directly on the oven rack.) Serve the meat and its broth with the roasted sweet potatoes. If desired, garnish with sprigs of fresh herbs.

RIGHT: *Huatía* is garnished with traditional native herbs and served with roasted sweet potatoes.

PASTEL DE CHOCLO
PERUVIAN CORN AND MEAT PIE

In all of the great corn cultures of the Americas, special dishes are prepared to celebrate the harvest of the first sweet young corn. In Peru, *Pastel de Choclo* is a favorite seasonal dish. The filling between the layers of fresh corn dough is usually beef, but it may also be made of lamb, chicken, or pork. Because *choclo* is higher in starch than the sweet corn sold in the United States, we have added some hominy to give the dough a better texture. Though it is best when made with fresh corn, we have used canned cream-style corn with acceptable results.

4½ tablespoons unsalted butter, plus additional for the baking dish

12 ears fresh corn or three 15-ounce cans cream-style corn

Two 14.5-ounce cans yellow or white hominy

1 teaspoon salt

1½ teaspoons sugar

4 cups *Pino* (Chilean spiced beef filling, page 194)

⅓ cup dark or golden raisins

2 ripe plum tomatoes, roasted (page 217), peeled, and coarsely chopped

2 hard-cooked eggs, sliced

8 Alfonso or Kalamata olives, pitted and chopped, or 2 tablespoons capers, drained

Preheat the oven to 375°F.

Butter an 8- or 9-inch square baking dish that is about 2½ inches deep, and set aside.

Using the coarse holes on a metal box grater, grate the kernels off the corn cobs into a large mixing bowl. You should have about 6 cups of pulp and juice. Drain the hominy and puree it in a blender or food processor.

Melt 3 tablespoons of the butter in a large skillet over medium heat. Add the grated fresh (or the canned) corn and the hominy, salt, and sugar. Cook over low heat, stirring often, until it becomes a thick paste, about 10 minutes. Remove from the heat and set aside.

In a mixing bowl combine the *Pino* with the raisins and tomatoes.

Spread half of the corn mixture in the bottom of the baking dish. Spoon the *Pino* mixture over the corn. Arrange the egg slices and olives over the beef. Top with the remaining corn mixture. Dot the top with the remaining 1½ tablespoons butter. Bake in the center of the oven until the top of the *pastel* is a light golden brown, 60 to 70 minutes. Allow it to cool for at least 10 minutes before cutting it into squares. Serve warm or at room temperature.

PAPAS RELLENAS
POTATOES STUFFED WITH CHILEAN SPICED BEEF

These stuffed potatoes are really mashed-potato croquettes with a spicy beef filling, molded into an oval "potato" shape. They are delicious and fun to make—as long as you use the right potatoes; otherwise they can be a sticky disaster. In our experience, the best potatoes for this purpose are Idaho potatoes. When riced they are moldable and don't stick to your hands. Make small "potatoes" for appetizers and larger ones as a main course, and serve them with *Salsa de Ají Amarillo* (page 148) or *Salsa de Mani* (page 149).

3 pounds Idaho potatoes, scrubbed

Salt and freshly ground black pepper to taste

2 cups *Pino* (Chilean spiced beef filling, page 194)

2 tablespoons raisins

1 tablespoon capers, drained

1 hard-cooked egg, coarsely chopped

½ cup all-purpose flour

2 eggs, lightly beaten

2 cups fresh bread crumbs, preferably from crusty French or Italian bread

3 to 4 cups vegetable oil, for frying

Place the potatoes in a large saucepan and add water to cover. Add 1 tablespoon salt and bring to a gentle boil. Cook the potatoes until tender when pierced with a knife, about 40 minutes. Drain the potatoes, and when they are cool enough to handle, peel them. Pass the potatoes through a ricer or food mill, or press them through a coarse sieve, into a bowl. Season to taste with salt and pepper.

Put the *Pino* in a bowl and gently fold in the raisins, capers, and chopped egg.

Divide the riced potatoes into 8 equal portions. While you are forming the stuffed potatoes, occasionally dip your hands into cold water to prevent the potatoes from sticking to them. Place one portion of mashed potatoes (about ⅔ cup) in the cupped palm of your hand and use the fingers of your other hand to form it into a "boat" shape. Place 2 tablespoons of the *Pino* mixture in the hollow, and press it down with your fingertips. Mold the sides of the "boat" up over the filling to enclose it. Use both hands to shape the stuffed potato to resemble a large egg. Repeat until all the potatoes and filling have been used.

Dredge the stuffed potatoes in the flour, gently shaking off any excess. Dip them into the beaten eggs and then roll them in the bread crumbs until they are evenly coated.

Preheat the oven to 300°F. Line a large baking sheet with slightly crumpled paper towels.

Fill a deep, heavy skillet with oil to a depth of 1 inch (or use a deep-fat fryer and fill as directed). Place the skillet over medium-high heat. When the oil reaches 375°F on a frying thermometer, or when a small cube of bread dropped into the oil turns golden brown in about 1 minute, the oil is ready. Using a slotted spoon, gently lower a stuffed and breaded potato into the hot oil. Cook 1 potato at a time, using the spoon to gently turn it, until golden brown on all sides, about 1 minute. As they are fried, transfer the potatoes to the baking sheet to drain. Keep them warm in the oven until all are cooked, and then serve.

NOTE: The *Papas Rellenos* may be prepared and fried in advance, then frozen for up to a month. To serve, reheat in a preheated 350°F oven for about 30 minutes, until crisp and hot.

THE INCA

PINO
CHILEAN SPICED BEEF FILLING

Slightly different versions of this versatile spicy meat filling are made throughout Latin America. It is used in both *Papas Rellenas* (page 193) and *Pastel de Choclo* (page 192).

2 tablespoons olive oil

1½ cups finely chopped onion

1½ teaspoons *Pasta de Ají Rojo* (chile paste, page 147) or Asian chile-garlic sauce (see Note, page 147), to taste

½ teaspoon ground cumin

¼ teaspoon dried oregano (preferably Mexican oregano)

1 pound lean ground beef

Salt

1 teaspoon sweet paprika

¼ teaspoon freshly ground black pepper

Pour the oil into a large skillet over medium heat. Add the onion, *ají* paste, cumin, and oregano, and sauté for 6 to 8 minutes, until the onion is softened and beginning to brown at the edges. Add the beef, 1½ teaspoons salt, the paprika, and the black pepper, and cook, stirring occasionally, until all the liquid has evaporated, 6 to 8 minutes. Taste, and add more salt if necessary.

CHARQUI
ANDEAN-STYLE JERKY

The word *charqui* derives from the Quechua word *cucharqui*, which means "dried meat" and is also the origin of the English word *jerky*. The arid climate of the Andes made drying a practical method of preserving meats. *Charqui* was often made from the meat of llamas and alpacas or of the wild *vicuña* and *guanaco*. The Andean deer, *buemúl*, also made tasty jerky. Though we were able to purchase llama *charqui* at Lima's large Mercado de Surquillo No. 1, the vendor, Herlinda Mendoza, told us that today, even in Peru, most *charqui* is made from beef or lamb.

2 pounds lean boneless beef or lamb, very thinly sliced with the grain of the meat

2 tablespoons coarse salt

1 to 2 tablespoons ground *ají amarillo* or other ground chiles (optional)

Rub the meat with the salt and chile (if using). Cover, and marinate in the refrigerator for 1 hour. Then put the meat in a dehydrator and dry it for 8 hours, or arrange the slices on a rack and dry them in a 150°F oven for 8 to 10 hours, or until very dry. Store in the refrigerator or freezer.

NOTE: Because of the concerns about E-coli and salmonella the USDA recommends using an oven thermometer to check the accuracy of the thermostat of either a dehydrator or a home oven. To be safe, the oven should maintain a steady temperature of at least 145°F when making jerky.

CHARQUEKAN
SAUTÉED JERKY SALAD

This ancient Bolivian dish is a bit like the warm salads that have become popular in the United States in recent years. Some of the ingredients are hot, some at room temperature. This version is served over hominy, which is similar, but not identical, to the traditional *mote*. It may also be served with hot rice. Some cooks garnish the plates with *chuño* (freeze-dried potato) that has been scrambled with eggs, as well as with boiled potatoes, and others add a layer of crumbled *queso fresco* or feta cheese between the *mote* and the jerky mixture—in which case the dish is called *charquetaca*.

¼ **pound *Charqui* (jerky, page 194) or prepared pepper-seasoned beef jerky**

2 **tablespoons mild cooking oil such as corn or canola**

1 **small yellow or white onion, chopped (about 1 cup)**

1 **large ripe tomato, diced**

½ **to 1 minced fresh *aji amarillo* or jalapeño chile**

1 **to 2 tablespoons minced fresh cilantro or parsley**

Salt to taste

2 **cups hot precooked or well-drained canned hominy**

4 **small potatoes, preferably yellow, boiled, peeled, and halved lengthwise**

½ **small red onion, peeled, slivered lengthwise, and soaked in cold water, or ½ to ¾ cup *Cebollas Encurtidas* (pickled onions, page 49)**

1 **or 2 hard-cooked eggs, cut into wedges**

Finely chop or shred the *Charqui*. Heat the oil in a large skillet over medium heat. Add the *Charqui* and chopped onion, and sauté until the *Charqui* is crisp and the onion is translucent, 5 to 6 minutes. Remove from the heat and add the tomato, chile, and cilantro. Toss gently. Taste, and add salt if needed. Place ½ cup of the hominy on each plate. Spoon the *Charqui* mixture over the hominy, and garnish with the potato halves, thoroughly drained red onion slivers, and egg wedges.

PAPAS A LA AREQUIPEÑA
PERUVIAN SCALLOPED POTATOES

The potato, *Solanum tuberosum,* is one of the greatest culinary treasures of the Americas. Originally from the mountainous regions of Peru, Bolivia, Ecuador, and Mexico, potatoes were probably gathered and eaten by Indian peoples on both continents as early as 8,000 years ago.

Potatoes are not only delicious, they are a nutritional bonanza. High in fiber and low in calories, one cooked medium-size potato contains about 800 milligrams of potassium and provides 50 percent of the recommended daily allowance of vitamin C. Potatoes are also rich in vitamins K and B6 and are a good source of iron, thiamine, and folic acid.

The Inca cultivated more than 3,000 varieties of potatoes, ranging from tiny to tremendous. They existed in a rainbow of colors and included all 250 varieties grown today. These potatoes were developed to suit the diverse soils and climatic conditions of the vast Inca empire.

The recipe that follows is typical of Arequipa, a southern Peruvian city famous for its spicy food. The use of cream and cheese shows a Spanish influence, and the intriguing addition of a chile filled with oil has direct links to the pre-Columbian past. Throughout South America, potato dishes are often served as a separate course before the main course.

2½ to 3 pounds all-purpose potatoes (preferably a combination of different colors)

½ pound feta or Muenster cheese, cut into ¼-inch cubes

¼ pound mozzarella cheese, cut into ¼-inch cubes

1 teaspoon coarse salt

¼ cup olive oil

½ cup heavy cream or evaporated milk

1 fresh *ají mirasol* or Anaheim chile (see Note)

1 tablespoon minced red bell pepper or minced fresh cilantro (optional)

Preheat the oven to 350°F.

Peel the potatoes and cut them into ¼-inch cubes. Keep them covered with cold water until ready to use. Drain the potatoes well and pat them dry with a kitchen towel. In a mixing bowl toss the potatoes with the cheeses, salt, and 1 tablespoon of the olive oil. Place the potato mixture in a shallow baking dish and drizzle the cream over the top.

Make a lengthwise slit in the chile to form a boatlike receptacle, and remove the seeds. Nestle the chile "boat" in the middle of the potato mixture, and fill it with the remaining oil.

Bake until the potatoes are tender, 1 to 1½ hours. Carefully spoon the hot oil from the chile over the potatoes, garnish with the bell pepper, and serve.

NOTE: To prepare this in 4 individual gratin dishes, place 1 fresh jalapeño chile in each dish and fill it with oil as described.

RIGHT: *Papas a la Arequipeña* is shown here in an individual gratin, topped with a jalapeño chile "boat" filled with oil.

CAUSA LIMEÑA
GOLDEN, SPICY MASHED-POTATO SALAD

Causa, Peru's national dish, is pre-Columbian in origin. The word itself is derived from the Quechua *kausac,* which means "that which sustains" or "that which nourishes." For anyone who likes potatoes, this interesting mashed-potato salad is great comfort food. At its simplest, *causa* is mashed yellow potatoes seasoned with pureed golden chiles, oil, salt, and vinegar or lemon juice. There are also more elaborate versions, filled with shrimp, chicken, tuna, or vegetable salad. The recipe has evolved over the centuries, and today most cooks add mayonnaise to make the potato mixture moister and fluffier.

Celia Bedia de Ustua grew up in a mountain town near Cuzco but has lived and worked in Lima for many years. She is a creative cook who maintains tradition while making full use of labor-saving devices like the electric blender. Depending on the occasion, and on how much time she has to spend in the kitchen, Celia's *causas* may be simple or fancy.

For a quick presentation, with deft lightly oiled hands, she either molds the potato mixture into individual potato-shaped *causas* or presses it into a lightly oiled ring mold or bowl. For a more formal occasion, Celia lines the mold with two-thirds of the potatoes and spoons in a filling—*Cebiche de Atún* (page 156) would work well. She then spreads the remaining potatoes over the filling and chills the *causa* for at least 30 minutes before unmolding it onto a serving platter. In either case, Celia garnishes the *causa* with hard-cooked eggs, olives, strips of roasted red bell pepper, and fresh herbs, and serves it with her own quick and easy interpretation of *Salsa Huancaina,* another Peruvian classic.

3 pounds yellow potatoes (such as Yukon Gold) (8 or 9 potatoes)

Salt to taste

4 to 6 tablespoons *Salsa de Ají Amarillo* (yellow chile sauce, page 148), or 2 to 3 teaspoons ground *ají amarillo*

1 tablespoon fresh lemon juice

3 to 6 tablespoons mayonnaise

Freshly ground black pepper to taste

1 or 2 hard-cooked eggs, sliced or quartered

6 to 8 pitted Kalamata olives

Red bell pepper strips, roasted (page 217)

Sprigs of fresh parsley, tarragon, or cilantro

Bibb or Boston lettuce leaves

***Salsa Huancaina* (recipe follows)**

Scrub the potatoes and place them in a saucepan with enough lightly salted cold water to cover by 2 inches. Bring to a boil, then reduce the heat and boil gently until the potatoes are tender when pierced with a knife, 30 to 40 minutes. Drain the potatoes and set them aside until they are cool enough to handle; peel the potatoes.

Put the peeled potatoes through a ricer, or use a wooden spoon to press them through a coarse sieve, into a bowl. Place the potatoes in the refrigerator to chill for at least 30 minutes.

Using your hands or a wooden spoon, gradually mix the *Salsa di Ají* and lemon juice into the cold potatoes. (If you are using ground chiles, combine it with the lemon juice and 3 tablespoons of the mayonnaise before mixing it into the potatoes.) When the salsa has been thoroughly incorporated, mix in enough mayonnaise to give the potatoes a nice rounded flavor but not enough to make the mixture too soft to mold. Season to taste with salt and pepper.

With lightly oiled hands, press the potato mixture into a

lightly oiled mold or bowl. Chill in the refrigerator for at least 30 minutes to set. (If it is unfilled, the *causa* may be covered and refrigerated for up to 1 day before serving.)

Carefully run a thin-bladed knife around the edge of the mold, and then invert it onto a serving platter. If it is very cold, place a warm damp kitchen towel over the mold to help warm the oil and loosen the *causa* without breaking it. Carefully lift off the mold. If necessary, smooth the surface of the *causa* with a spatula. Garnish the *causa* with the sliced eggs, olives, roasted pepper, and parsley sprigs. Cut it into wedges and serve on luncheon plates lined with lettuce leaves. Pass the *Salsa Huancaina* separately.

SALSA HUANCAINA

Makes
about
1⅓ cups

¾ cup crumbled *queso fresco*

4 to 5 tablespoons *Salsa de Ají Amarillo* (yellow chile sauce, page 148), or 1 to 3 teaspoons ground *ají amarillo*

2 t o3 tablespoons evaporated milk, heavy cream, or half-and-half

2 to 3 tablespoons salad oil or light olive oil

Salt and freshly ground black pepper, to taste

Place the cheese and *Salsa de Ají* in a blender or food processor and blend until smooth. With the machine running, gradually add 2 tablespoons of the milk and 2 tablespoons of the oil. If the sauce seems too thick, add a little more milk and oil. Season to taste with salt and pepper. Pour the sauce into a small bowl, and serve.

PAPAS A LA HUANCAINA
BOILED POTATOES WITH CREAMY CHILE AND CHEESE SAUCE

This spicy but soothing potato dish is a typical first course from Huancayo, a Peruvian city located in the Sierra at 11,000 feet. Like many Andean dishes it is "golden," tinted the color of the sun with fiery golden chiles and *palillo*, a local herb that is not readily available in other countries but may be replaced with turmeric. This sauce is a variation of *Salsa Huancaina* (page 199). The dish usually is served as a first course, with one whole potato with its sauce and garnishes per person.

Juice of 1 lemon (¼ cup)

1 dried *hontaka* chile, seeded and crushed (see Note), or ⅛ teaspoon "Chile Caribe" or other hot red pepper flakes

Salt and freshly ground black pepper to taste

1 red onion, peeled and thinly sliced into rings

6 all-purpose potatoes, preferably Yukon Gold

Boston or Bibb lettuce leaves

1 to 3 fresh *ají mirasol*, or other medium-hot orange, yellow, or red chiles, or 1 to 3 teaspoons dried ground *ají amarillo*

2 cups coarsely chopped *queso fresco* or Muenster cheese

½ to 1 teaspoon *palillo* or turmeric

1 cup heavy cream

½ cup safflower or mild olive oil

3 hard-cooked eggs, quartered

2 ears fresh or frozen corn, cooked and cut into 1-inch rounds

12 Alfonso, Kalamata, or other black olives, pitted

In a bowl combine the lemon juice, dried chile, ¼ teaspoon salt, and a pinch of black pepper. Add the onion and set aside to marinate at room temperature while you prepare the rest of the dish.

Put the potatoes in a large saucepan and add lightly salted water to cover. Bring to a boil, then reduce the heat and boil gently until tender when pierced with a knife, 20 to 30 minutes. Drain the potatoes and peel them. Line a platter with the lettuce leaves and arrange the potatoes on the lettuce.

If you are using fresh chiles, stem, seed, and coarsely chop them. Place the fresh or ground chiles, cheese, *palillo*, and cream in a blender or food processor and puree.

Heat the oil in a large skillet over medium heat. Add the cheese mixture, reduce the heat to low, and cook, stirring constantly with a wooden spoon, until the sauce is smooth and creamy. Taste, and add salt if needed.

Spoon the sauce over the potatoes and arrange the quartered eggs, corn, and olives between them. Drain the marinated onions and scatter the rings over the top. Serve slightly warm or at room temperature.

NOTE: A *hontaka* is a small, hot, dried red chile. Cayenne or another small, hot, dried Mexican or Asian chile can be substituted as well.

PASTEL DE PAPAS
ANDEAN POTATO AND CHEESE PIE

For the Quechua and Aymara people, the first cutting of a child's hair is an important rite of passage—the transition from infant to child—that is celebrated at a *rutuchi* ceremony. The child's hair is plaited into many tiny braids, each tied with a ribbon, red for girls and blue for boys. With family and friends gathered, the godparents ask Pachamama (Mother Earth) to protect and guide the child through life. They then present a gift, perhaps a baby alpaca if the child lives in the Sierra and money or clothing if the family lives in town. Using special scissors adorned with satin ribbons, each godparent cuts off one of the braids. Then other relatives and friends are invited to step forward, and after offering a gift, each cuts off a braid. When all the gifts are given and all of the ribbon-festooned braids have been gathered in a bundle to be cherished as a keepsake or given as an offering to Pachamama, dinner is served and the fiesta continues long into the night.

This rich, dense Andean potato pie was one of the dishes served at the *rutuchi* ceremony for a little girl named Tamia Ni'An—"rain" in Quechua—which was held in Sicuani, a town high in the Peruvian Andes near the border with Bolivia.

Pastel de Papas is a great side dish to serve with roasted meat or fowl. For a variation, or to make it a main course, spread 2 cups of *Pino* (page 194) between the layers of potatoes and cheese.

Salt

2 pounds all-purpose potatoes, peeled and thinly sliced

3 tablespoons butter, plus additional for the baking dish

1¼ cups shredded mozzarella cheese

¼ cup grated Parmesan or Romano cheese

2 extra-large eggs

One 12-ounce can evaporated milk or 1½ cups half-and-half

¼ teaspoon freshly ground black pepper

⅛ teaspoon grated nutmeg

Preheat the oven to 375°F.

Bring a large pot of lightly salted water to a boil. Add the potatoes, and when the water returns to a boil remove it from the heat and drain the potatoes. Set aside.

Butter an 8-inch square baking dish. Arrange one-third of the potato slices, slightly overlapping, in the dish. Dot with 1 tablespoon of the butter, and sprinkle with one-third of the cheese. Add two more layers of potatoes, butter, and cheese.

In a mixing bowl whisk together the eggs, evaporated milk, 1 teaspoon salt, the pepper, and the nutmeg. Pour the egg mixture over the potatoes. Bake until the potatoes are tender and most of the liquid has been absorbed, 45 to 60 minutes. Cut the *pastel* into squares, and serve.

LLAPINGACHOS
ECUADORIAN MASHED-POTATO CAKES

Cutting into these luscious little mashed-potato cakes and finding a melted cheese center is a delightful surprise. Like many Andean potato dishes, they are often served as a first course, usually on a platter garnished with lettuce leaves and slices of avocado, tomato, and red onion. We also like to eat them for breakfast or brunch, topped with a fried egg, or as a side dish with fish or meat. They are not difficult to make, but to simplify the preparation you may mix the cheese directly into the potatoes instead of putting it in the center of each cake. Some cooks we know omit the red onion. Serve this dish with *Salsa de Maní* (page 149).

---

2 pounds Idaho or other good mashing potatoes, peeled and sliced

Salt to taste

3 to 4 tablespoons butter

1½ cups finely chopped white or yellow onion

Freshly ground black pepper to taste

¾ to 1 cup shredded mozzarella cheese

2 to 4 tablespoons vegetable oil

½ cup all-purpose flour

Dash of cayenne pepper

1 small head romaine lettuce

2 ripe avocados, peeled, pitted, and thinly sliced

3 or 4 ripe plum tomatoes, sliced

1 small red onion, peeled and thinly sliced (optional)

Put the sliced potatoes in a large saucepan and add lightly salted water to cover. Bring to a boil, then reduce the heat and boil gently until tender, 15 to 20 minutes. Drain the slices well and pass them through a ricer or mash them by hand. (Do not use a food processor; it makes potatoes like glue.)

Melt the butter in a large skillet over medium heat. Add the onion and cook, stirring occasionally, until translucent, about 5 minutes. Add the onion to the potatoes, mix well, and season to taste with salt and pepper.

Divide the potato mixture into 12 portions, and roll them into balls. Place a potato ball in the palm of your hand. Form a well in the center, and place about 1 tablespoon of the cheese in the well. Bring the potato around the cheese to enclose it, and flatten the ball between the palms of your hands to make a cake the size of a large biscuit. Form the remaining cakes in the same manner, and place them on a platter or baking sheet. Chill the cakes in the refrigerator for

at least 15 minutes, or make the cakes in advance and chill, covered, for several hours.

Preheat the oven to 300°F. Line a baking sheet with paper towels.

Pour enough oil into a large nonstick or well-seasoned skillet to cover the bottom. Place the skillet over medium heat. Stir together the flour, salt and black pepper to taste, and the cayenne.

Lightly dust the potato cakes with this mixture, shaking off any excess. Sauté the cakes, in batches, until golden brown on both sides, about 5 minutes total. Transfer them to the baking sheet and keep them warm in the oven until all are cooked. Add more oil to the skillet as needed.

Line 6 plates with lettuce leaves, and arrange 2 potato cakes on each plate. Garnish with the avocados, tomatoes, and onion, and serve.

TORREJAS DE QUINOA
QUINOA GRIDDLE CAKES

Torrejas are often served for breakfast or sent along with schoolchildren to eat as a midmorning snack. They are also an excellent accompaniment to roasted or grilled meats. Though they are usually made with leftover quinoa, they are so good that it's worth preparing the quinoa just to have *torrejas!*

2 cups cooked quinoa

¾ to 1 cup grated carrot

1 small yellow onion, finely chopped

¼ cup chopped fresh Italian parsley

2 eggs, beaten

1 to 1¼ teaspoons salt, to taste

¼ to ½ teaspoon freshly ground black pepper to taste

¼ to ⅓ cup all-purpose flour

2 to 4 tablespoons canola or other mild oil

In a mixing bowl combine the quinoa, carrot, onion, parsley, eggs, salt, pepper, and ¼ cup of the flour. Toss together to combine thoroughly. Add more flour if needed to hold the mixture together.

Heat 1 tablespoon of the oil in a nonstick or well-seasoned skillet or griddle over medium-high heat. In batches, spoon heaping tablespoons of the quinoa mixture onto the preheated skillet. Using a spatula, flatten each spoonful to form a 3½- to 4-inch round patty. Fry the *torrejas* for 2 to 3 minutes on each side, until golden brown. Brush the skillet with more oil as needed. Serve hot or at room temperature.

NOTE: To cook quinoa, first place the quinoa in a sieve and rinse it well under cold running water. Rub it between your hands while you rinse it, to remove any bitter residue.

Place the quinoa in a 1½-quart saucepan, add the water, and bring to a boil. Reduce the heat to maintain a simmer, cover, and cook until all of the water has been absorbed, about 15 minutes. You will know the quinoa is done when all the grains have turned from white to transparent and the spiral germ has separated.

QUINOA CON QUESO
QUINOA AND POTATO GRATIN

Quinoa con Queso is a popular dish in Peru and Bolivia. It combines two of the most important crops of the High Andes—potatoes and quinoa—with tomatoes, onions, and chiles, foods that originated in the lower semitropical regions of the vast Inca empire.

This recipe is adapted from one we found in a booklet distributed by the Central de Cooperativas Agropecuarias, "Operacion Tierra," in southern Bolivia. The cooperative is located in a dry, cool area of salt flats at an elevation of 10,000 feet. The average yearly rainfall is only 10 inches, and quinoa is the only agricultural crop. Operacion Tierra was formed to promote this crop and the organization puts on an annual quinoa festival, which includes, among other things, quinoa-cooking contests.

1 cup uncooked quinoa

2 cups cold water

1 cup evaporated milk or light cream

1 pound all-purpose potatoes, preferably a mixture of yellow, purple, and red

Salt

2 tablespoons butter or vegetable oil, plus additional for the baking dish

1 yellow onion, peeled and chopped

1½ teaspoons minced garlic

One 8-ounce can tomato sauce

1 or 2 fresh Anaheim or New Mexican chiles, peeled, seeded, and chopped, or one 4-ounce can mild green chiles, drained and chopped

1½ to 2 tablespoons minced fresh cilantro or Italian parsley

Freshly ground black pepper to taste

8 ounces (about 2 cups) shredded Muenster, Monterey Jack, or mild cheddar cheese

Place the quinoa in a sieve and rinse it well under cold running water. Rub it between your hands while you rinse it, to remove any bitter residue.

Place the quinoa in a 1½-quart saucepan, add the water, and bring to a boil. Reduce the heat to maintain a simmer, cover, and cook until all of the water has been absorbed, about 15 minutes. You will know the quinoa is done when all the grains have turned from white to transparent and the spiral germ has separated. Stir in the evaporated milk and set aside.

Meanwhile, put the potatoes in a saucepan and add lightly salted water to cover. Bring to a boil, then reduce the heat and boil gently until just tender, about 20 minutes. Drain the potatoes, peel them, and cut them into 1-inch chunks.

Preheat the oven to 350°F. Butter a 9 x 12 x 2½-inch baking dish and set aside.

Melt the butter in large deep skillet over medium-high heat. Add the onion and garlic and sauté until golden, 3 to 5 minutes. Stir in the tomato sauce, chiles, and cilantro. Add the quinoa mixture and the potatoes, and fold together gently. Season to taste with salt and pepper. Fold in half of the cheese, and transfer the mixture to the baking dish. Top with the remaining cheese, and bake until the casserole is bubbling and the cheese on top has melted, about 20 minutes. Serve hot.

NOTE: For a simpler version, fold all of the cheese into the mixture in the skillet, heat it briefly, and serve directly from the skillet.

RIGHT: *Quinoa con Queso* combines two of the most important crops of the Andea: quinoa and potatoes.

CHAPANAS DE CAÑETE
SWEET YUCA TAMALES WITH GOLDEN RAISINS

MAKES 12 TO 15 TAMALES

If you wander through the market in Cañete, a small Peruvian town south of the bustling metropolis of Lima, you are apt to see vendors sitting behind beautifully stacked pyramids of *chapanas*—sweet and spicy yuca tamales filled with liqueur-soaked golden raisins, a local specialty. Passersby stop and purchase a *chapana* to eat out of hand or to take home to enjoy later with a cup of coffee. We like to serve them for dessert with a dollop of lightly sweetened whipped cream. As a variation, *chapanas* may be made smaller and wrapped in dried corn husks following the directions for making *Humintas Dulces*, opposite.

- 2 tablespoons annatto (*achiote*) seeds
- ⅔ cup Pisco or light rum
- ½ cup water
- ½ cup golden raisins
- 2 ½ pounds fresh yuca root (also called cassava or manioc)
- 1 cup sugar
- ½ teaspoon ground cinnamon
- ¼ teaspoon ground cloves
- ¼ teaspoon ground nutmeg
- ⅛ teaspoon cayenne pepper
- One 1-pound package frozen banana leaves

In a small saucepan, combine the annatto seeds, Pisco, and water. Set aside to soak for about 15 minutes, while you peel and grate the yuca.

Scrub the yuca root with a vegetable brush under cold running water. Cut it into pieces 4 to 5 inches long. With a sharp paring knife, cut a slit through the skin down the length of each piece of yuca. With the point of the knife, loosen the skin and peel it off in one piece, like the bark on a tree. Using a metal box grater, finely grate the white flesh of the yuca into a mixing bowl. Discard the woody core.

Place the annatto mixture over medium heat and bring to a boil. Reduce the heat to low and simmer, stirring occasionally, until the liquid has reduced to about ¾ cup, 5 to 7 minutes. Pour the liquid through a small strainer into a bowl. Discard the seeds. Place the raisins in the liquid to soak for 30 minutes. Add the reserved liquid and raisins, the sugar and the spices to the grated yuca and stir well to combine.

Rinse the banana leaves under hot running water. Wipe the leaves along the grain with a paper towel. If they are whole, use sharp scissors to cut along both sides of the center rib to divide them in half lengthwise. Reserve the center ribs or cut strips of the leaves to use as ties for the *champanas;* or use kitchen twine if you prefer (page 219). Cut the banana leaf halves into 10 x 12-inch pieces.

Place a leaf section on the work surface with the grain running horizontally in front of you. (Try to select pieces without splits or tears; if there is a tear, place a piece of leaf on top of it as a patch.) Place 3 tablespoons of the yuca mixture about 2 inches from the near edge of the leaf. Fold that edge up over the filling, then roll the enclosed filling away from you to form a neat tube. Gently squeeze the filling in from the ends, and twist and tie the ends to form a cylindrical tamale that looks like Christmas cracker.

Arrange the *chapanas* in the top of a steamer over boiling water. If desired, arrange a layer of banana leaves over the *chapanas*—it will help to keep them moist during the long steaming time. Cover tightly and steam for 2½ hours. Check occasionally and add more boiling water to the bottom of the steamer of needed. (If you don't have a steamer, improvise by placing the *chapanas* on a rack in a roasting pan. Fill the bottom of the pan with boiling water, being careful not to let it touch the *chapanas*, and cover it tightly with aluminum foil. Steam in a preheated 350°F oven for 2½ hours.)

Remove the *chapanas* from the steamer and allow them to cool thoroughly on a wire rack. Serve at room temperature.

NOTES: Drop a coin in the steamer water. When you no longer hear the coin rattling, it is time to add more hot water.

The steamed *chapanas* may be stored in the refrigerator for several days. Allow them to come to room temperature before serving.

THE INCA

MAKES ABOUT 30 TAMALES

Humintas are fresh corn tamales typical of Bolivia, Chile, and Peru. Similar breads have been made since pre-Columbian times throughout the great corn cultures of the Americas. Traditionally this special kind of tamale is eaten as part of the celebration of the first tender green corn of the season. *Humintas* may be either savory or sweet. In Bolivia and Chile the savory version is traditional. In Peru, sweet *humintas* filled with caramel are more popular. We add *masa harina* to the dough to compensate for the lower starch content of American sweet corn.

As a quick substitute for caramel filling, we sometimes use the caramel sheets sold for making caramel apples. Cut each sheet into 3 or 4 pieces and roll them around a few pieces of chopped nuts to make small cylinders.

FILLING

1 ¼ cups sweetened condensed milk

1 small cinnamon stick (preferably Mexican cinnamon)

2 tablespoons dark rum (optional)

1 teaspoon pure vanilla extract

⅛ teaspoon ground cayenne pepper

Finely grated zest of ½ lemon

¼ cup chopped lightly toasted walnuts, peanuts, or pecans

1 tablespoon unsalted butter

CORN HUSKS AND DOUGH

8 ears fresh corn, with husks, or two 15-ounce cans cream-style corn plus one 8-ounce package dried corn husks

½ cup sweetened condensed milk

2 cups *masa harina*

2 teaspoons baking powder

½ teaspoon salt

1 cup (2 sticks) unsalted butter, softened

⅓ cup dried currants or raisins

2 teaspoons pure vanilla extract

Prepare the filling: In a heavy-bottomed saucepan combine the condensed milk, cinnamon, rum (if using), vanilla, and cayenne. Place the saucepan over very low heat and cook, stirring often, until the mixture thickens and turns a rich caramel color, about 30 minutes.

Remove the pan from the heat. Scrape off the cinnamon stick and discard it. Stir in the lemon zest, nuts, and butter, and beat vigorously until the caramel mixture is cool. Divide the caramel into 30 portions. With lightly buttered hands, roll each portion into a small cylinder about 2 inches long and ⅓ inch in diameter. Set aside in a cool, dry place.

Prepare the corn husks: Using a sharp chef's knife cut the base off each ear of corn and carefully remove the husks. Rinse the fresh or dried husks, and place them in a large pot with enough water to cover. Place the pot over high heat and bring to a boil. Remove the pot from the heat, but leave the husks in the water while you prepare the dough.

Remove and discard the silk from the ears of corn. Using the large holes on a metal box grater, grate the corn off the fresh ears into a large mixing bowl. You should have about 4 cups of combined juice and pulp. Stir in the condensed milk (or combine the canned corn and milk), and transfer to a saucepan. Cook, stirring, over medium-low heat for about 10 minutes, until the mixture thickens slightly. Set aside and allow the mixture to cool completely, about 30 minutes.

Sift the *masa harina*, baking powder, and salt into a bowl. In a separate large bowl, beat the butter with an electric mixer until smooth and fluffy. Alternately beat in the corn and *masa harina* mixtures, ½ cup at a time, beating until the mixture forms a fluffy, moist, but fairly stiff dough. Stir in the currants and vanilla.

Remove the corn husks from the saucepan. Wipe them off with a kitchen towel and discard any that are discolored. Reserve narrow pieces to tie the tamales (page 219).

(continued on page 209)

THE INCA

Place a large untorn corn husk on the work surface, with the wide end nearest you and the point facing away. Place 2 tablespoons of the corn dough in the middle of the husk. Push a caramel cylinder into the dough and lift up the long sides of the husk to bring the dough up over the caramel, forming a small tamale (about 1½ inches wide and 3 inches long) with the caramel in the center. Fold in the long sides, then fold up the bottom of the husk to cover the tamale. Fold down the pointed end so that the tamale is completely enclosed in a neat package. Use a strip of corn husk or a length of kitchen string to tie the tamale in the center. (If the husks are small or torn, you may have to overlap them. For extra security, you may wish to double-wrap the *humintas* to prevent them from leaking as they steam and expand.) Continue to make *humintas* until all the husks, dough, and filling have been used.

Arrange the *humintas* in the top of a steamer over boiling water. Steam for 45 to 50 minutes, or until they feel fairly firm to the touch. Check occasionally and add more boiling water to the bottom of the steamer if needed. (If you don't have a steamer, improvise by placing the *humintas* on a rack in a roasting pan. Fill the bottom of the pan with boiling water, being careful not to let it touch the *humintas,* and cover it tightly with aluminum foil. Steam in a preheated 350°F oven for 45 to 50 minutes.) Let the *humintas* cool to room temperature before serving.

NOTE: Drop a coin in the steamer water. When you no longer hear the coin rattling, it is time to add more hot water.

LEFT: *Champanas de Cañete* (page 206) and *Humintas Dulces* are traditional sweet dessert tamales.

MAZAMORRA DE QUINOA
QUINOA PUDDING

Quinoa is delicious and extremely versatile. It may be used in place of almost any other grain, including rice, to make everything from appetizers to desserts. If you like rice pudding, you will like this dessert.

1 cup uncooked quinoa

3 cups cold water

**One 2-inch cinnamon stick
(preferably Mexican cinnamon)**

3 or 4 whole cloves

Finely grated zest of ½ lime or lemon

½ cup raisins

¼ to ⅓ cup rum (optional)

2 egg yolks

½ cup sugar

**One 12-ounce can evaporated milk,
or 1½ cups half-and-half**

1 teaspoon pure vanilla extract

Pinch of salt

Place the quinoa in a sieve and rinse it well under cold running water. Rub it between your hands while you rinse it, to remove any bitter residue.

Place the quinoa, water, cinnamon, cloves, and lime zest in a saucepan and bring to a boil over high heat. Reduce the heat to low, cover, and simmer until the quinoa has turned translucent, about 20 minutes.

While the quinoa is cooking, place the raisins in a small bowl. Add rum or hot water to cover, and set aside to soak until the raisins have plumped. Drain the raisins.

Remove the quinoa from the heat and discard the cinnamon and cloves. If there seems to be a lot of liquid, drain the quinoa, but do not rinse.

In a small mixing bowl whisk together the egg yolks and sugar until well combined and pale yellow. Whisk in the evaporated milk. Stir the milk mixture, vanilla, salt, and raisins into the quinoa in the saucepan. Cook, stirring, over low heat until the pudding is thickened and uniformly combined, 10 to 12 minutes. Spoon into serving dishes and serve warm or chilled.

VARIATIONS: Add ½ cup drained pineapple tidbits in place of, or along with, the raisins. Fold in or sprinkle the top of the pudding with ¼ cup shredded coconut.

API DE QUINOA
HOT QUINOA BREAKFAST DRINK

On cold winter mornings, mothers in Peru and Bolivia prepare mugs of warm nourishing *api de quinoa* for their children before sending them off to school. Adults often enjoy a cup of *api* fortified with a shot of Pisco or rum if they feel a chill coming on.

While staying with our friends Irma Bacigalupo de Henderson and Mike Henderson in Lima, we were spoiled by their wonderful cook, Celia Bedia de Ustua, who took us into her kitchen and under her wing. When asked about quinoa recipes, Celia offered to make *api de quinoa* for breakfast the next day. We were anxious to try it but unsure of what to expect. When the *api* arrived, lightly sweetened and fragrant with cinnamon, cloves, and vanilla, we were hooked, and bet you will be too.

½ cup uncooked quinoa

5 cups water

One 2- to 3-inch cinnamon stick
    (preferably Mexican cinnamon)

3 whole cloves

1 cup evaporated milk or half-and-
    half

4 to 6 tablespoons sugar, to taste

¾ teaspoon pure vanilla extract

Pinch of salt

Rinse the quinoa well in two or three changes of cold water, then drain. Put it in a blender with 1 cup of the fresh water, and liquefy it.

Combine the remaining 4 cups water, the cinnamon, and the cloves in a saucepan and bring to a boil. Gradually whisk in the quinoa mixture. Reduce the heat to low and simmer for 15 minutes, stirring often so that it doesn't stick to the pan.

Stir in the evaporated milk, sugar, vanilla, and salt, and continue to cook until hot. Pour the *api* through a strainer into a pitcher or directly into 4 to 6 mugs.

NOTE: *Api de quinoa* may be made in advance and stored in the refrigerator for 2 to 3 days. Just reheat it before serving.

CAMOTILLO
BAKED SWEET POTATO ROLL

MAKES ABOUT 24 CAMOTILLOS

The sweet potato was called *apichu* by the early Quechua, but it is now more commonly known as *camote*. Anthropologists tell us that it has been cultivated along the coast of Peru since at least 2400 B.C.

An ancient way of preparing *camotes* as a dessert was to expose them to the sun for a few days so that their sugars would concentrate, then place them directly in the embers of the fire to cook until they were sweet and syrupy. This dessert, called *camotes pavitos*, or little turkey sweet potatoes, is still prepared in the highlands today.

Camotillo is another old Peruvian dessert that is simple to make, interesting, and very good. When baked, the "little potatoes" remind us of small freestanding, crustless sweet potato pies.

3 to 4 sweet potatoes, baked and peeled

½ cup heavy cream

½ cup light or dark brown sugar

2 eggs, beaten

4 tablespoons butter, softened

½ teaspoon ground cinnamon (optional)

¼ teaspoon ground nutmeg (optional)

Finely grated zest of 1 small lime

Juice of ½ lime

¼ cup coarse "natural" sugar

½ cup chopped walnuts or pecans

Rice the sweet potatoes or press them through a coarse metal strainer into a mixing bowl. You should have 4 cups of potatoes. Beat in the cream, brown sugar, eggs, butter, cinnamon, nutmeg, lime zest, and lime juice. Allow the potato mixture to sit for about 30 minutes to thicken.

Meanwhile, preheat the oven to 325°F. Butter a large baking sheet.

Using a kitchen spoon, place scoops of the sweet potato mixture about 1 inch apart on the baking sheet. Use a moistened table knife to smooth the edges so that the *camotillos* have an oval shape and a rounded top. Sprinkle them lightly with the sugar and chopped nuts. Bake for 40 minutes, until a crust forms and the bottoms of the *camotillos* are lightly browned. With a spatula, carefully transfer them to a wire rack. Allow them to cool thoroughly before serving.

appendix

TRADITIONAL COOKING EQUIPMENT

GRINDING IMPLEMENTS

The Maya and Aztec ground chiles, herbs, and spices with a *molcajete* and *tejolote* (volcanic-stone mortar and pestle). For grinding corn or large quantities of other ingredients, they used a *metate,* a sloping, rectangular piece of volcanic stone supported on three legs. It was paired with a *metapil* or *mano* (a stone rolling pin). In Central Mexico, these implements are still in use and are usually made of basalt, a dark gray or black volcanic rock; the better-quality ones are smooth textured and not too porous. The lowland Maya prefer fine-grained light-colored stone grinders.

The Inca ground foods with a *batan,* which today may be either a small stone mortar and pestle for grinding chiles, herbs, and spices, or a large slab somewhat similar to the Mesoamerican *metate.* The major difference is that the large *batan* is paired with an extremely heavy, crescent-shaped grinding stone, ergonomically designed to crush corn and other hard foods by rocking back and forth. They also used a metal knife with a crescent-shaped blade, called a *tumi,* for everyday food chopping as well as for ceremonial purposes.

To season and use stone implements, smooth the stone surface and season the implement by mixing a handful of wet raw rice with a tablespoon of coarse salt and then rubbing it into the stone with the pestle or rolling pin. When the rice mixture is finely ground, discard it and repeat the process with additional rice and salt. Continue until the rough edges of the stone have become smooth, and newly ground rice no longer looks dirty or covered with grit. When grinding ingredients for a sauce, grind the hardest ingredients first, then gradually add the softer ones such as onions and tomatoes.

Both the Aztec and the Inca also used small earthenware mortars and pestles. Today, as in the past, the inside of the bowl is ridged, which helps in the grinding process.

COOKING POTS AND PANS

Many traditional cooks in Mesoamerica and South America prefer to use clay cookware, and indeed these pots give a wonderfully "earthy" flavor to the foods prepared in them. The downside is that they are fragile and the glazes often contain lead. Make sure that any pottery to be used for cooking or serving does not have a lead-based glaze.

To season a clay piece before using it for the first time, rub the outside of the pot with a cut garlic clove and fill the inside up to the rim with warm soapy water. Place the pot over direct heat and let most of the water boil away. Remove the pot from the heat and let it sit for about 30 minutes to seal the clay. After a thorough rinsing, the pottery is ready to be used both for cooking over direct heat and for baking. If you have not used the pot for a long time, repeat the seasoning process.

To season an unglazed clay comal (*griddle*), rub both sides with a thick paste made of slaked lime (available at pharmacies and hardware stores) and water. Heat the *comal* over direct heat until the lime has dried and browned. Use a stiff brush to remove the lime mixture. The *comal* should now be ready to use. If it is not used often, repeat the seasoning process periodically.

SUGGESTED MODERN EQUIPMENT

For many cooks the electric blender and a small electric spice grinder or coffee grinder have replaced traditional grinders. Enameled iron, well-seasoned cast iron, and nonstick cookware are becoming popular alternatives to earthenware. Our Maya friend Juanita Velasco likes to bake tortillas on a nonstick griddle. Other useful pieces of equipment are a metal tortilla press, a heavy Dutch oven for soups and stews, a medium-size steamer to use for smaller tamales and a roasting pan with a flat rack to use for large Maya tamales, a grilling basket for whole fish, a few wooden spoons and spatulas, a pair of long-handled metal tongs and a wood-handled barbecue or fondue fork for flame-roasting vegetables, and a large medium-mesh sieve for straining sauces.

BASIC COOKING TECHNIQUES

HANDLING CHILES

The heat of chiles is often rated on a scale of 1 to 10 with "1" being mild and "10" being the hottest. If possible, wear rubber gloves when handling hot chiles. An alternative is to apply a thin layer of lard or vegetable shortening to your hands. If your mouth is burning, drink milk or eat a tortilla, bread, or rice. If chile gets on your skin, rinse with cold salted water or tomato juice, or rub on a mixture of toothpaste and water to put out the fire. *Never touch your eyes or face when working with chiles.*

ROASTING FRESH CHILES AND VEGETABLES

To flame-roast: Using tongs or a barbecue fork, hold the chile, tomato, or unpeeled onion or head of garlic directly over the burner of a gas stove, and roast until it is thoroughly charred all over.

For larger amounts of ingredients or with an electric stove: Place the vegetables on a hot griddle over medium heat. Roast, turning with tongs, until the skin is blackened.

After roasting: Immediately place roasted chiles in a plastic bag and close it tight. Let the chiles steam for a few minutes, so the skin will loosen. Then remove the skin—it's not a problem if a few patches of skin remain. Remove the stem and the spicy seeds and ribs, if desired.

PREPARING DRIED CHILES

Rinse dried chiles in cold water. Yucatecan and Mexican recipes often call for toasting the rinsed chiles on a hot griddle or in a heavy skillet over medium heat just until the moisture is gone and the skin begins to puff slightly, usually less than 1 minute. Be careful to keep turning the chiles and not to burn them, or the flavor will be bitter. The chiles are then stemmed, seeded if desired, and soaked. Submerge them in boiling water or broth, then cover and allow to soak for 30 minutes to 1 hour, until softened. Some of the soaking liquid from the toasted chiles may be added to the recipe. Be sure to taste the liquid before using; if it is bitter, discard it.

Peruvian and Bolivian cooks don't usually toast dried *ajíes*, but they do rinse, seed, and soak them as described above. They also often include some of the soaking liquid, provided it is not bitter, in their recipes.

RENDERING LARD

To make about 3 cups of lard, you will need 3 pounds of fresh pork fat trimmings, leaf fat, or fat back (not salt pork). Fat with a little meat attached produces tasty cracklings and lard that has a good roasted pork flavor but is a little darker in color. Thoroughly chill the fat in the freezer, then chop it into small pieces (a food processor works well for this). Place the pieces of fat in a heavy Dutch oven, spreading them out evenly so they will melt quickly. Preheat the oven to 350°F. Place the pan in the oven and cook, stirring frequently, until the fat begins to render, about 15 minutes. Then reduce the oven temperature to 225°F. Continue to cook, stirring occasionally, until all the fat is rendered and any cracklings are crisp, about 1 hour. (Rendering also may be done on top of the stove, starting over medium heat, then reducing the heat to medium-low or low.) Remove the fat from the heat and allow it to cool slightly. Ladle it through a strainer into clean jars. Refrigerate, and when chilled, cover tightly. The lard may be stored in the refrigerator for up to 1 week or in the freezer for several months.

BANANA-LEAF PACKAGE WRAP:

1. Place the *masa* and filling in the middle of a 12 x 15-inch piece of banana leaf.

2. Fold in the long sides to cover the filling.

3. Fold up the ends to form a neat rectangular or square package.

4. Tie the tamale like a package with a string made from a strip of banana leaf or with kitchen string.

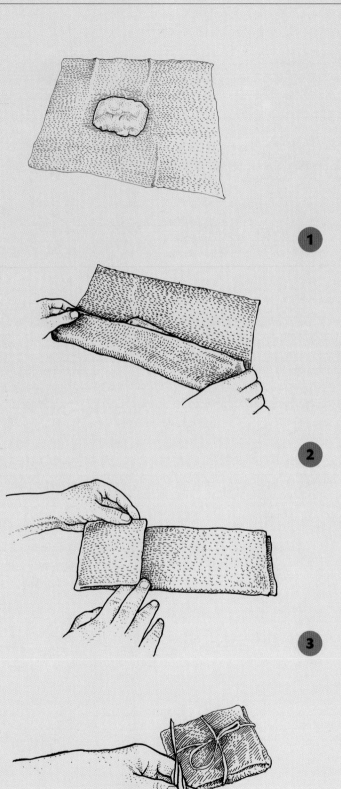

1

2

3

4

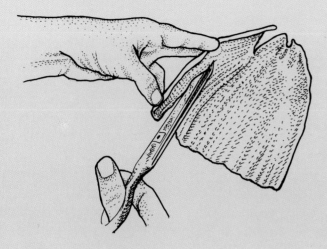

TO MAKE A CORN HUSK STRING

1. Cut a ½-inch-wide strip the length of the corn husk.

2. Tie a knot at the narrowest end of the strip.

3. Starting at the wider end, cut down the length of the strip in the middle almost to the knot. You should now have a ¼-inch-wide string, double the length of the husk.

1

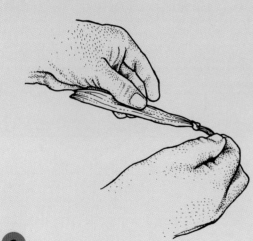

2

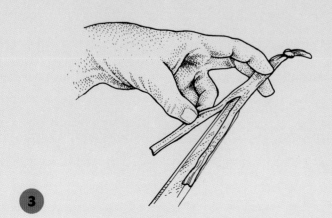

3

FRESH OR DRIED CORN HUSK "CANOE" WRAP

1. **Arrange two husks with the wide ends overlapping by 1 inch to make a canoe shape.**

2. **Place a third husk on top, in the middle, to cover the overlap.**

3. **Place the *masa* and the filling on top of the third husk.**

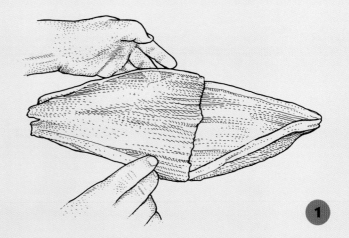

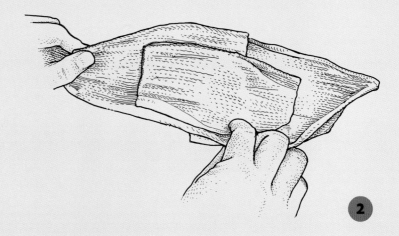

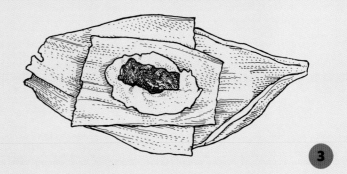

4. **Fold in the long sides of the "canoe" to cover the filling.**

5. **Fold up the two pointed ends to form a neat rectangular package.**

6. **Tie like a package with a string made from a strip of corn husk or with kitchen string.**

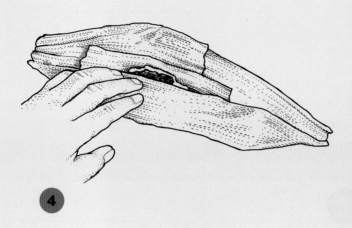

4

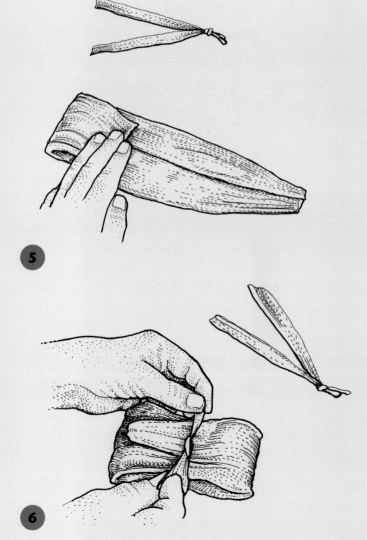

5

6

FRESH OR DRIED CORN HUSK OPEN-ENDED WRAP

1. **Place the masa about 1½ inches from the wide end of a corn husk, and top it with the filling.**

2. **Fold in the long sides of the husk to enclose the tamale.**

3. **Fold up the pointed end of the husk to form a package with one open end.**

4. **Tie the tamale in the middle with a string made from a dried strip of corn husk or with kitchen string.**

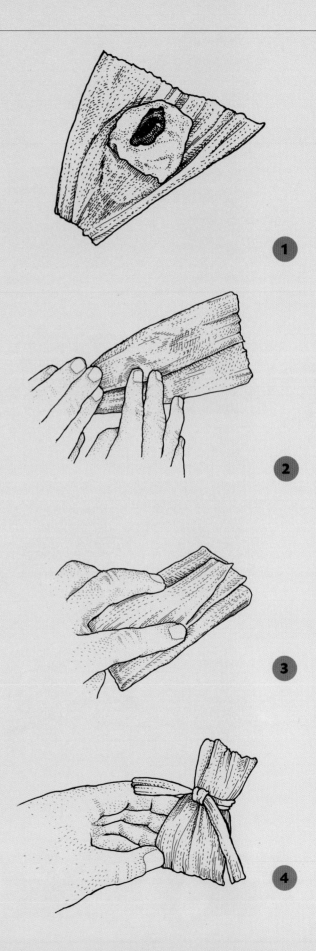

MESOAMERICAN AND SOUTH AMERICAN INGREDIENTS AND COOKING TERMS

ACHIOTE: Also called *annatto*. The small, hard, brick-red seeds of *Bixa orellana*, a tropical tree. Used by the Maya, Aztec, and Inca, both as a condiment and ceremonially. Sold either in the form of seeds or ground into a paste and formed into small bricks. The paste from the Yucatán contains herbs and other seasonings; the Oaxacan paste is usually pure. The flavor of *achiote* is subtle; its main use in cooking is to give a beautiful red or golden color to other foods. Available in the United States in food markets catering to Latin Americans and through mail order (see Sources).

AJÍES: The generic name for Peruvian and Bolivian chiles. The term *ají* is also is used to describe several dishes in which *ajíes* are an important seasoning, for example *Ají de Pollo* ("Chicken Ají"). See also *Chiles*.

VARIETIES OF *AJÍ* USED IN THE INCA RECIPES IN THIS BOOK

AJÍES AMARILLO AND COLORADO (or *ROJO*): Rated 7 to 8 on the heat scale (of 1 to 10), with a slightly fruity flavor, these slender yellow (*amarillo*) or red (*colorado/rojo*) chiles are 3 to 5 inches long and about ¼ inch in diameter. Sold fresh, dried, and as powder or puree. Available in some specialty stores in the United States and through mail order (see Sources). Though the flavor is not the same, fresh yellow Hungarian banana peppers, Mexican güero chiles, and dried *costeño amarillo* chiles are a possible substitute for yellow *ajíes*, as they have a similar golden color. Possible substitutions for red *ajíes* might include red serrano chiles, red jalapeños, red Hungarian wax peppers, or dried *guajillos*.

AJÍ MIRASOL: Rated 2.5 to 3 on the heat scale, this fruity orange-yellow chile tapers to a point and is 3 to 5 inches long and 1 to 1½ inches wide. Sold fresh or dried, and as a powder or puree. Available in some specialty stores in the United States and through mail order. Possible substitutions might include: New Mexico Sunrise chiles, yellow Hungarian wax peppers, Sandia chiles, and dried *costeño amarillos*.

AJÍ PANCA: Rated 1.5 on the heat scale, this mild reddish brown chile is 3 to 5 inches long and 1 to 1½ inches wide. Available in some specialty stores in the United States and through mail order. It is usually sold dried or ground into powder. Possible substitutions might include red Anaheim chiles, dried mild New Mexico chiles, and dried ancho or *guajillo* chiles.

AJÍ ROCOTO (OR LOCOTO): Rated 9 to 10 on the heat scale, these very hot chiles have a rounded shape somewhat like a bell pepper. They may be green, yellow, or red and vary in size from 2 to 4 inches long and 2 to 4 inches in diameter. They are used in ceviches and salsas, and the larger varieties are often stuffed after first being blanched in several changes of boiling sugared water to remove some of the heat. Possible substitutions might include habaneros, jalapeños, or serranos for ceviches and salsas, and poblanos or Anaheim chiles for stuffing.

ALEGRÍAS: A ceremonial Aztec sweet made with puffed amaranth bound with honey or blood and formed into the shape of gods. Modern *alegrías* are bound with honey or sugar syrup and usually made into rounds, squares, or rectangles.

AMARANTH: Called *amaranto* in Mexico and *kiwicha* or *achita* in South America. An annual flowering plant. Both the tender young leaves and the seeds are eaten throughout Central and South America. The tiny seeds are high in protein and lysine and rich in calcium, iron, phosphorus, potassium, zinc, and vitamins B and E. The Aztec bound popped amaranth seeds together with honey or blood and formed them into the shape of gods as a ceremonial offering. This practice was denounced by the Spanish, who then forbade all native peoples under their domination to grow amaranth. For hundreds of years this nutritious plant was largely forgotten, but its value is now being rediscovered.

AVOCADO FRUIT AND LEAVES: "Avocado" derives from *ahuacatl,* the Nahuatl (Aztec) word for "testicle." It is called *palta* in South America. Pits of wild avocados, dating back to 8000 to 7000 B.C. have been found in archaeological sites in Mexico. Avocados were an important source of fat in the pre-Columbian diet; they are also rich in protein and vitamins. Both the flesh and the leaves of the small Mexican *crillo* variety have a fennel-like flavor. These leaves are sold and used as a flavoring. They are available in some Mexican markets in the United States and may also be mail ordered (see Sources). The best North American variety to use in Mexican cooking is the California or Hass avocado.

BANANA LEAVES: used as wrappers for tamales and other foods throughout Latin America. If using fresh leaves, slowly pass them over a gas flame until soft and shiny-looking, or steam them for 20 minutes to soften. The leaves available in the United States are usually pre-cut into rectangles and sold frozen in 1-pound packages. Look for them in Latin American, Caribbean, and Asian food stores. When using frozen leaves, defrost them overnight in the refrigerator. Rinse the thawed leaves thoroughly in hot water and wipe off any mold. With scissors, cut along the sides of the tough center rib and remove it. Then, before using, soak the leaves in hot water, or roll them up and steam them for about 20 minutes, until softened. If banana leaves are not available, our friend Margoth Giron suggests wrapping tamales in cooking parchment and tying them with unflavored "ribbon" dental floss, or simply wrapping them in aluminum foil.

BEAN: referring to the genus of beans native to the Americas, which includes kidney beans, string beans, snap beans, the Mexican *frijole,* the common bean, butter bean, lima bean, navy bean, and pole bean. An important staple in the diet of the Maya, Inca, and Aztec, beans are usually combined with corn to make a complete protein.

CACTUS PADDLES (*nopales* and *nopalitos*): The paddle-shaped stems of prickly pear cactus plants used in the cooking of west-central and central Mexico. They are sold fresh in many supermarkets and Mexican food markets in the United States. Look for firm, unwrinkled paddles; if loosely wrapped and refrigerated, they will last for at least one week. *Nopalitos* are also available in cans or jars; after draining and rinsing, they are ready to eat. Clean fresh cactus paddles shortly before using. Wearing gloves, trim off the outer edge of the paddle with kitchen scissors or a sharp knife. Then use the point of a paring knife to dig out and discard any remaining stickers. The cleaned paddles may be grilled whole or cut into strips and boiled. After boiling, drain and rinse first under hot water and then under cold to remove the sticky juices. Recent findings suggest that including *nopalitos* in their diet may help diabetics to control their condition and may even help to prevent the onset of diabetes.

CANCHA: Large kernels of toasted corn, similar to the "corn nuts" sold in the United States. In Peru, Bolivia, and Ecuador, *cancha* is eaten as a snack or used as a garnish for ceviches and other dishes.

CEVICHE (cebiche, seviche, sebiche): Most people think that ceviche is raw or lightly blanched fish or seafood that is "cooked" in a marinade of acidic fruit juice and hot chiles. This is true, but there are other ceviches, especially in Peru, made with marinated meat or poultry that is then cooked. Since citrus fruits were first introduced by the Spanish in the sixteenth century, it has been argued that ceviche must be a post-Conquest innovation. However, recent studies of pre-Columbian foods suggest that the first ceviches may well have been made with the acidic juice of a native Peruvian fruit called tumbo.

CHARQUI (jerky): Dried meat. Its name derives from the Quechua word *cusharqui.* The Andean civilizations are thought to be the inventors of jerky. It is used in cooking both in South and Central America. In Mexico it is called *carne seca.*

CHAYOTE: Derives from the Nahuatl (Aztec) word *chayotli*. This pale green, smooth-skinned squash was first domesticated in Mexico. Unwrapped and refrigerated, chayotes last for at least one week. They may be boiled, fried, or stuffed and baked. Their flavor and texture fall somewhere between a zucchini and a potato. The starchy root and tender young leaves are also eaten.

CHEESE: Cheese was not known in pre-Columbian Mexico, Central and South America. Cheese-making was first introduced by the Spanish, and different local cheeses have developed over the years as have Latin American versions of Old World cheeses. Those most often used in recipes in this book are the *queso blanco* (white cheese), similar in taste and texture to mozzarella or Muenster and lightly salted, and *queso fresco* (fresh cheese), which may be similar in texture to Italian *ricotta salata* or may be more like fresh ricotta or cream cheese, and *panella*, which is a mild, creamy, white cheese. There are also aged cheeses, *queso anejo* or *queso seco* (dry cheese), that are often grated like Parmesan. Oaxaca is famous for its *queso de hebra* (string cheese), which is usually wound into a flattened ball. It is a versatile cheese that may be fried, shredded, or melted.

CHICHA: The traditional beverage of the Inca and their Quechua and Aymara descendants. It may or may not be fermented. *Chicha* is often made from corn, but it may also be made from quinoa and other grains, and also from peanuts or fruit.

CHICHARRONES: Crisp fried strips of pork rind, a favorite snack in Mexico. They are often served for dipping with guacamole, instead of tortilla chips, and are also ground with onion and other seasoning and made into fillings for *tlatloyos* (page 100). They are sold at Mexican food markets in the United States and are also available in packages at most supermarkets, labeled "cracklings."

CHILES: Pepper, chile, chili, *ají*—all are among the common names used around the world for the various species plants of the genus *capsicum*, and members of the *Solanaceae* (Nightshade) family, which also includes tomatoes, potatoes, tobacco, and petunias. Chiles have been a staple of the native Meso- and South American diet for thousands of years; introduced to Europe by Columbus, their use spanned the globe in less than 100 years. (See also *Ajíes*.)

VARIETIES OF CHILES USED IN THE MAYA AND AZTEC RECIPES IN THIS BOOK

ANAHEIM: Rated 2 to 3 on the heat scale (of 1 to 10), this fairly mild California chile may be green or red. An Anaheim is usually about 6 inches long and 2 to 3 inches in diameter. It is often cut into strips (*rajas*) and are also good stuffed. It may also be sold as a "long green" or New Mexico chile. It is a good substitute in recipes calling for Oaxacan *chiles de agua*.

ANCHO: is the dried version of a fresh poblano chile. It is rated 3 to 5 on the heat scale. When dried, the ancho is a deep burgundy color, almost black. They are usually about 4 inches long and 2½ inches wide at the top. *Anchos* are sometimes lightly toasted on a griddle, then soaked in hot water to soften, and then pureed. The puree is used in many Mexican sauces; it has a rich, almost sweet flavor with a hint of bitterness.

CHILCOSTLE: a reddish orange dried Oaxacan chile that is rated 4 to 5 on the heat scale. The puree is medium-hot and slightly sweet, with a hint of orange and anise. It is used in moles and other sauces.

CHIPOTLE: derives from the Nahuatl word for "smoked chile." *Chipotles* are smoke-dried jalapeños. They are rated 5 to 6 on the heat scale and are sold either dried or, more commonly in the United States, canned in adobo sauce. They are hot, smoky, and slightly sweet.

COSTEÑO AMARILLO: a dried Oaxacan variety that is rated 4 to 5 on the heat scale. It is used to make traditional yellow mole. *Costeño amarillos* are a deep amber color, with subtle heat and a light, crisp, citrus flavor.

GUAJILLO: usually sold in dried form, *guajillos* are a deep burgundy color. The large ones are about 4½ inches long and 2 inches wide at the top. There is also a smaller, more slender and hotter variety called a *guajillo pulpulla* ("taunting" or "teasing" chile). The puree is bright red and ranges in heat from 4, fairly mild, to 6, medium-hot; the flavor is bright and clean with just a hint of smokiness. This is one of the most widely used and most versatile Mexican chiles.

HABANERO: A favorite chile in Yucatecan cooking, habaneros range in color from yellow and green to red. They are small but fiercely hot—30 to 50 times hotter than a jalapeño—a definite 10+ on the heat scale. Handle and taste with caution! Used in salsas, soups, and marinades.

JALAPEÑO: the best known and most available fresh hot chile in the United States, named after Xalapa (Jalapa), the capital of the state of Veracruz. Jalapeños are usually 2 to 3 inches long and 1 to 1½ inches in diameter. They are fairly hot, 5 to 6 on the heat scale, but very versatile. Red (fully ripened) jalapeños are sweeter than the green ones.

POBLANO: One of the most widely used fresh chiles in Mexico, poblanos are fairly mild, 2.5 to 3 on the heat scale. They are usually dark green, 4 to 5 inches long, and 2½ to 3 inches in diameter. They are used to make *rajas* (thin strips for sautéing) and are also good for stuffing.

SERRANO: Similar to the jalapeño in availability and versatility, these slender fresh green or red chiles are usually 1½ to 2 inches long and ½ to ¾ inch in diameter. They are medium-hot to hot, about a 7 on the heat scale.

PASILLA: the dried version of a *chile chilaca*. Pasillas are a deep burgundy, almost black. They are 3 to 5 on the heat scale and range from 4 to 6 inches in length and are 1 to 1½ inches wide. Pasilla puree is a deep reddish brown color, medium-hot to hot, with an intriguingly complex flavor.

CHILIPÍN (*Crotolaria vitellina*): A Central American herb with a tart, refreshing taste somewhere between watercress and sorrel. It is also very fragrant. Maya cooks use it in fillings for tamales, and it is also used by the Zoque people of Chiapas as a pot herb and for soup. *Chilipín* is sold frozen in 6-ounce containers in some Latin American grocery stores in the United States. The leaves should be thawed and the stems removed before using. Though the flavor is not the same, watercress and/or sorrel leaves may be substituted with good results.

CHOCLO: The Peruvian and Bolivian word for fresh corn on the cob. It refers to a large-kerneled white variety with ears 12 to 14 inches long.

CHOCOLATE: A sacred drink. It was used ceremonially and medicinally and usually consumed only by the upper classes. Cocoa beans were the primary form of currency of both the Maya and the Aztec.

CHUÑO: freeze-dried potatoes that are widely used in Andean cooking. They are often combined in the same dish with fresh potatoes. *Chuño* are sold dried or canned and most often available in food markets catering to local Bolivian or Peruvian populations in the United States.

CINNAMON (*canela*): Also called "Mexican cinnamon," "soft-stick cinnamon," or "Ceylon cinnamon," it is the bark of *Cinnamomun zeylanicum*. It is more delicate in flavor, softer, and easier to grind than *Cinnamomum Cassia*, the hard, tightly rolled variety more commonly sold under the name cinnamon.

CITRUS FRUITS: Citrus fruits were first introduced to the new world by the Spanish in the sixteenth century. In Mexico the most important varieties used in cooking are the Seville orange (*Citrus aurantium*), also called bitter or sour orange, and a variety of lime (*Citrus aurantiifolia*). In South America the *limón sutíl* (*Citrus limonium*), a fruit closer in flavor to the North American lime or Key lime than to a lemon, is used to make ceviche and other dishes.

CORIANDER, FRESH (*cilantro* or *culantro*): This flavorful herb is used extensively in Mexican and South American cooking. Cilantro keeps well if stored in the refrigerator, with the stems in a jar of cold water and the leaves loosely covered with a plastic bag.

CORN (Maize): The most sacred crop of the Maya, Aztec, and Inca. Since the varieties cultivated in South America before the Conquest were quite different from the Mexican, it is thought that the first domestication may have taken place in Mexico and South America simultaneously.

CORN HUSKS (*hojas de maiz*): The large dried husks of field corn are commonly used to wrap tamales and other foods in Central and South America. Dried husks should be thoroughly rinsed with hot water and soaked in hot water for at least 30 minutes before using. When the green corn is harvested, fresh husks are also used as wrappers.

ELOTE: The Mexican word for fresh corn, usually on the cob.

EPAZOTE (*Chenopodium ambrosioides*): Considered an essential ingredient when cooking beans, epazote is a pungent-smelling herb with jagged leaves that grows about 2 feet tall. It also grows wild and is known as pigweed. It is sometimes sold in the produce departments of markets with a large Mexican clientele, and is available either fresh or dried through mail order.

HIERBA BUENA: The generic name for several different varieties of mint used in Latin American cooking.

HOJA SANTA (*Piper sanctum*): Large soft leaves that are used both for their peppery aniselike flavor and as a wrapper for other foods. If chopping the leaves to use in cooking remove the center rib as it tends to be bitter. Both live plants and fresh or dried leaves are available through mail order (see Sources). Though they are not as intense in flavor, chopped fresh fennel leaves are a reasonable substitute.

HONEY: The Maya were skilled beekeepers. Honey was an important offering to their gods and the principal ingredient in the sacred beverage *balché*. It was also used as an article of trade in pre-Columbian America.

HUCATAY (*Huacataya, Tagetes minuta*): An herb with a strong tarragon-anise flavor, used in Peruvian and Bolivian cooking. *Tagetes lucida*, Mexican mint marigold, is from the same genus and is somewhat similar in flavor. Fresh tarragon, or a combination of tarragon and fresh fennel greens, can be a good substitute.

HUITLACOCHE (*Cuitlacoche*): Maize smut fungus (*Usilago maydis*), a strange-looking but delicious fungus that grows on ears of corn. Usually considered a blight in the United States, it was a great delicacy for the Aztec and remains so for their modern descendants. It is very expensive, even in Mexico—almost like buying truffles.

JÍCAMA: A root vegetable that resembles a round, thick-skinned potato. Its name derives from the Nahuatl (Aztec) word *xicamatl*. The white flesh has a flavor and texture somewhere between a potato and a water chestnut. It may be eaten raw or cooked. The Maya like to roast unpeeled jícamas in a *pib* (earth oven).

LARD AND COOKING OILS: The diet of most pre-Columbian civilizations in Mesoamerica and South America was low in fat. Lard and vegetable oils were introduced after the Spanish Conquest, along with the technique of frying. Lard has been adopted by the native peoples of these regions and is widely used, especially in Mexico. Though some people are hesitant to cook with lard, according to the USDA, it has less than half the cholesterol of butter. Mexican lard has far better flavor than the commercial product sold in the United States. We recommend that you render your own lard for tamales and other dishes in which lard is an important ingredient or flavoring (page 217). Modern Peruvian and Bolivian cooks often use corn oil or peanut oil.

LIME, SLAKED (calcium hydroxide): Used during the process of nixtamalization to treat tough-hulled varieties of field corn so that the kernels will swell and the hull may be removed. The whole hulled kernels are then cooked as *pozole* (hominy) or ground into dough for tortillas or tamales. Chunks of *tequexquite*, quicklime (calcium oxide), are sold in markets in Mexico for the same purpose. It must first be treated by putting it in water. In some areas, wood ashes are used in a similar manner.

MASA: Means "dough" in Spanish. In Mexico it is generally understood to mean the dough made from ground nixtamalized corn that is used to make tortillas and tamales.

MASA HARINA: Flour made from fresh corn *masa,* which is dried and then ground into powder. Sold in most supermarkets.

MEXICAN CINNAMON. See *canela.*

MOTE: An Andean preparation of corn similar to hominy, made with *maíz patazca,* a large-kerneled white Peruvian variety. *Mote* is used in many soups and stews. Food markets in South America sell *mote* pre-soaked in water; in the United States, canned hominy in the best substitute.

NIXTAMALIZATION: Discovered by the Maya and Aztec, a process used to remove the hulls, or pericarps, from the tough-skinned varieties of corn. This is done by first soaking and then boiling the kernels in a solution of water and slaked lime (or wood or plant ashes) until the hulls are loosened. The corn is then rinsed in fresh water until the hulls come off and the taste of lime or ashes is removed. The corn (hominy or *pozole*) is then ready to cook whole or to be ground for tortillas or tamales. Nixtamalization makes corn easier to grind, but the major benefit is that it greatly enhances the protein value of the corn. Where or when this process originated is not known for certain, but household equipment used to make nixtamal dated at 1550 B.C. has been found in an archaeological site on the southern coast of Guatemala.

OREGANO: There are several different herbs that are called oregano in Latin America. One variety, often sold as "Mexican oregano" in the United States, is *Lippia berlandieri* 'Shawer', a member of the verbena family. Dried Mexican oregano is sold in many supermarkets. Live plants are available through mail order (see Sources).

PEANUTS (*Arachis hypogaea*): Native to South America, but known as far north as Mexico by A.D. 500. Peanuts are an ingredient in many dishes in Peru and Bolivia, where they are called *maní.*

PILONCILLO: The old-fashioned brown sugar cones used in Mexican cooking. The small (¾-ounce) cones are often sold in the United States in 5-ounce packages. *Piloncillos* are very hard; we usually wrap them in a kitchen towel or heavy plastic bag and smash them into small pieces with a meat pounder. Do not attempt to chop a whole cone in a food processor; it may break the blade.

PISCO: A traditional aged fermented drink made from the Muscatel grape, originally produced in Pisco, Peru.

PLANTAIN (*plátano macho*): These large, thick-skinned cooking bananas were introduced by the Spanish and have thrived in the New World. A staple for people in the tropical regions of Central and South America, they are eaten like a vegetable when green and used in desserts when fully ripe and sweet.

POZOLE (*Posole, Posolli*): A stew or drink made with nixtamalized corn.

PRICKLY PEAR CACTUS FRUIT (*tuna*): Early Spanish chronicles mention thirteen different varieties of cactus fruit eaten by the Aztec in Mexico. Those most often sold in the United States are a mildly sweet red-fleshed variety. When handling *tunas*, be mindful of the tiny spines on the outside of the skin. Choose smooth, unblemished fruit. Loosely wrapped, they will keep for up to one month in the refrigerator.

PULQUE: The ritual drink of the Aztec, made from the fermented sap of a large greenish gray variety of the maguey plant. *Pulque* has a fairly low alcohol content and is high in nutrients.

PUMPKIN SEEDS (*pepitas*): Pumpkin seeds were used by the Maya and the Aztec to enrich and thicken sauces. They are an important ingredient in *pipiánes*, stews thickened with ground seeds, of the Yucatán Peninsula and Central Mexico.

QUINOA (*Chenopodium Quinoa*): An extremely nourishing Andean plant. The tender young leaves, which unfortunately seldom reach the consumer, may be eaten raw in salads or cooked like spinach. They are high in vitamin A. The white or beige seeds should be rinsed thoroughly to remove any trace of the bitter-tasting saponin, which protects them from insects. They are cooked like rice and are versatile and delicious. Quinoa seeds are rich in protein, high in fiber, and particularly rich in the amino acid lysine. The seeds are also a good source of calcium, phosphorus, and vitamins B and E.

RECADOS OR RECAUDOS: Maya mixtures of herbs and spices that have been compared to the curries of India. For more information see page 36.

SHRIMP, dried: An important ingredient in the native cooking of Oaxaca and Central Mexico. The shrimp are first boiled, then salted and dried. Those that are available in the United States are usually tiny and are sold in 1- to 2-ounce packets in the dried spice section of Mexican supermarkets.

SQUASH: Most squash varieties eaten today originated in the Americas. The Maya, Aztec, and Inca all ate squash and squash blossoms, but it was the oil-rich seeds that were most valued by pre-Columbian cooks. When ground, the seeds were used to thicken and enrich sauces.

TOMATILLO (*Physalis*): The green-husked tomato that was first domesticated in Mexico. Tomatillos are not really tomatoes, but a relative of the Cape gooseberry and the ground-cherry. In Central Mexico they are called *tomate verde* or *miltomate*. When green, their flavor is tart; as they ripen to yellow it becomes sweeter. To prepare, remove the papery husk and rinse the tomatillo with cold water to remove any stickiness.

TOMATO (*Lycopersicon*): Tomatoes are indigenous to Mexico and South America. They were first cultivated in Mexico, where they are known as *jitomates*. In Peru and Bolivia they are called *tomates*.

VANILLA (*Vanilla planifolia*): The fruit of a climbing orchid indigenous to southeastern Mexico, the West Indies, Central America, and northern South America. The Totonac people of Veracruz are credited with being the first to discover wild vanilla and then to cultivate it. Vanilla is the most labor-intensive agricultural product in the world. Demand is far greater than supply. The average retail price of a high-quality bean is between two and three dollars, which may sound like an extravagance, but a bean may be used more than once. After steeping, simply remove the bean, rinse, and dry it. Beans may be stored in an airtight bottle, or in canister of sugar. Keep vanilla extract capped in a cool dark place. When traveling abroad, beware of bargain vanilla extract, even if it is labeled "pure." Labeling laws vary from one country to another. Synthetic vanilla extract, particularly in Mexico and the Caribbean, may contain coumarin, which is used in blood-thinning medicines as an anticoagulant.

YUCA (manioc, cassava): An important food in the tropics of Central America and South America. This woody-looking root is native to the Amazon and has been cultivated along the coast of Peru since about 2000 B.C. Usually sold in produce departments in the United States as "yuca root." When buying yuca, look for roots that are firm and not wrinkled. If in doubt, ask the produce clerk to cut off a piece of the root; the flesh should be firm and white.

SOURCES

ADRIAN VILLADA CHILE SEEDS

Apartado Postal No. 64
Atlacomulco, Estado De Mexico
Mexico C.P. 50450
Website:
www.ushotstuff.com/amxcatalog.htm
Sells almost 20 varieties of chile
seeds from Central America including *rocoto*, serrano, jalapeño,
guajillo, and habanero. All orders
and sales via the Internet. Villada
will also seek out special requests
in local markets.

THE CMC COMPANY

P.O. Box 322
Avalon, NJ 08202
Phone: 800-CMC-2780
Fax: 609-861-3065
Website: www.thecmccompany.com
Avocado leaves, dried and canned
chiles, *masa harina*, canned tomatil-
los, *piloncillo*, Mexican chocolate,
Mexican oregano, *achiote* paste.
Equipment: tortilla presses, *molca-
jetes, comales*.

THE CHILE SEED COMPANY

Stoney Bridge, Cark in Cartmel,
Grange over Sands
Cumbria LA11 7PE England
Phone: 01 5395 58110
Fax: 01 5395 59100
E-mail: enquiries@chileseeds.co.uk
Website: www.chileseeds.co.uk
Specialist seed supplier of chile
seeds in the United Kingdom. On-
line catalog features more than 50
varieties from around the world.

THE CHILE WOMAN

1704 S. Weimer Rd.
Bloomington, IN 47403-2869
E-mail:
chilewomn@thechilewoman.com
Website: www.thechilewoman.com
Extensive selection of organically
grown chile, sweet pepper, and
tomatillo plants.

COMPANION PLANTS

7247 N. Coolville Ridge Rd.
Athens, OH 45701
Phone: 740-592-4643
Fax: 740-593-3092
Website:
www.companionplants.com
Catalog: $3.00
Mexican oregano plants, *hoja santa*
plants, epazote plants, and *Tagetes
minuta* (Peruvian *huacatay* or
Bolivian *huacataya*).

CROSS COUNTRY NURSERIES

P.O. Box 170
199 Kingwood-Locktown Rd.
Rosemont, NJ 08556-0170
Phone: 908-996-4646
Fax: 908-996-4638
E-mail: janie@chileplants.com
Website: www.chileplants.com
More than 400 varieties of organi-
cally grown chile and sweet pepper
plants. Fresh chiles also available.

DEAN & DELUCA

Catalog Department
560 Broadway
New York, NY 10012
Phone: 800-221-7714
Fax: 800-781-4050
Website: www.deandeluca.com
Dried chiles, canned chipotles,
Mexican chocolate, *masa harina*,
pumpkin seeds, unusual dried
beans, orange flower water.

ECKERTON HILL FARM

130 Far View Rd.
Hamburg, PA 19526
Phone: 610-562-2591
E-mail: eckerton@enter.net
Fresh and dried Peruvian chiles,
including *ají amarillo, ají mirasol,
ají colorado (rojo)*, and *rocotos*. Also
some hot sauces made with
Peruvian chiles.

FIREWORKS FOODS

450 Queensbury St.
North Melbourne, 3051
Australia
Fax: 61 3 9329 2977
Phone: 61 3 9329 6950
E-mail: info@fireworksfoods.com.au
More than 200 varieties of chile
seeds (rated by heat), as well as an
extensive selection of hot sauces
from around the world; dried,
canned, and pickled chiles;
Mexican cooking chocolate

FRIEDA'S BY MAIL

P.O. Box 58488
Los Angeles, CA 90058
Phone: 800-241-1771
Website: www.friedas.com
Wide selection of dried and fresh chiles, including Oaxacan varieties, Peruvian *ajíes* (special order), twenty-five varieties of squash including *chayotes,* avocado leaves, cactus paddles and prickly pears, yuca, colored potatoes, dried beans, *piloncillos,* corn husks, and banana leaves.

GENERATION FARMS

1109 N. McKinney
Rice, TX 75155
Phone: 903-326-4263
Fax: 903-326-6511
E-mail: generationfarms@pflash.com
Freshly cut epazote, *hoja santa,* and Mexican mint marigold (similar to Peruvian *huacatay,* tastes like strong tarragon) sent overnight via Federal Express.

THE HUITLACOCHE PATCH

1345 Bay Lake Loup
Groveland, FL 34736
Phone: 352-429-4048
Owner Roy Burns grows and sells *huitlacoche.* It is shipped frozen and packed in dry ice.

IT'S ABOUT THYME

11726 Manchaca Rd.
Austin, Texas 78748
Phone: 512-280-1192
Fax: 512-280-6356
E-mail: itsaboutthyme@evi.net
Website: www.itsaboutthyme.com
Diane Winslow has an excellent selection of herb plants including *hoja santa,* epazote, cilantro, *hierba buena,* Mexican Mint Marigold (similar to Peruvian *hucatay*) and *Lippia dulces,* the sweet herb of the Aztecs (a few flowers will sweeten a whole pitcher of iced tea).

KITCHEN MARKET

218 Eighth Ave.
New York, NY 10011
Phones: 212-243-4433,
888-HOT-4433
E-mail: mail@kitchenmarket.com
Outstanding source for dried chiles and pure chile powders, including Oaxacan and Peruvian varieties; also sells jars of some ready-to-use chile purees, moles, and pipiánes. Also available: *canela* (Mexican cinnamon), Mexican oregano, canned *huiltlacoche,* white *chuño "tinta,"* and *chuño negro* (in cans), and *chuño* flour.

LA PERLA SPICE CO.

555 N. Fairview
Santa Ana, CA 92703
Phones: 800-DEL MAYAB, 714-543-5533
Fax: 714-543-4421
E-mail: delmayab@aol.com
Website: www.Delmayab.com
Recado colorado (*achiote* paste) made according to an old Yucatecan family recipe.

MOZZARELLA COMPANY

2944 Elm St.
Dallas, TX 75226
Phone: 800-798-2954
Fax: 214-741-4076
E-mail: mozzaco@aol.com
Queso fresco and cheeses flavored with ancho chile and epazote.

NATIVE SEEDS/ SEARCH

526 North Fourth Ave.
Tucson, AZ 85705
Phone: 520-622-5561
Fax: 520-622-5591
E-mail: nss@azstarnet.com
Website: www.nativeseeds.org
Native Seeds/SEARCH works to conserve the traditional crops, seeds, and farming methods that have sustained native peoples throughout the southwestern United States and northern Mexico. It is a leader in the heirloom seed movement with more than 1,900 collections in its seed bank. It specializes in both domestic and wild crops.

A good source for dried chiles and pure chile powders, including many from Peru and Mexico. Also seeds, for those who want to grow their own chiles.

NU-WORLD AMARANTH

Consumer Orders
P.O. Box 2202
Napierville, IL 60567
Phone: 630-369-6819
Fax: 630-369-6851
E-mail:
sales@nuworldamaranth.com
A variety of amaranth and quinoa products, including both puffed amaranth and puffed quinoa.

PENZEYS SPICES

P.O. Box 933
W19362 Apollo Dr.
Muskego, WI 53150
Phones: 262-679-7207,
800-741-7787
Fax: 262-679-7878
Website: www.penzeys.com
High-quality whole or ground
spices, including Mexican oregano,
epazote, annatto (*achiote*) seeds,
Mexican vanilla beans, dried chiles.

ROCOTO.COM

E-mail: Joe@rocoto.com
Joe Carrasco's website is a good
source of infomration about South
American chiles. While not a retail
outlet, the site is dedicated to col-
lecting, trading, growing, preserving
(and eating!) *ajíes.*

SECRETS TO COOKING TEX-MEX

6515 Redbird Ln.
San Antonio, TX 78240
Phone: 850-682-3272
Orders: 877-243-8839
Website: www.texmex.net
Fresh corn and flour tortillas by
mail (including large quantities for
parties). Also lard, MASECA corn
flour, corn husks, canned beans and
peppers, salsas and spice mixes,
comal, large and small tortilla
presses, *molcajete,* and other food
and cooking items.

SHARFFEN BERGER CHOCOLATE
MAKER

250 South Maple Avenue, Unit C
South San Francisco, CA 94080
Phone: 800-930-4528
Website: www.scharffen-berger.com
Top-quality chocolate from hand-
selected South American, African,
and Caribbean beans. Products
include roasted cocoa nibs with
husks removed, 99-percent pure
unsweetened chocolate bars, as
well as bittersweet and semisweet
chocolate.

SUR LA TABLE

1765 Sixth Avenue South
Seattle, WA 98134-1608
(Mail order and internet catalogs
with retail stores across the United
States)
Phone: 800-243-0852
Fax: 206-682-1026
E-mail:
customerservice@surlatable.com
Website: www.surlatable.com
Extensive selection of cooking
equipment, including lava *molca-
jete,* traditional tortilla press, tortilla
basket, tortilla warmer, oval *comal,*
and stovetop rack for roasting veg-
etables.

WHITE MOUNTAIN FARM

8890 Lane 4 North
Mosca, CO 81146
Phone: 800-364-3019
Fax: 719-378-2897
Website:
www.whitemountainfarm.com
Organically grown quinoa and
exotic-colored potatoes.

METRIC CONVERSION CHART

WEIGHT EQUIVALENTS

The metric weights given in this chart are not exact equivalents, but have been rounded up or down slightly to make measuring easier.

AVOIRDUPOIS	METRIC
¼ oz	7 g
½ oz	15 g
1 oz	30 g
2 oz	60 g
3 oz	90 g
4 oz	115 g
5 oz	150 g
6 oz	175 g
7 oz	200 g
8 oz (½ lb)	225 g
9 oz	250 g
10 oz	300 g
11 oz	325 g
12 oz	350 g
13 oz	375 g
14 oz	400 g
15 oz	425 g
16 oz (1 lb)	450 g
1½ lb	750 g
2 lb	900 g
2¼ lb	1 kg
3 lb	1.4 kg
4 lb	1.8 kg

VOLUME EQUIVALENTS

These are not exact equivalents for American cups and spoons, but have been rounded up or down slightly to make measuring easier.

AMERICAN	METRIC	IMPERIAL
¼ t	1.2 ml	
½ t	2.5 ml	
1 t	5.0 ml	
½ T (1.5 t)	7.5 ml	
1 T (3 t)	15 ml	
¼ cup (4 T)	60 ml	2 fl oz
⅓ cup (5 T)	75 ml	2½ fl oz
½ cup (8 T)	125 ml	4 fl oz
⅔ cup (10 T)	150 ml	5 fl oz
¾ cup (12 T)	175 ml	6 fl oz
1 cup (16 T)	250 ml	8 fl oz
1¼ cups	300 ml	10 fl oz (½ pt)
1½ cups	350 ml	12 fl oz
2 cups (1 pint)	500 ml	16 fl oz
2½ cups	625 ml	20 fl oz (1 pint)
1 quart	1 liter	32 fl oz

OVEN TEMPERATURE EQUIVALENTS

OVEN MARK	F	C	GAS
Very cool	250-275	130-140	½-1
Cool	300	150	2
Warm	325	170	3
Moderate	350	180	4
Moderately hot	375	190	5
	400	200	6
Hot	425	220	7
	450	230	8
Very hot	475	250	9

BIBLIOGRAPHY

HISTORY AND GENERAL INFORMATION

Coe, Michael D. *The Maya*. 5th ed. New York: Thames and Hudson, 1993

————*Mexico: From the Olmecs to the Aztecs*. 4th ed. New York: Thames and Hudson, 1994

Coe, Michael D., Dean Snow, and Elizabeth Benson. *Atlas of Ancient America*. Oxford, England: Andromedia Oxford Limited, 1980.

Coe, Sophie D. *America's First Cuisines*. Austin: University of Texas Press, 1994.

Davies, Nigel. *The Aztecs*. London, England: Sphere Books, 1977.

Elorrieta-Salazar, Fernando E., and Edgar Elorrieta. *The Sacred Valley of the Incas: Myths and Symbols*. Cuzco, Peru: Sociedad Pacaritanpu Hatha, 1996.

Foster, Nelson, and Linda S. Cordel, *Chiles to Chocolate*. Tucson: University of Arizona Press, 1992.

Fussell, Betty. *The Story of Corn*. New York: Alfred A. Knopf, 1992.

Horcasitas, Fernando. *The Aztecs Then and Now*. Mexico City: Minutiae, 1979.

Lanning, Edward P. *Peru Before the Incas*. Englewood Cliffs, N.J.: Prentice-Hall, 1967.

Martin, Luis. *The Kingdom of the Sun*. New York: Charles Scribner's Sons, 1974.

Miller, Mark. *The Great Chile Book*. Berkeley, Calif.: Ten Speed Press, 1991.

McFarren, Peter. *An Insider's Guide to Bolivia*. La Paz, Bolivia: Fundacion Cultural Quipus, 1988.

Pettit, Florence H., and Robert M. Pettit. *Mexican Folk Toys*. New York: Hasting House, 1978.

Viola, Herman, J. *After Columbus, The Smithsonian Chronicle of the North American Indians*. Washington, D.C.: Smithsonian Books, 1990.

Weatherford, Jack. *Indian Givers*. New York: Crown Publishers, 1988.

Weston, Rosario Olivas. *Cultura Indentidad y Cocina en el Perú*. Lima, Peru: Universidad de San Martin de Porres, 1996.

————*La Cocina en el Virreinato del Perú*. Lima, Peru: Universidad de San Martin de Porres, 1998.

MAYA

Hamman, Cherry. *Mayan Cooking: Recipes from the Sun Kingdoms of Mexico*. New York: Hippocrene Books, 1997.

Morton, Lyman. *Yucatán Cook Book: Recipes and Tales*. Santa Fe, N.M.: Red Crane Books, 1996.

Rosado, Renan Irigoyen. *Guisos y Postres Tradicionales de Yucatán*. 4th ed. Mérida, Yucatán, Mexico: Maldonada Editores, 1993.

INCA

Aguirre, Jorge Stanbury. *Great Peruvian Recipes*. Lima, Peru: Jonathan Cavanagh, 1997.

Alvarez, Isabel. *Huellas y Sabores del Perú*. Lima, Peru: Universidad de San Martin de Porres, 1997.

American Women's Literary Club. *Cook Book*. Lima, Peru: American Women's Literary Club, 1990.

Cabieses, Fernando. *Cien Siglos de Pan*. 2nd ed. Lima, Peru: Universidad de San Martin de Porres, 1995.

Canedo, Gabby Vallejo. *Comida y Bebida Indígenas en Cochabamba*. Cochabamba, Bolivia: Impresores Colorgraf, 1999.

Clausen de Molina, Gloria Hinostroza. *Cocina Limeña*. Lima, Peru: Universidad de San Martin de Porres, 1999.

La Cocina Colombiana, Volumen 2. Colombia. Circulo de Lectores S.A.

de la Guerra, Josie Sison Porras. *El Peru y Sus Manjares*. Lima, Peru: n.p., 1994.

de Jordan, Nelly. *Nuestras Comidas*. 8th ed. Cochabamba, Bolivia: n.p., 1997.

de Prada, Teresa, Wilma W. Velasco, Peggy Palza, and Susan Gisbert. *Epicuro Andino*. 6th ed. La Paz, Bolivia: Sierpe Publicaciones, 1995.

de Velasco, Emilia Romero, and Carole Guttentag de Muzevich. *Cocina Tradicional Boliviana*. Cochabamba, Peru: "Los Amigos del Libro" Werner Guttentag, 1999.

Gainsborg, Aida (v. de Aguirre Achá). *La Cocina en Bolivia*. 13th ed. La Paz, Bolivia: n.p., 1996.

Karoff, Barbara. *South American Cooking*. Reading, Mass.: Addison-Wesley, 1989.

Paredes-Candia, Antonio. *La Comida Popular Boliviana, Segunda Edicion,* La Paz. Bolivia: Antonio Paredes-Candia, 1990.

Rivas, Heriberto Garcia. *Cocina Prehispánica Mexicana.* Mexico City: Panorama Editorial, 1991.

Rojas-Lombardi, Felipe. *The Art of South American Cooking.* New York: HarperCollins, 1991.

Rossells, Beatriz. *La Gastronmía en Potosí y Charcas.* La Paz, Bolivia: Editora "Khana Cruz", 1995.

Umaña-Murray, Mirtha. *Three Generations of Chilean Cuisine.* Los Angeles, Calif.: Lowell House, 1996.

Waldo, Myra. *The Art of South American Cookery.* New York: Hippocrene Books, 1996.

AZTEC

Bayless, Richard. *Mexican Kitchen.* New York: Scribner, 1996.

Bayless, Richard, and Deann Groen. *Authentic Mexican.* New York: William Morrow, 1987.

Booth, George, C. *The Food and Drink of Mexico.* New York: Dover, 1964.

de Benitez, Ana M. *Pre-Hispanic Cooking. Mexico City:* Ediciones Euroamericanas Klaus Thiele, 1974.

Guzman de Vasquez Colmenares, Ana Maria. *Tradiciones Gastronomicas Oaxaqueñas.* 2nd ed. Oaxaca, Mexico: n.p., 1992.

Howard, Josefina. *Rosa Mexicano.* New York: Viking, 1998.

Kennedy, Diana. *The Tortilla Book.* New York: HarperCollins, 1991.

Lomelí, Arturo. *El Chile y Otros Picantes.* Mexico City: Editorial Prometeo Libre, 1987.

Martinez, Zarela. *The Food and Life of Oaxaca.* New York: Macmillan, 1997.

Quintana, Patricia. *The Taste of Mexico.* New York: Stewart, Tabori & Chang, 1986.

Ramos Galicia, Yolanda. *Así se Come en Tlaxcala.* Tlaxcala, Mexico: Instituto Nacional de Anthropología y Historia, 1992

Carolyn Margolis is chief of exhibition design and development for the National Museum of Natural History, Smithsonian Institution. Margolis was assistant director for Quincentenary Programs for the National Museum of Natural History. She co-curated *Seeds of Change,* a major exhibition that examined the consequences of the cultural and biological exchanges between Old World America and Old World Europe that were the result of Columbus's voyages of exploration. Her publications include *Seeds of Change,* co-edited with Herman J. Viola (Smithsonian Institution Press, 1991). In her spare time, Ms. Margolis is a member of the board of the National Capital Chapter of the American Institute of Wine and Food and past program chair/vice chairman of the National Board of The American Institute of Wine and Food.

Michael D. Coe is professor emeritus of anthropology at Yale University and Curator at the Peabody Museum of Natural History. His many books include *America's First Civilization: Discovering the Olmec; The Maya; Mexico: From Olmecs to Aztecs;* and *The True History of Chocolate,* co-authored with Sophie Coe.

Jack Weatherford is professor of anthropology at Macalester College in St. Paul, Minnesota. His previous books include *Indian Givers: How the Indians of the Americas Transformed the World; Native Roots: How the Indians Enriched America;* and *Tribes on the Hill.*

INDEX